HEATHCLIFF

Major Literary Characters

**THE ANCIENT WORLD THROUGH
THE SEVENTEENTH CENTURY**

ACHILLES
Homer, *Iliad*

CALIBAN
William Shakespeare, *The Tempest*
Robert Browning, *Caliban upon Setebos*

CLEOPATRA
William Shakespeare, *Antony and
    Cleopatra*
John Dryden, *All for Love*
George Bernard Shaw, *Caesar and
    Cleopatra*

DON QUIXOTE
Miguel de Cervantes, *Don Quixote*
Franz Kafka, *Parables*

FALSTAFF
William Shakespeare, *Henry IV, Part I,
    Henry IV, Part II, The Merry Wives
    of Windsor*

FAUST
Christopher Marlowe, *Doctor Faustus*
Johann Wolfgang von Goethe, *Faust*
Thomas Mann, *Doctor Faustus*

HAMLET
William Shakespeare, *Hamlet*

IAGO
William Shakespeare, *Othello*

JULIUS CAESAR
William Shakespeare, *Julius Caesar*
George Bernard Shaw, *Caesar and
    Cleopatra*

KING LEAR
William Shakespeare, *King Lear*

MACBETH
William Shakespeare, *Macbeth*

ODYSSEUS/ULYSSES
Homer, *Odyssey*
James Joyce, *Ulysses*

OEDIPUS
Sophocles, *Oedipus Rex, Oedipus
    at Colonus*

OTHELLO
William Shakespeare, *Othello*

ROSALIND
William Shakespeare, *As You Like It*

SANCHO PANZA
Miguel de Cervantes, *Don Quixote*
Franz Kafka, *Parables*

SATAN
The Book of Job
John Milton, *Paradise Lost*

SHYLOCK
William Shakespeare, *The Merchant
    of Venice*

THE WIFE OF BATH
Geoffrey Chaucer, *The Canterbury
    Tales*

**THE EIGHTEENTH AND
NINETEENTH CENTURIES**

AHAB
Herman Melville, *Moby-Dick*

ISABEL ARCHER
Henry James, *Portrait of a Lady*

EMMA BOVARY
Gustave Flaubert, *Madame Bovary*

DOROTHEA BROOKE
George Eliot, *Middlemarch*

CHELSEA HOUSE PUBLISHERS

Major Literary Characters

DAVID COPPERFIELD
Charles Dickens, *David Copperfield*

ROBINSON CRUSOE
Daniel Defoe, *Robinson Crusoe*

DON JUAN
Molière, *Don Juan*
Lord Byron, *Don Juan*

HUCK FINN
Mark Twain, *The Adventures of
Tom Sawyer, Adventures of
Huckleberry Finn*

CLARISSA HARLOWE
Samuel Richardson, *Clarissa*

HEATHCLIFF
Emily Brontë, *Wuthering Heights*

ANNA KARENINA
Leo Tolstoy, *Anna Karenina*

MR. PICKWICK
Charles Dickens, *The Pickwick Papers*

HESTER PRYNNE
Nathaniel Hawthorne, *The Scarlet Letter*

BECKY SHARP
William Makepeace Thackeray, *Vanity Fair*

LAMBERT STRETHER
Henry James, *The Ambassadors*

EUSTACIA VYE
Thomas Hardy, *The Return of the Native*

TWENTIETH CENTURY

ÁNTONIA
Willa Cather, *My Ántonia*

BRETT ASHLEY
Ernest Hemingway, *The Sun Also Rises*

HANS CASTORP
Thomas Mann, *The Magic Mountain*

HOLDEN CAULFIELD
J. D. Salinger, *The Catcher in the Rye*

CADDY COMPSON
William Faulkner, *The Sound and the Fury*

JANIE CRAWFORD
Zora Neale Hurston, *Their Eyes Were
Watching God*

CLARISSA DALLOWAY
Virginia Woolf, *Mrs. Dalloway*

DILSEY
William Faulkner, *The Sound and the Fury*

GATSBY
F. Scott Fitzgerald, *The Great Gatsby*

HERZOG
Saul Bellow, *Herzog*

JOAN OF ARC
William Shakespeare, *Henry VI*
George Bernard Shaw, *Saint Joan*

LOLITA
Vladimir Nabokov, *Lolita*

WILLY LOMAN
Arthur Miller, *Death of a Salesman*

MARLOW
Joseph Conrad, *Lord Jim, Heart of
Darkness, Youth, Chance*

PORTNOY
Philip Roth, *Portnoy's Complaint*

BIGGER THOMAS
Richard Wright, *Native Son*

CHELSEA HOUSE PUBLISHERS

Major Literary Characters

HEATHCLIFF

**Edited and with an introduction by
HAROLD BLOOM**

CHELSEA HOUSE PUBLISHERS
New York ◊ Philadelphia

Jacket illustration: Wood engraving by Clare Leighton from *Wuthering Heights* (London: Duckworth, 1931) (Courtesy of The New York Public Library, Astor, Lenox and Tilden Foundations). *Inset:* Title page of the first edition of *Wuthering Heights* (London: Thomas Cautley Newby, 1847) (Courtesy of Henry W. and Albert A. Berg Collection, The New York Public Library, Astor, Lenox and Tilden Foundations).

Chelsea House Publishers

Editor-in-Chief   Richard S. Papale
Managing Editor   Karyn Gullen Browne
Picture Editor   Adrian G. Allen
Art Director   Nora Wertz
Manufacturing Manager   Gerald Levine

Major Literary Characters

Senior Editor   S. T. Joshi
Copy Chief   Philip Koslow
Designer   Maria Epes

Staff for HEATHCLIFF

Picture Researcher   Ellen Barrett
Production Coordinator   Marie Claire Cebrián

©1993 by Chelsea House Publishers, a division of Main Line Book Co.

Introduction © 1993 by Harold Bloom.

Printed and bound in the United States of America

3   5   7   9   8   6   4   2

Library of Congress Cataloging-in-Publication Data

Heathcliff / edited and with an introduction by Harold Bloom.
p.   cm.—(Major literary characters)
Includes bibliographical references and index.
ISBN 0-7910-0942-4.—ISBN 0-7910-0997-1 (pbk.)
1. Brontë, Emily, 1818–1848. Wuthering Heights.   2. Brontë, Emily, 1818–1848—Characters—Heathcliff.   3. Heathcliff (Fictitious character)
I. Bloom, Harold.   II. Series.
PR4172.W7   1992
823'.8—dc20
92-17992
CIP

CONTENTS

THE ANALYSIS OF CHARACTER

Harold Bloom

"Character," according to our dictionaries, still has as a primary meaning a graphic symbol, such as a letter of the alphabet. This meaning reflects the word's apparent origin in the ancient Greek *charactēr*, a sharp stylus. *Charactēr* also meant the mark of the stylus' incisions. Recent fashions in literary criticism have reduced "character" in literature to a matter of marks upon a page. But our word "character" also has a very different meaning, matching that of the ancient Greek *ēthos*, "habitual way of life." Shall we say then that literary character is an imitation of human character, or is it just a grouping of marks? The issue is between a critic like Dr. Samuel Johnson, for whom words were as much like people as like things, and a critic like the late Roland Barthes, who told us that "the fact can only exist linguistically, as a term of discourse." Who is closer to our experience of reading literature, Johnson or Barthes? What difference does it make, if we side with one critic rather than the other?

Barthes is famous, like Foucault and other recent French theorists, for having added to Nietzsche's proclamation of the death of God a subsidiary demise, that of the literary author. If there are no authors, then there are no fictional personages, presumably because literature does not refer to a world outside language. Words indeed necessarily refer to other words in the first place, but the impact of words ultimately is drawn from a universe of fact. Stories, poems, and plays are recognizable as such because they are human utterances within traditions of utterances, and traditions, by achieving authority, become a kind of fact, or at least the sense of a fact. Our sense that literary characters, within the context of a fictive cosmos, indeed are fictional personages is also a kind of fact. The meaning and value of every character in a successful work of literary representation depend upon our ideas of persons in the factual reality of our lives.

Literary character is always an invention, and inventions generally are indebted to prior inventions. Shakespeare is the inventor of literary character as we know it; he

ix

reformed the universal human expectations for the verbal imitation of personality, and the reformation appears now to be permanent and uncannily inevitable. Remarkable as the Bible and Homer are at representing personages, their characters are relatively unchanging. They age within their stories, but their habitual modes of being do not develop. Jacob and Achilles unfold before us, but without metamorphoses. Lear and Macbeth, Hamlet and Othello severely modify themselves not only by their actions, but by their utterances, and most of all through *overhearing themselves,* whether they speak to themselves or to others. Pondering what they themselves have said, they will to change, and actually do change, sometimes extravagantly yet always persuasively. Or else they suffer change, without willing it, but in reaction not so much to their language as to their relation to that language.

I do not think it useful to say that Shakespeare successfully imitated elements in our characters. Rather, it could be argued that he compelled aspects of character to appear that previously were concealed, or not available to representation. This is not to say that Shakespeare is God, but to remind us that language is not God either. The mimesis of character in Shakespeare's dramas now seems to us normative, and indeed became the accepted mode almost immediately, as Ben Jonson shrewdly and somewhat grudgingly implied. And yet, Shakespearean representation has surprisingly little in common with the imitation of reality in Jonson or in Christopher Marlowe. The origins of Shakespeare's originality in the portrayal of men and women are to be found in the *Canterbury Tales* of Geoffrey Chaucer, insofar as they can be located anywhere before Shakespeare himself. Chaucer's savage and superb Pardoner overhears his own tale-telling, as well as his mocking rehearsal of his own spiel, and through this overhearing he is emboldened to forget himself, and enthusiastically urges all his fellow-pilgrims to come forward to be fleeced by him. His self-awareness, and apocalyptically rancid sense of spiritual fall, are preludes to the even grander abysses of the perverted will in Iago and in Edmund. What might be called the character trait of a negative charisma may be Chaucer's invention, but came to its perfection in Shakespearean mimesis.

The analysis of character is as much Shakespeare's invention as the representation of character is, since Iago and Edmund are adepts at analyzing both themselves and their victims. Hamlet, whose overwhelming charisma has many negative components, is certainly the most comprehensive of all literary characters, and so necessarily prophesies the labyrinthine complexities of the will in Iago and Edmund. Charisma, according to Max Weber, its first codifier, is primarily a natural endowment, and implies a primordial and idiosyncratic power over nature, and so finally over death. Hamlet's uncanniness is at its most suggestive in the scene of his long dying, where the audience, through the mediation of Horatio, itself is compelled to meditate upon suicide, if only because outliving the prince of Denmark scarcely seems an option.

Shakespearean representation has usurped not only our sense of literary character, but our sense of ourselves as characters, with Hamlet playing the part of the largest of these usurpations. Insofar as we have an idea of human disinterestedness, we tend to derive it from the Hamlet of Act V, whose quietism has about it a ghostly authority. Oscar Wilde, in his profound and profoundly witty dialogue, "The Decay of Lying," expressed a permanent insight when he insisted that art shaped every era, far more than any age formed art. Life imitates art, we imitate Shakespeare, because without Shakespeare we would perish for lack of images. Wilde's grandest audacity demystifies Shakespearean mimesis with a Shakespearean vivaciousness: "This unfortunate aphorism about art holding the mirror up to Nature is deliberately said by Hamlet in order to convince the bystanders of his absolute insanity in all art-matters." Of *Hamlet*'s influence upon the ages Wilde remarked that: "The world has grown sad because a puppet was once melancholy." "Puppet" is Wilde's own deconstruction, a brilliant reminder that Shakespeare's artistry of illusion has so mastered reality as to have changed reality, evidently forever.

The analysis of character, as a critical pursuit, seems to me as much a Shakespearean invention as literary character was, since much of what we know about how to analyze character necessarily follows Shakespearean procedures. His hero-villains, from Richard III through Iago, Edmund, and Macbeth, are shrewd and endless questers into their own self-motivations. If we could bear to see Hamlet, in his unwearied negations, as another hero-villain, then we would judge him the supreme analyst of the darker recalcitrances in the selfhood. Freud followed the pre-Socratic Empedocles, in arguing that character is fate, a frightening doctrine that maintains the fear that there are no accidents, that overdetermination rules us all of our lives. Hamlet assumes the same, yet adds to this argument the terrible passivity he manifests in Act V. Throughout Shakespeare's tragedies, the most interesting personages seem doom-eager, reminding us again that a Shakespearean reading of Freud would be more illuminating than a Freudian exegesis of Shakespeare. We learn more when we discover Hamlet in the Freudian Death Drive, than when we read *Beyond the Pleasure Principle* into *Hamlet.*

In Shakespearean comedy, character achieves its true literary apotheosis, which is the representation of the inner freedom that can be created by great wit alone. Rosalind and Falstaff, perhaps alone among Shakespeare's personages, match Hamlet in wit, though hardly in the metaphysics of consciousness. Whether in the comic or the modern mode, Shakespeare has set the standard of measurement in the balance between character and passion.

In Shakespeare the self is more dramatized than theatricalized, which is why a Shakespearean reading of Freud works out so well. Character-formation after the passing of the Oedipal stage takes the place of fetishistic fragmentings of the self. Critics who now call literary character into question, and who proclaim also the death of the author, invariably also regard all notions, literary and human, of a stable character as being mere reductions of deeper pre-Oedipal desires. It becomes clear that the fortunes of literary character rise and fall with the prestige of normative conceptions of the ego. Shakespeare's Iago, who wars against being, may be the first deconstructionist of the self, with his proclamation of "I am not what I am." This constitutes the necessary prologue to any view that would regard a fixed ego as a virtual abnormality. But deconstructions of the self are no more modern than Modernism is. Like literary modernism, the decentered ego came out of the Hellenistic culture of ancient Alexandria. The Gnostic heretics believed that the psyche, like the body, was a fallen entity, mechanically fashioned by the Demiurge or false creator. They held however that each of us possessed also a spark or pneuma, which was a fragment of the original Abyss or true, alien God. The soul or psyche within every one of us was thus at war with the self or pneuma, and only that sparklike self could be saved.

Shakespeare, following after Chaucer in this respect, was the first and remains still the greatest master of representing character both as a stable soul and a wavering self. There is a substance that endures in Shakespeare's figures, and there is also a quicksilver rendition of the unsettling sparks. Racine and Tolstoy, Balzac and Dickens, follow in Shakespeare's wake by giving us some sense of pre-Oedipal sparks or drives, and considerably more sense of post-Oedipal character and personality, stabilizations or sublimations of the fetish-seeking drives. Critics like Leo Bersani and René Girard argue eloquently against our taking this mimesis as the only proper work of literature. I would suggest that strong fictions of the self, from the Bible through Samuel Beckett, necessarily participate in both modes, the sublimation of desire, and the persistence of a primordial desire. The mystery of Hamlet or of Lear is intimately invested in the tangled mixture of the two modes of representation.

Psychic mobility is proposed by Bersani as the ideal to which deconstructions of the literary self may yet guide us. The ideal has its pathos, but the realities of literary representation seem to me very different, perhaps destructively so. When a novelist like D. H. Lawrence sought to reduce his characters to Eros and the Death Drive, he still had to persuade us of his authority at mimesis by lavishing upon the figures of *The Rainbow* and *Women in Love* all of the vivid stigmata of normative personality. Birkin and Ursula may represent antithetical and uncanny drives, but they develop and change as characters pondering their own pronouncements and reactions to self and others. The cost of a non-Shakespearean representation is enormous. Pynchon, in *The Crying of Lot 49* and *Gravity's Rainbow*, evades the burden of the normative by resorting to something like Christopher Marlowe's art of caricature in *The Jew of Malta*. Marlowe's Barabas is a marvelous rhetorician, yet he is a cartoon alongside the troublingly equivocal Shylock. Pynchon's personages are deliberate cartoons also, as flat as comic strips. Marlowe's achievement, and Pynchon's, are beyond dispute, yet they are like the prelude and the postlude to Shakespearean reality. They do not wish to engage with our hunger for the empirical world and so they enter the problematic cosmos of literary fantasy.

No writer, not even Shakespeare or Proust, alters the available stock that we agree to call reality, but Shakespeare, more than any other, does show us how much of reality we could encounter if only we retained adequate desire. The strong literary representation of character is already an analysis of character, and is part of the healing work of a literary culture, which implicitly seeks to cure violence through a normative mimesis of ego, *as if it were stable,* whether in actuality it is or is not. I do not believe that this is a social quest taken on by literary culture, but rather that we confront here the aesthetic essence of what makes a culture *literary,* rather than metaphysical or ethical or religious. A culture becomes literary when its conceptual modes have failed it, which means when religion, philosophy, and science have begun to lose their authority. If they cannot heal violence, then literature attempts to do so, which may be only a turning inside out of the critical arguments of Girard and Bersani.

I conclude by offering a particular instance or special case as a paradigm for the healing enterprise that is at once the representation and the analysis of literary character. Let us call it the aesthetics of being outraged, or rather of successfully representing the state of being outraged. W. C. Fields was one modern master of such representation, and Nathanael West was another, as was Faulkner before him. Here also the greatest master remains Shakespeare, whose Macbeth, himself a bloody outrage, yet retains our imaginative sympathy precisely because he grows increasingly outraged as he experiences the equivocation of the fiend that lies like truth. The double-natured promises and the prophecies of the weird sisters finally induce in Macbeth an apocalyptic version of the stage actor's anxiety at missing cues, the horror of a phantasmagoric stage fright of missing one's time, of always reacting too late. Macbeth, a veritable monster of solipsistic inwardness but no intellectual, counters his dilemma by fresh murders, that prolong him in time yet provoke him only to a perpetually freshened sense of being outraged, as all his expectations be-come still worse confounded. We are moved by Macbeth, however estrangedly, because his terrible inwardness is a paradigm for our own solipsism, but also because none of us can resist a strong and successful representation of the human in a state of being outraged.

The ultimate outrage is the necessity of dying, an outrage concealed in a multitude of masks, including the tyrannical ambitions of Macbeth. I suspect that our outrage at being outraged is the most difficult of all our affects for us to represent to ourselves, which is why we are so inclined to imaginative sympathy for a character who strongly conveys that affect to us. The Shrike of West's *Miss Lonely-hearts* or Faulkner's Joe Christmas of *Light in August* are crucial modern instances, but such figures can be located in many other works, since the ability to represent this extreme emotion is one of the tests that strong writers are driven to set for themselves.

However a reader seeks to reduce literary character to a question of marks on a page, she will come at last to the impasse constituted by the thought of death, her death, and before that to all the stations of being outraged that memorialize her own drive towards death. In reading, she quests for evidences that are strong representations, whether of her desire or her despair. Such questings constitute the necessary basis for the analysis of literary character, an enterprise that always will survive every vagary of critical fashion.

EDITOR'S NOTE

This book brings together a representative selection of the best criticism that has been devoted to Heathcliff, the vivid hero, or hero-villain, of Emily Brontë's novel, *Wuthering Heights*. The extracts and essays each are reprinted here in the chronological order of their original publication. I am indebted to the erudition and acumen of S. T. Joshi in assisting my editing of this volume.

My introduction considers the uncanny revisions of the Byronic hero that are involved in the portrayal of Heathcliff. The critical extracts begin with Charlotte Brontë, and go on to the very varied company of A. C. Swinburne, W. D. Howells, E. M. Forster, Georges Bataille, Q. D. Leavis, and the feminist duo of Gilbert and Gubar.

Full-scale essays begin with Miriam Allott's speculation upon dialectical elements in the only apparent "rejection of Heathcliff," whether by the elder Catherine or by Emily Brontë. Walter L. Reed emphasizes childlike elements in Heathcliff, while Ronald B. Hatch relates Heathcliff's suicidal death to Schopenhauer's sense of how the will to live might be defied.

Whether there is authentic love for Heathcliff on the part of "his" Catherine is questioned by John Beversluis. Walter E. Anderson works through some of the consequences for the representation of Heathcliff's character that ensue from the novel's form as dramatic lyric.

The effect of generational complexities upon Heathcliff's nature is the subject of Mary Burgan's essay, while John T. Matthews provides a formal consideration of Heathcliff's debt to Emily Brontë's narrative art of "framing." The "erotic faith" incarnated in Heathcliff is expounded by Robert M. Polhemus, after which W. David Shaw concludes this volume by ascribing Heathcliff's resistance to analysis to Emily Brontë's venture into what is nearly unutterable.

INTRODUCTION

Palpably Byronic, Heathcliff nevertheless is neither a repetition of the Byronic hero (Lara, Manfred, Cain) nor a portrait, however distorted, of Lord Byron himself. Despite his lineage, Heathcliff's greatest distinction as a literary character consists in his originality. As Dorothy Van Ghent strongly emphasized, moral judgment—his own, that of others, or ours—is irrelevant to Heathcliff. A daemonic changeling, Heathcliff emanates from a realm beyond good and evil. His sublimity somehow excludes pathos; his sufferings impress us, but they scarcely move us, so little do they resemble our own. As a representative of what seems before or beyond nature, Heathcliff belongs to the essentially Gnostic cosmos of Emily Brontë's Gondal poems, or of her handful of mature and powerful lyrics. Freedom, for Heathcliff as for his author, resides in the primal Abyss, stationed before the Fall into Creation or our nature. The mutual solitude finally achieved by Heathcliff and the first Catherine, after his death, is at once a wildness and a restoration, and so a freedom very different from that of societal or normative vision.

Melville's Ahab resembles Heathcliff neither in character nor in situation, and yet there is an affinity, possibly because *Moby-Dick*, like *Wuthering Heights*, and like Shakespeare's *Macbeth*, is set in a Gnostic cosmos. Gnostic protagonists manifest a continuous sense of having been outraged; in our time one thinks of Faulkner's Joe Christmas in *Light in August*, or the entire Bundren clan in *As I Lay Dying*. Thomas Pynchon, who appears to be the authentic seer of our contemporary Gnosis, conveys the aesthetics of outrage so persuasively that outrage scarcely seems extreme or uncommon. But there is still a normative and natural world in *Wuthering Heights*; it breaks Catherine Earnshaw, and reduces Heathcliff to the role of anomaly, who can disrupt for a while, but finally is subsumed by the union of the Earnshaws and Lintons in Hareton and the second Catherine. Yet even as an anomaly, Heathcliff is fiercely memorable, and is as High Romantic as Ahab or as Shelley's Prometheus. All these are questers *contra naturam*, breakers of metaphysical absolutes, who desire what the ruined creation can never give them.

1

Heathcliff dies by being startled out of life, so distracted by the ghastly presence of Catherine Earnshaw that he can neither eat nor sleep. He is scarcely thirty-eight, but has already been essentially posthumous during the eighteen years that have passed since his Catherine's death. No one lives for very long in *Wuthering Heights,* or in the Brontë family. My first thought always, when I remember the novel, is that everyone marries very young because they know, on some curious level, that they will die young. Even at his death, the uncanny Heathcliff essentially is an overgrown child, still questing for the union with Catherine he had in his infancy. There are no "mature values" for Emily Brontë, whose imagination, in *Wuthering Heights* and the best poems, identifies transcendent reality with a child's yearnings. Byron's peculiar mixture of sin and guilt, blended from his aristocratic misreadings both of Calvinism and Catholicism, is alien to Emily Brontë, who was not a Christian visionary. Her Gnosticism, very much her own, ignores the stranger God of the ancient heretics, and worships only the God within her own breast. Heathcliff is a follower of that God, whom he calls Catherine Earnshaw.

There are therefore few relevant terms available for describing Heathcliff, since his only quest is for Catherine, alive or dead. But this is not the Shelleyan quest for an epipsyche. Extreme as that was, Shelley remained urbane and ironical enough to acknowledge *some* limits to the name and nature of desire. Heathcliff and Catherine regard themselves as *being* one another, an identification that is neither a metaphor nor a reality. Yet to call it either a delusion or a pathological obsession would be a reduction of Emily Brontë's novel. We are confronted again by the originality of Heathcliff as a fictive character. Frank Kermode wisely remarks of *Wuthering Heights* that: "Dreams, visions, ghosts—the whole pneumatology of the book is only indeterminately related to the natural narrative." There will always be something missing in any critical account of Heathcliff, and of his place in the novel. Emily Brontë, with authentic audacity, declined to provide any bridge except for the fragile though fierce Catherine Earnshaw between the occult and realistic realms in her novel. We lack any certain route into the mystery of Heathcliff.

Aesthetically, this seems to me more of a gain than not, since it saves Heathcliff from psychoanalytic or sociological reductions. His precisely timeless quality is felt in his peculiar relations to present time, where he seems never to be, whether longing for the past, or anticipating a timeless future. The Byronic hero suffers always the crisis of the present, fallen away from the ideal, but Heathcliff has no ideal, not even Catherine, who is too close for idealization. *Wuthering Heights* is of no genre, even as Heathcliff evades the hero-villain category of Shakespeare's Edmund (in *King Lear*) or of Byron's Cain. As a protagonist of a kind of daemonic romance, Heathcliff would incarnate some mode of guilt, but even the daemonic is not an adequate descriptive mode for encompassing him. He is so much a negation of every received tradition that he can be seen only as an undoing figure, presumably a blocking agent set against male representations, like Byron's or Shelley's, of the infinite nature of desire. Feminist criticism doubtless will help solve the dilemma of Heathcliff, when some day its instruments of analysis become more refined, but for now, as with all other criticisms, it meets a limit in Emily Brontë's severe modification of the male Romantic tradition. Heathcliff wanders into the nineteenth-century English novel from some unwritten visionary epic, darker and larger than the Gondal saga of Emily Brontë's childhood.

—H. B.

CRITICAL EXTRACTS

CHARLOTTE BRONTË

Heathcliffe, again, of *Wuthering Heights* is quite another creation. He exemplifies the effects which a life of continued injustice and hard usage may produce on a naturally perverse, vindictive, and inexorable disposition. Carefully trained and kindly treated, the black gipsy-cub might possibly have been reared into a human being, but tyranny and ignorance made of him a mere demon. The worst of it is, some of his spirit seems breathed through the whole narrative in which he figures: it haunts every moor and glen, and beckons in every fir-tree of the Heights.

—CHARLOTTE BRONTË, Letter to W. S. Williams (August 14, 1848), in Clement K. Shorter, *The Brontës: Life and Letters* (London: Hodder & Stoughton, 1908), Vol. I, p. 446

[EDWIN P. WHIPPLE]

Acton, when left altogether to his own imaginations, seems to take a morose satisfaction in developing a full and complete science of human brutality. In *Wuthering Heights* he has succeeded in reaching the summit of this laudable ambition. He appears to think that spiritual wickedness is a combination of animal ferocities, and has accordingly made a compendium of the most striking qualities of tiger, wolf, cur, and wild-cat, in the hope of framing out of such elements a suitable brute-demon to serve as the hero of his novel. Compared with Heathcote, Squeers is considerate and Quilp humane. He is a deformed monster, whom the Mephistopheles of Goethe would have nothing to say to, whom the Satan of Milton would consider as an object of simple disgust, and to whom Dante would hesitate in awarding the honor of a place among those whom he has consigned to the burning pitch. This epitome of brutality, disavowed by man and devil, Mr. Acton Bell attempts in two whole volumes to delineate, and certainly he is to be congratulated on his success. As he is a man of uncommon talents, it is needless to say that it is to his subject and

5

his dogged manner of handling it that we are to refer the burst of dislike with which the novel was received. His mode of delineating a bad character is to narrate every offensive act and repeat every vile expression which are characteristic. Hence, in *Wuthering Heights,* he details all the ingenuities of animal malignity, and exhausts the whole rhetoric of stupid blasphemy, in order that there may be no mistake as to the kind of person he intends to hold up to the popular gaze. Like all spendthrifts of malice and profanity, however, he overdoes the business. Though he scatters oaths as plentifully as sentimental writers do interjections, the comparative parsimony of the great novelists in this respect is productive of infinitely more effect. It must be confessed that this coarseness, though the prominent, is not the only characteristic of the writer. His attempt at originality does not stop with the conception of Heathcote, but he aims further to exhibit the action of the sentiment of love on the nature of the being whom his morbid imagination has created. This is by far the ablest and most subtle portion of his labors, and indicates that strong hold upon the elements of character, and that decision of touch in the delineation of the most evanescent qualities of emotion, which distinguish the mind of the whole family. For all practical purposes, however, the power evinced in *Wuthering Heights* is power thrown away. Nightmares and dreams, through which devils dance and wolves howl, make bad novels.

—[EDWIN P. WHIPPLE], "Novels of the Season," *North American Review*
No. 141 (October 1848): 358–59

CHARLOTTE BRONTË

Heathcliff, indeed, stands unredeemed; never once swerving in his arrow-straight course to perdition, from the time when "the little black-haired swarthy thing, as dark as if it came from the Devil," was first unrolled out of the bundle and set on its feet in the farmhouse kitchen, to the hour when Nelly Dean found the grim, stalwart corpse laid on its back in the panel-enclosed bed, with wide-gazing eyes that seemed "to sneer at her attempt to close them, and parted lips and sharp white teeth that sneered too."

Heathcliff betrays one solitary human feeling, and that is *not* his love for Catherine; which is a sentiment fierce and inhuman: a passion such as might boil and glow in the bad essence of some evil genius; a fire that might form the tormented centre—the ever-suffering soul of a magnate of the infernal world: and by its quenchless and ceaseless ravage effect the execution of the decree which dooms him to carry Hell with him wherever he wanders. No; the single link that connects Heathcliff with humanity is his rudely-confessed regard for Hareton Earnshaw—the young man whom he has ruined; and then his half-implied esteem for Nelly Dean. These solitary traits omitted, we should say he was child neither of Lascar nor gipsy, but a man's shape animated by demon life—a Ghoul—an Afreet.

Whether it is right or advisable to create beings like Heathcliff, I do not know: I scarcely think it is. But this I know: the writer who possesses the creative gift owns something of which he is not always master—something that, at times, strangely wills and works for itself. He may lay down rules and devise principles, and to rules and principles it will perhaps for years lie in subjection; and then, haply without any warning of revolt, there comes a time when it will no longer consent to "harrow the valleys, or be bound with a band in the furrow"—when it "laughs at the multitude of the city, and regards not the crying of the driver"—when, refusing absolutely to make ropes out of sea-sand any longer, it sets to work on statue-hewing, and you have a Pluto or a Jove, a Tisiphone or a Psyche, a Mermaid or a Madonna, as Fate or Inspiration direct. Be the work grim or glorious, dread or divine, you have little choice left but quiescent adoption. As for you—the nominal artist—your share in it has been to work passively under dictates you neither delivered nor could question—that would not be uttered at your prayer, nor suppressed nor changed at your caprice. If the result be attractive, the World will praise you, who little deserve praise; if it be repulsive, the same World will blame you, who almost as little deserve blame.

—CHARLOTTE BRONTË, "Preface" to Wuthering Heights (London:
Smith, Elder & Co., 1850)

PETER BAYNE

Touching the character of Heathcliff, moreover, and, with less expressness, of that of Cathy Earnshaw, we have a remark to make, which will extend to certain of the characters of Currer Bell, and which might, we think, go far to point out a psychological defence, to be urged with some plausibility, of much that is extravagant and revolting in either case. The power over the mind of what Mr. Carlyle calls "fixed idea," is well known; the possession of the whole soul of one belief or aim produces strange and unaccountable effects, commingling strength and weakness, kindness and cruelty, and seeming, at first sight, to compromise the very unity of nature. Ellis Bell, in *Wuthering Heights,* deals with a kindred, though somewhat different phenomenon. She has not to do with intellect, but emotion. She paints the effects of one overmastering feeling, the maniac actings of him who has quaffed one draught of maddening passion. The passion she has chosen is love. There is still a gleam of nobleness, of natural human affection, in the heart of Heathcliff in the days of his early love for Cathy, when he rushes manfully at the bull-dog which has seized her, and sets himself, after she is safe in Thrushcross Grange, on the window ledge, to watch how matters go on, "because," says he, "if Catherine had wished to return, I intended shattering their great glass panes to a million fragments, unless they let her out." But we watch that boyish heart, until, in the furnace of hopeless and agonizing passion, it becomes as insensible to any tender emotion, to any emotion save one, as a mass of glowing iron to trickling dew. Heathcliff's original nature is seen only in the outgoing of his love towards Cathy; there he is human, if he is frenzied; in all other cases, he is a devil. As his nature was never good, as there were always in it the hidden elements of the sneak and the butcher, the whole of that semi-vital life which he retains towards the rest of the world is ignoble and revolting. His sorrow has been to him moral death. With truly diabolic uniformity, every exercise of power possible to him upon any creature, rational or irrational, Cathy, of course, excepted, is made for its torment. He seems in one half of his nature to have lost all sensibility, to be unconscious that human beings suffer pain. The great agony of passion has burned out of his bosom the chords of sympathy which linked him to his kind, and left him in that ghastly and fiendish solitude, which it is awful to dream of as a possible element in the punishment of hell. However frightful the love-scenes in the death chamber of Cathy—and we suppose there is nothing at all similar to these in the range of literature—we feel that we are in the presence of a man. When we think on his early roamings with his lost and dying love on the wild moors, we can even perceive, stealing over the heart, a faint breath of sympathy. But when he leaves the world of his real existence—the world of his love for Cathy, whether as a breathing woman, or as the wraith which he still loves on—we shrink from him as from a corpse, made more ghastly by the hideous movements of galvanism. Somewhat different is the effect of the same passion upon Cathy. Hers was originally a brave, beautiful, essentially noble nature; through all her waywardness, we love her still; and though her passion for Heathcliff costs her her life, it never scathes and sears her soul into a calcined crag like his. To the last, her heart and imagination can bear her to the wild flowers she used to gather amid the heath; strange and wraith-like as she grows in the storm of that resistless passion, we know full well that no mean, or cruel, or unwomanly thought could enter her breast. Viewed as a psychological study of this sort, a defense might, we say, be set up for the choice of these two characters; and when thus confessedly morbid, their handling will be allowed to be masterly. Nor can it be alleged that instances of similar passion, attended by like results, are not to be met with in real life. Madness, idiocy, and death, are acknowledged to follow misguided or hopeless affection. In the case both of Cathy and Heathcliff, there was unquestionably a degree of the first. But the defense can at best be partial, for, we submit, bedlam is no legitimate sphere of art. Of one thing, however, there can be no doubt. The girl's hand which drew Heathcliff and Cathy, which never shook as it brought out those lines of agony on cheek and brow, which never for a moment lost its strength and sweep in flourish or bravura, was such as has seldom wielded either pen or pencil.

—PETER BAYNE, "Currer Bell," *Essays in Biography and Criticism*
(Boston: Gould & Lincoln, 1857), pp. 400–402

ALGERNON CHARLES SWINBURNE

A graver and perhaps a somewhat more plausible charge is brought against the author of *Wuthering Heights* by those who find here and there in her book the savage note or the sickly symptom of a morbid ferocity. Twice or thrice especially the details of deliberate or passionate brutality in Heathcliff's treatment of his victims make the reader feel for a moment as though he were reading a police report or even a novel by some French 'naturalist' of the latest and brutallest order. But the pervading atmosphere of the book is so high and healthy that the effect even of those 'vivid and fearful scenes' which impaired the rest of Charlotte Brontë is almost at once neutralized—we may hardly say softened, but sweetened, dispersed, and transfigured—by the general impression of noble purity and passionate straightforwardness, which removes it at once and for ever from any such ugly possibility of association or comparison. The whole work is not more incomparable in the effect of its atmosphere or landscape than in the peculiar note of its wild and bitter pathos; but most of all is it unique in the special and distinctive character of its passion. The love which devours life itself, which devastates the present and desolates the future with unquenchable and raging fire, has nothing less pure in it than flame or sunlight. And this passionate and ardent chastity is utterly and unmistakably spontaneous and unconscious. Not till the story is ended, not till the effect of it has been thoroughly absorbed and digested, does the reader even perceive the simple and natural absence of any grosser element, any hint or suggestion of a baser alloy in the ingredients of its human emotion than in the splendour of lightning or the roll of a gathered wave. Then, as on issuing sometimes from the tumult of charging waters, he finds with something of wonder how absolutely pure and sweet was the element of living storm with which his own nature has been for awhile made one; not a grain in it of soiling sand, not a waif of clogging weed. As was the author's life, so is her book in all things: troubled and taintless, with little of rest in it, and nothing of reproach. It may be true that not many will ever take it to their hearts; it is certain that those who do like it will like nothing very much better in the whole world of poetry or prose.

—ALGERNON CHARLES SWINBURNE, "Emily Brontë" (1883), *Miscellanies* (London: Chatto & Windus, 1886), pp. 269–70

MRS. HUMPHRY WARD

Wuthering Heights ⟨. . .⟩ is the product of romantic imagination, working probably under influences from German literature, and marvellously fused with local knowledge and a realistic power which, within its own range, has seldom been surpassed. Its few great faults are soon enumerated. The tendency to extravagance and monstrosity may, as we have seen, be taken to some extent as belonging more to a literary fashion than to the artist. Tieck and Hoffmann are full of raving and lunatic beings who sob, shout, tear out their hair by the roots, and live in a perpetual state of personal violence both towards themselves and their neighbors. Emily Brontë probably received from them an additional impulse towards a certain wildness of manner and conception which was already natural to her Irish blood, to a woman brought up amid the solitudes of the moors and the ruggedness of Yorkshire life fifty years ago, and natural also, alas! to the sister of the opium-eater and drunkard Branwell Brontë.

To this let us add a certain awkwardness and confusion of structure; a strain of ruthless exaggeration in the character of Heathcliff; and some absurdities and contradictions in the character of Nelly Dean. The latter criticism indeed is bound up with the first. Nelly Dean is presented as the faithful and affectionate nurse, the only good angel both of the elder and the younger Catherine. But Nelly Dean does the most treacherous, cruel, and indefensible things, simply that the story may move. She becomes the go-between for Catherine and Heathcliff; she knowingly allows her charge Catherine, on the eve of her confinement, to fast in solitude and delirium for three days and nights, without saying a word to Edgar Linton, Catherine's affectionate husband, and her master, who was in the house all the time. It is her breach of trust which brings about Catherine's dying scene with Heathcliff, just as it is her disobedience and unfaith which really betray Catherine's child into the hands of her enemies. Without these lapses and indiscretions indeed the story could not maintain itself; but the clumsiness or carelessness of them is hardly to be denied. In the case of Heathcliff, the blemish lies rather in a certain deliberate and passionate defiance of the reader's sense of humanity and possibility; partly also in the innocence of the writer, who, in a world of sex and passion, has invented a situation charged with the full forces of both, without any true realization of what she has done. Heathcliff's murderous language to Catherine about the husband whom she loves with an affection only second to that which she cherishes for his hateful self; his sordid and incredible courtship of Isabella under Catherine's eyes; the long horror of his pursuit and capture of the younger Catherine, his dead love's child; the total incompatibility between his passion for the mother and his mean ruffianism towards the daughter; the utter absence of any touch of kindness even in his love for Catherine, whom he scolds and rates on the very threshold of death; the mingling in him of high passion with the vilest arts of the sharper and the thief:—these things o'erleap themselves, so that again and again the sense of tragedy is lost in mere violence and excess, and what might have been a man becomes a monster. There are speeches and actions of Catherine's, moreover, contained in these central pages which have no relation to any life of men and women that the true world knows. It may be said indeed that the writer's very ignorance of certain facts and relations of life, combined with the force of imaginative passion which she throws into her conceptions, produces a special poetic effect—a strange and bodiless tragedy—unique in literature. And there is much truth in this; but not enough to vindicate these scenes of the book, from radical weakness and falsity, nor to preserve in the reader that illusion, that inner consent, which is the final test of all imaginative effort.

—MRS. HUMPHRY WARD, "Introduction" to *Wuthering Heights*
(New York: Harper & Brothers, 1900), pp. xxviii–xxx

W. D. HOWELLS

The heroines of Emily Brontë have not the artistic completeness of Charlotte Brontë's. They are blocked out with hysterical force, and in their character there is something elemental, as if, like the man who beat and browbeat them, they too were close to the savagery of nature. The sort of supernaturalism which appears here and there in their story wants the refinement of the telepathy and presentiment which play a part in Jane Eyre, but it is still more effectual in the ruder clutch which it lays upon the fancy.

In her dealing with the wild passion of Heathcliff for the first Catharine, Emily Brontë does not keep even such slight terms with convention as Charlotte does in the love of Rochester and Jane Eyre; but this fierce longing, stated as it were in its own language, is still farther from anything that corrupts or tempts; it is as wholesome and decent as a thunder-storm, in the consciousness of the witness. The perversities of the mutual attraction of the lovers are rendered without apparent sense on the part of the author that they can seem out of nature, so deeply does she feel them to be in nature, and there is no hint from her that they need any sort of proof. It is vouchsafed us to know that Heathcliff is a foundling of unknown origin, early fixed in his hereditary evils by the cruelty of Hindley Earnshaw, whose father has adopted him; but it is not explained why he should have his malign power upon Catharine. Perhaps it is enough that she is shown a wilful, impetuous, undisciplined girl, whose pity has been moved for the outcast before her fancy is taken. After that we are told what happens and are left to account for it as we may.

We are very badly told, in terms of autobiography thrice involved. First, we have the narrative of Heathcliff's tenant, then within his the narrative of the tenant's housekeeper, as she explains the situation she has witnessed at Heathcliff's house, and then within hers the several narratives of the actors in the tragedy. Seldom has a great romance been worse contrived, both as to generals and particulars, but the essentials are all there, and the book has a tremendous vitality. If it were of the fashion of any other book, it might have passed away, but it is of its own fashion solely, and it endures like a piece of the country in which its scenes are laid, enveloped in a lurid light and tempestuous atmosphere of its own. Its people are all of extreme types, and yet they do not seem unreal, like the extravagant creations of Dickens's fancy; they have an intense and convincing reality, the weak ones, such as Heathcliff's wife and son, equally with the powerful, such as Heathcliff himself and the Catharines, mother and daughter. A weird malevolence broods over the gloomy drama, and through all plays a force truly demoniacal, with scarcely the relief of a moment's kindliness. The facts are simply conceived, and stated without shadow of apology or extenuation; and the imagination from which they sprang cannot adequately be called morbid, for it deals with the brute motives employed without a taint of sickly subjectiveness. The author remains throughout superior to her material; her creations have all a distinct projection, and in this Emily Brontë shows herself a greater talent than Charlotte, who is never quite detached from her heroine, but is always trammelled in sympathy with Jane Eyre, with whom she is united by ties of a like vocation and experience, as governess. You feel that she is present in all Jane's sufferings, small and great, if not in her raptures; but Emily Brontë keeps as sternly aloof from both her Catharines as from Heathcliff himself. She bequeathed the world at her early death a single book of as singular power as any in fiction; and proved herself, in spite of its defective technique, a great artist, of as realistic motive and ideal as any who have followed her.

—W. D. HOWELLS, "The Two Catherines of Emily Brontë," *Heroines of Fiction* (New York: Harper & Brothers, 1901), Vol. 1, pp. 229–31

MAY SINCLAIR

Hindley Earnshaw is brutal to the foundling, Heathcliff, and degrades him. Heathcliff, when his hour comes, pays back his wrong with the interest due. He is brutal beyond brutality to Hindley Earnshaw, and he degrades Hareton, Hindley's son, as he himself was degraded; but he is not brutal to him. The frustrated passion of Catherine Earnshaw for Heathcliff, and of Heathcliff for Catherine, hardly knows itself from hate; they pay each other back torture for torture, and pang for hopeless pang. When Catherine marries Edgar Linton, Heathcliff marries Isabella, Edgar's sister, in order that he may torture to perfection Catherine and Edgar and Isabella. His justice is more than poetic. The love of Catherine Earnshaw was all that he possessed. He knows that he has lost it through the degradation that he owes to Hindley Earnshaw. It is because an Earnshaw and a Linton between them have robbed him of all that he possessed, that, when his hour comes, he pays himself back by robbing the Lintons and the Earnshaws of all that *they* possess, their Thrushcross Grange and Wuthering Heights. He loathes above all loathly creatures, Linton, his own son by Isabella. The white-blooded thing is so sickly that he can hardly keep it alive. But with an unearthly cruelty he cherishes, he nourishes this spawn till he can marry it on its death-bed to the younger Catherine, the child of Catherine Earnshaw and of Edgar Linton. This supreme deed accomplished, he lets the creature die, so that Thrushcross Grange may fall into his hands. Judged by his bare deeds, Heathcliff seems a monster of evil, a devil without any fiery infernal splendour, a mean and sordid devil.

But—and this is what makes Emily Brontë's work stupendous—not for a moment can you judge Heathcliff by his bare deeds. Properly speaking, there are no bare deeds to judge him by. Each deed comes wrapt in its own infernal glamour, trailing a cloud of supernatural splendor. The whole drama moves on a plane of reality superior to any deed. The spirit of it, like Emily Brontë's spirit, is superbly regardless of the material event. As far as material action goes Heathcliff is singularly inert. He never seems to raise a hand to help his vengeance. He lets things take their course. He lets Catherine marry Edgar Linton and remain married to him. He lets Isabella's passion satisfy itself. He lets Hindley Earnshaw drink himself to death. He lets Hareton sink to the level of a boor. He lets Linton die. His most overt and violent action is the capture of the younger Catherine. And even there he takes advantage of the accident that brings her to the door of Wuthering Heights. He watches and bides his time with the intentness of a brooding spirit that in all material happenings seeks its own. He makes them his instruments of vengeance. And Heathcliff's vengeance, like his passion for Catherine, is an immortal and immaterial thing. He shows how little he thinks of sordid, tangible possession; for, when his vengeance is complete, when Edgar Linton and Linton Heathcliff are dead and their lands and houses are his, he becomes utterly indifferent. He falls into a melancholy. He neither eats nor drinks. He shuts himself up in Cathy's little room and is found dead there, lying on Cathy's bed.

—MAY SINCLAIR, *The Three Brontës* (London: Hutchinson, 1912), pp. 244–46

JOHN COWPER POWYS

One cannot help feeling aware, as we follow the story of Heathcliff, how Emily Brontë has torn and rent at her own soul in the creation of this appalling figure. Heathcliff, without father or mother, without even a Christian name, becomes for us a sort of personal embodiment of the suppressed fury of Emily Brontë's own soul. The cautious prudence and hypocritical reserves of the discreet world of timid, kindly, compromising human beings has got upon the nerves of this formidable girl, and, as she goes tearing and rending at all the masks which cover our loves and our hates, she seems to utter wild discordant cries, cries like those of some she-wolf rushing through the herd of normal human sheep.

Heathcliff and Cathy, what a pair they are! What terrifying lovers! They seem to have arisen from some remote unfathomed past of the world's earlier and less civilised passions. And yet, one occasionally catches, as one goes through the world, the Heathcliff look upon the face of a man and the Cathy look upon the face of a woman.

In a writer of less genius than Emily Brontë Heathcliff would never have found his match; would never have found his mate, his equal, his twin-soul.

It needed the imagination of one who had both Heathcliff and Cathy in her to dig them both out of the same granite rock, covered with yellow gorse and purple ling, and to hurl them into one another's arms.

From the moment when they inscribed their initials upon the walls of that melancholy room, to the moment when, with a howl like a madman, Heathcliff drags her from her grave, their affiliation is desperate and absolute.

This is a love which passes far beyond all sensuality, far beyond all voluptuous pleasure. They get little good of their love, these two—little solace and small comfort.

But one cannot conceive their wishing to change their lot with any happier lovers. They are what they are, and they are prepared to endure what fate shall send them.

When Cathy admits to the old servant that she intends to marry Linton because Heathcliff was unworthy of her and would drag her down, "I love Linton," she says—"but *I am* Heathcliff!" And this "*I am* Heathcliff" rings in our ears as the final challenge to a chaotic pluralistic world full of cynical disillusionment, of the desperate spirit of which Emily Brontë was made.

—JOHN COWPER POWYS, "Emily Brontë," *Suspended Judgments: Essays on Books and Sensations* (New York: G. Arnold Shaw, 1916), pp. 327–29

E. M. FORSTER

⟨. . .⟩ the emotions of Heathcliffe and Catherine Earnshaw function differently to other emotions in fiction. Instead of inhabiting the characters, they surround them like thunder clouds, and generate the explosions that fill the novel from the moment when Lockwood dreams of the hand at the window down to the moment when Heathcliffe, with the same window open, is discovered dead. *Wuthering Heights* is filled with sound—storm and rushing wind—a sound more important than words and thoughts. Great as the novel is, one cannot afterwards remember anything in it but Heathcliffe and the elder Catherine. They cause the action by their separation: they close it by their union after death. No wonder they "walk"; what else could such beings do? even when they were alive their love and hate transcended them.

Emily Brontë had in some ways a literal and careful mind. She constructed her novel on a time chart even more elaborate than Miss Austen's, and she arranged the Linton and Earnshaw families symmetrically, and she had a clear idea of the various legal steps by which Heathcliffe gained possession of their two properties. Then why did she deliberately introduce muddle, chaos, tempest? Because in our sense of the word she was a prophetess: because what is implied is more important to her than what is said; and only in confusion could the figures of Heathcliffe and Catherine externalize their passion till it streamed through the house and over the moors. *Wuthering Heights* has no mythology beyond what these two characters provide: no great book is more cut off from the universals of Heaven and Hell. It is local, like the spirits it engenders, and whereas we may meet Moby Dick in any pond, we shall only encounter them among the harebells and limestone of their own county.

—E. M. FORSTER, "Prophecy," *Aspects of the Novel* (New York: Harcourt, Brace & World, 1927), pp. 209–11

DAVID CECIL

The setting is a microcosm of the universal scheme as Emily Brontë conceived it. On the one hand, we have Wuthering Heights, the land of storm; high on the barren moorland, naked to the shock of the elements, the natural home of the Earnshaw family, fiery, untamed children of the storm. On the other, sheltered in the leafy valley below, stands Thrushcross Grange, the appropriate home of the children of calm, the gentle, passive, timid Lintons. Together each group, following its own nature in its own sphere, combines to compose a cosmic harmony. It is the destruction and re-establishment of this harmony which is the theme of the story. It opens with the arrival at Wuthering Heights of an extraneous element— Heathcliff. He, too, is a child of the storm; and the affinity between him and Catherine Earnshaw makes them fall in love with each other. But since he is an extraneous element, he is a source of discord, inevitably disrupting the working of the natural order. He drives the father, Earnshaw, into conflict with the son, Hindley, and as a result Hindley into conflict with himself, Heathcliff. The order is still further dislocated by Catherine, who is seduced into uniting herself in an "unnatural" marriage with Linton, the child of calm. The shock of her infidelity and Hindley's ill-treatment of him now, in its turn, disturbs the natural harmony of Heathcliff's nature, and turns him from an alien element in the established order, into a force active for its destruction. He is not therefore, as usually supposed, a wicked man voluntarily yielding to his wicked impulses. Like all Emily Brontë's characters, he is a manifestation of natural forces acting involuntarily under the pressure of his own nature. But he is a natural force which has been frustrated of its natural outlet, so that it inevitably becomes destructive; like a mountain torrent diverted from its channel, which flows out on the surrounding country, laying waste whatever may happen to lie in its way. Nor can it stop doing so, until the obstacles which kept it from its natural channel are removed.

Heathcliff's first destructive act is to drive Hindley to death. Secondly, as a counterblast to Catherine's marriage, and actuated not by love, but by hatred of the Lintons, he himself makes another "unnatural" marriage with Isabella. This, coupled with the conflict induced in her by her own violation of her nature, is too much for Catherine; and she dies. Heathcliff, further maddened by the loss of his life's object, becomes yet more destructive, and proceeds to wreak his revenge on the next generation, Hareton Earnshaw, Catherine Linton and Linton Heathcliff. These—for Hindley, like Heathcliff and Catherine, had married a child of calm—cannot be divided as their parents were into children of calm or storm; they are the offspring of both and partake of both natures. But there is a difference between them. Hareton and Catherine are the children of love, and so combine the positive "good" qualities of their respective parents: the kindness and constancy of calm, the strength and courage of storm. Linton, on the other hand, is a child of hate, and combines the negative "bad" qualities of his two parents—the cowardice and weakness of calm, the cruelty and ruthlessness of storm. Heathcliff obtains power over all three children. Catherine is married to her natural antipathy, Linton; so that her own nature, diverted from its purpose, grows antagonistic to her natural affinity—Hareton. The natural order is for the time being wholly subverted: the destructive principle reigns supreme. But at this, its high-water mark, the tide turns. From this moment the single purpose that directs the universe begins to reassert itself, to impose order once more. First of all Linton Heathcliff dies. Negative as his nature is, it has not the seed of life within it. Then, freed from the incubus of his presence, the affinity between Hareton and Catherine begins to override the superficial antagonism that Heathcliff's actions have raised between them; they fall in love. The only obstacle left to the re-establishment of harmony is Heathcliff's antagonism; finally this, too, changes. His nature could never find fulfillment in destruction; for it was not—as we have seen—primarily destructive, and has become so only because it was frustrated of its true fulfillment—union with its affinity, Catherine Earnshaw. Heathcliff's desire for this union never ceased to torment him. Even at his most destructive, her magnetic power dragged at his heart, depriving him of any sense of satisfaction his revenge might have obtained for him. Now it grows so strong that it breaks through the veil of mortality to manifest itself to his physical eye in the shape of her ghost. The actual sight of her gives him strength at last to defeat the forces that had upset his equilibrium; with a prodigious effort the stream breaks through the obstacles that had so long stood in its way, and flows at last in a torrent down its rightful channel. He forgets his rage, he forgets even to satisfy the wants of physical nature; he wants only to unite himself with Catherine. Within two days his wish is satisfied. He dies. His death removes the last impediment to the re-establishment of harmony. Hareton and Catherine settle down happy and united at Thrushcross Grange. Wuthering Heights is left to its rightful possessors, the spirits of Heathcliff and the first Catherine. The wheel has come full circle; at length the alien element that has so long disturbed it has been assimilated to the body of nature; the cosmic order has been established once more.

—DAVID CECIL, "Emily Brontë," *Early Victorian Novelists*
(Indianapolis: Bobbs-Merrill, 1935), pp. 174–77

V. S. PRITCHETT

If Emily Brontë saw her leading characters as elemental spiritual types, she did not leave them simple and boring. We can see exactly the superstructure of character. We know quite well why Catherine became Catherine. An unflinching Northern shrewdness marked the duality of her character and saw that the duality gave her wilfulness, her caprice and her power to wound. Heathcliff is an understandable monster. There is a faint suggestion of the Victorian social conscience in the creation of him. He is the slum orphan. He represents, in a sense perhaps remote, the passion of the outraged poor. So utterly crushed, he will crush utterly if he arises. He has the exorbitant will to power. He would—indeed he does—run a concentration camp. In a sense the struggle between Catherine and himself is a class struggle. This is a point worth keeping at the back of one's mind because it is too easy to regard Emily Brontë as a writer who was mystical in the void. But there is another aspect of him. Compare him with Charlotte Brontë's portrait of Rochester. Charlotte's desired villain is a feminine day-dream; Emily's Heathcliff is not a day-dream at all. His ancestor in literature is Lovelace, the superb male in full possession of the power of conspiracy and seduction. Heathcliff's appalling words to the housekeeper in front of his wife, Isabella, recalls the letters of Lovelace:

> But at last, I think she begins to know me: I don't perceive the silly smiles and grimaces that provoked me at first; and the senseless incapability of discerning that I was in earnest when I gave her my opinion of her infatuation and herself. It was a marvellous effort of perspicacity to discover that I did not love her. I believed, at one time, no lessons could teach her that! And yet it is poorly learnt; for this morning she announced, as a piece of appalling intelligence, that I had actually succeeded in making her hate me! . . . Are you

sure you hate me? If I let you alone for half a day, won't you come sighing and wheedling to me again? I dare say she would rather I had seemed all tenderness before you: it wounds her vanity to have the truth wholly exposed.

But Heathcliff is not so admirable a villain as Lovelace; Heathcliff lacks the force of the male intellect. He is Lucifer without the mind and with a mere appetite for property; though, here again, it is interesting to note that he, like Lovelace, is moved to act by the desire for revenge upon the woman's family. Yet, if he is inferior to Lovelace, like Lovelace he is deified by his passion. The destinies of Lovelace and Clarissa are spiritually linked for ever by Clarissa's death; the destinies of Heathcliff and Catherine are linked for ever, not spiritually, but as it were by natural law; not by the immortality of the soul only but by the immortality of the earth:

> My love for Linton is like the foliage in the woods: time will change it, I'm well aware, as winter changes the trees. My love for Heathcliff resembles the eternal rocks beneath: a source of little visible delight, but necessary. Nelly, I *am* Heathcliff. He's always, always in my mind; not as a pleasure, any more than I am always a pleasure to myself, but as my own being.

The power of *Wuthering Heights* grows and is sustained by its plain language and because, at no point, does the writer forget the detail of house or moorland. The storm is intolerable because we have to stand resisting it with our feet clinging to the earth; Emily Brontë would be lost if that storm became rhetorical. But I am one of those who are not carried on by the second part of the story. I can see its moral necessity, but I do not *feel* its logic. Grotesque elements bob up at the break between the two tales. To hear afterwards that Catherine was in advanced pregnancy during the wonderful last scene with Heathcliff, which seems to me the highest moment in the English literature of passionate love, is a physical offence. And then in the beating-up scene later, when Heathcliff breaks in and starts his Dachau act, there are descriptive excesses. One grins back at his "cannibal face" with its "sharp teeth" at the window; and when, on top of all this, Hareton comes in and announces he has been hanging puppies, one lets out the laugh one had reserved for the murder of the children in *Jude the Obscure*. This is just Gothic stuff. The second Catherine has her captivation, but you feel she is a poor creature to fall for Hareton whose long history as a problem-child will take a lot of living down. We have entered the field of psychological realism and social allegory and we are not sure that we have the proper guide. I do not mean that this part of the book is less well written. The characters, the incident, the scene are just as well done as in the earlier part, which is to say that they are beautifully done; and there is always the irresistible pleasure of seeing the wheel turn full circle. But the high power has gone, the storm has spent its force, Heathcliff has become a set character; the devil—and this is surely a decline—has become vicious instead of diabolical. Only, in the last pages, when he fancies he sees the first Catherine again and when, starving himself to death, he begins to relive that ineluctable love, does the power return. And those last pages reconcile us to the moral necessity of the second part of a novel which is not, as some have said, carelessly constructed, but unevenly felt.

—V. S. PRITCHETT, "Books in General," *New Statesman and Nation,*
June 22, 1946, p. 453

DOROTHY VAN GHENT

There is still the difficulty of defining, with any precision, the quality of the daemonic that is realized most vividly in the conception of Heathcliff, a difficulty that is mainly due to our tendency always to give the "daemonic" some ethical status— that is, to relate it to an ethical hierarchy. Heathcliff's is an archetypal figure, untraceably ancient in mythological thought—an imaged recognition of that part of nature which is "other" than the human soul (the world of the elements and the animals) and of that part of the soul itself which is "other" than the conscious part. But since Martin Luther's revival of this archetype for modern mythology, it has tended to forget its relationship with the elemental "otherness" of the outer world and to identify itself solely with the dark functions of the soul. As an image of soul work, it is ethically relevant, since everything that the soul does—even unconsciously, even "ignorantly" (as in the case of Oedipus)—offers itself for ethical judgment, whereas the elements and the animals do not. Puritanism perpetuated the figure for the imagination; Milton gave it its greatest aesthetic splendor, in the fallen angel through whom the divine beauty still shone; Richardson introduced it, in the person of Lovelace, to an infatuated middle class; and always the figure was ethically relevant through the conception of "sin" and "guilt." (Let us note here, however, the ambivalence of the figure, an ambivalence that the medieval devil does not have. The medieval devil is a really ugly customer, so ugly that he can even become a comedy figure—as in the medieval moralities. The daemonic archetype of which we are speaking here is deeply serious in quality because of his ambivalence: he is a fertilizing energy and profoundly attractive, and at the same time horribly destructive to civilized institutionalism. It is because of his ambivalence that, though he is the "enemy," ethically speaking, he so easily takes on the stature and beauty of a hero, as he does in the Satan of *Paradise Lost.*) In Byron's *Manfred,* the archetype underwent a rather confusing sea-change, for Manfred's crime is, presumably, so frightful that it cannot be mentioned, and the indefinable nature of the crime blurs the edges of the figure and cuts down its resonance in the imagination (when we guess that the crime might be incest, we are disposed to find this a rather paltry equation for the Byronic incantation of guilt); nevertheless, the ethical relevancy of the figure remains. Let us follow it a little further, before returning to Emily Brontë's Heathcliff. In the later nineteenth century, in the novels of Dostoevski, it reappears with an enormous development of psychological subtlety, and also with a great strengthening and clarification of its ethical significance. In the work of André Gide, it undergoes another sea-change: the archetypal daemonic figure now becomes the principle of progress, the spirit of free investigation and creative experience; with this reorientation, it becomes positively ethical rather than negatively so. In Thomas Mann's *Doctor Faustus,* it reverts to its earlier and more constant significance, as the type of the instinctive part of the soul, a great and fertilizing power, but ethically unregenerate and therefore a great danger to ethical man.

Our interest in sketching some phases of the history of this archetype has been to show that it has had, in modern mythology, constantly a status in relation to ethical thought. The exception is Heathcliff. Heathcliff is no more ethically relevant than is flood or earthquake or whirlwind. It is as impossible to speak of him in terms of "sin" and "guilt" as it is to speak in this way of the natural elements or the creatures of the animal world. In him, the type reverts to a more ancient mythology and to an earlier symbolism. *Wuthering Heights* so baffles and confounds the ethical sense because it is not informed with that sense at all: it is profoundly informed with the attitudes of "animism," by which the natural world—that world which is "other" than and "outside of" the consciously individualized human—*appears* to act with an energy similar to the energies of the soul; to be permeated with soul energy but of a mysterious and alien kind that the conscious human soul, bent on securing itself through civilization, cannot identify itself with as to purpose; an energy that can be propitiated, that can at times be canalized into humanly purposeful channels, that *must* be given religious recognition both for its enormous fertility and its enormous potential destructiveness. But Heathcliff does have human shape and human relationships; he is, so to speak, "caught in" the human; two kinds of reality intersect in him—as they do, with a somewhat different balance, in Catherine; as they do, indeed, in the other characters. Each entertains, in some degree, the powers of darkness—from Hindley, with his passion for self-destruction (he, too, wants to get "out"), to Nelly Dean, who in a sense "propitiates" those powers with the casuistry of her actions, and even to Lockwood, with his sadistic dream. Even in the weakest of these souls there is an intimation of the dark Otherness, by which the soul is related psychologically to the inhuman world of pure energy, for it carries within itself an "otherness" of its own, that inhabits below consciousness.

> —DOROTHY VAN GHENT, "On *Wuthering Heights," The English Novel: Form and Function* (New York: Rinehart & Co., 1953), pp. 163–65

GEORGES BATAILLE

As Jacques Blondel pointed out, we must always keep in mind that 'the feelings are formed during Catherine's and Heathcliff's childhood'. But even if children have the power to forget the world of adults for a time, they are nevertheless doomed to live in this world. Catastrophe ensues. Heathcliff, the foundling, is obliged to flee from the enchanted kingdom where he raced Catherine on the heath, while Catherine, though she remains as rugged as ever, denies her wild childhood: she allows herself to be seduced by the easy life personified by a young, rich and sensitive gentleman. Her marriage with Edgar Linton does, admittedly, retain an element of ambiguity. It is not a true decline. The world of Thrushcross Grange, where Catherine lives with Linton near Wuthering Heights, is far from being a sedentary world in Emily Brontë's eyes. Linton is a generous man. He has not lost the natural pride of youth, but he is settling down. His sovereignty goes beyond the material conditions from which he benefits, but if he were not in profound agreement with the well-established world of reason, he could not benefit from it. So, when he returns rich from a long journey, Heathcliff is prepared to believe that Catherine has betrayed the sovereign kingdom of childhood to which, body and soul, she *belonged* with him.

This, then, is a somewhat clumsy synopsis of a story in which Heathcliff's unbridled violence is recounted calmly and simply. The subject of the book is the revolt of the man accursed, whom fate has banished from his kingdom and who will stop at nothing to regain it. I have no intention of giving a detailed account of a series of fascinating episodes. I am simply going to recall that there is no law or force, no convention or restraining pity which can curb Heathcliff's fury for a single instant— not even death itself, for he is the remorseless and passionate cause of Catherine's disease and death, though he believes her to be his. For I intend to deal with the moral significance of the revolutionary nature of Emily Brontë's imagination and dreams.

It is the revolt of Evil against Good. Formally it is irrational. What does the kingdom of childhood, which Heathcliff demoniacally refuses to give up, signify if not the *impossible* and ultimate death? There are two ways to revolt against the real world, dominated as it is by reason and based on the will to survive. The most common and relevant is the rejection of its rationality. It is easy to see that the underlying principle of the real world is not really reason, but reason which has come to terms with that arbitrary element born of the violence and puerile instincts of the past. Such a revolt exposes the struggle of Good against Evil, represented by violence or by puerility. Heathcliff passes judgement on the world to which he is opposed. He cannot identify it with Good because he is fighting it. But even if he is fighting it furiously, he is doing so lucidly: he knows that he represents Good and reason. He hates the humanity and goodness which provoke his sarcasm. If we imagine him outside the story, bereft of the charm of the story, his character seems artificial and contrived. But he is conceived in the dreams, not the logic, of the author. There is no character in romantic literature who comes across more convincingly or more simply than Heathcliff, although he represents a very basic state—that of the child in revolt against the world of Good, against the adult world, and committed, in his revolt, to the side of Evil.

In this revolt there is no law which Heathcliff does not enjoy breaking. He sees that Catherine's sister-in-law is in love with him, so he marries her in order to do Catherine's husband as much harm as he can. He abducts her and, as soon as they are married, scoffs her. He then proceeds to drive her to despair by his callous treatment of her. Jacques Blondel is right to compare the following two passages from Sade and Emily Brontë: 'How sensual is the act of destruction,' says one of the executioners in *Justine*, 'I can think of nothing which excites me more deliciously.

There is no ecstasy similar to that which we experience when we yield to this divine infamy.' 'Had I been born where laws are less strict and tastes less dainty,' says Heathcliff, 'I should treat myself to a slow vivisection of those two, as an evening's amusement.'

—GEORGES BATAILLE, "Emily Brontë," *Literature and Evil* [1957], tr. Alastair Hamilton (London: Calder & Boyars, 1973), pp. 6–8

J. HILLIS MILLER

Heathcliff's situation after Cathy's death is different from hers while she lived, and his reaction to that situation is not the despairing acceptance of separateness, but the attempt to regain his lost fullness of being. The universal human desire is for union with something outside oneself. People differ from one another only in the intensity of their desire, and in the diversity of the ways they seek to assuage it.

After Cathy's death Heathcliff's whole life is concentrated on the suffering caused by his loss, and on the violence of his desire to get her back, for she is his soul, and without her he grovels in an abyss of nothingness. Why does Heathcliff spend so much of his time in an elaborate attempt to destroy Thrushcross Grange and Wuthering Heights, with all their inhabitants? Why does he take delight in torturing Hindley, Isabella, Hareton, the second Cathy, his son Linton? Why does he, both before Cathy's death and after, enter on a violent career of sadistic destruction? Is it because he is, as Cathy says, a "fierce, pitiless, wolfish man," or does his sadism have some further meaning?

During the violent scene of mutual recrimination between Heathcliff and Cathy which ends in the fight between Heathcliff and Edgar, Heathcliff tells Cathy that she has treated him "infernally" by betraying him and marrying Edgar. He will not, he says, "suffer unrevenged." But, says Heathcliff, "I seek no revenge on you . . . The tyrant grinds down his slaves and they don't turn against him, they crush those beneath them— You are welcome to torture me to death for your amusement, only, allow me to amuse myself a little in the same style . . ." Heathcliff's cruelty toward others is a mode of relation to Cathy. Though his appearance at Wuthering Heights in itself disrupts the Earnshaw family, Heathcliff's relation to Cathy forms the basis of his defiance of everyone else, and his destructive hatred attains its full development only after he is separated from her. His sadistic treatment of others is the only kind of revenge against Cathy he can take, for the person who most controls events in *Wuthering Heights* is not Heathcliff. It is Cathy herself.

Heathcliff's sadism is more than an attempt to take revenge indirectly on Cathy. It is also a strange and paradoxical attempt to regain his lost intimacy with her. If Cathy can say, "I am Heathcliff," Heathcliff could equally well say, "I am Cathy," for she is, as he says, his "soul." Possession of Heathcliff gives Cathy possession of the entire universe. If she were to lose Heathcliff, "the universe would turn to a mighty stranger," just as Heathcliff becomes an alien and outcast from all the world after he loses Cathy. If his childhood relation to Cathy gave him possession of the whole world through her, perhaps now that Cathy is lost he can get her back by appropriating the world. The sadistic infliction of pain on other people, like the destruction of inanimate objects, is a way of breaking down the barriers between oneself and the world. Now that he has lost Cathy, the only thing remaining to Heathcliff which is like the lost fusion with her is the destructive assimilation of other people or things. So he turns sadist, just as, in the Gondal poems, Julius Brenzaida turns on the world in war when he has been betrayed by Augusta. Heathcliff's violence against everyone but Cathy plays the same role in *Wuthering Heights* as does the theme of war in the poems. In both cases there is an implicit recognition that war or sadism is like love because love too is destructive, since it must break down the separateness of the loved one. Augusta too is a sadist. She moves quickly from inspiring her lovers to abandon honor for her sake to betraying them and causing them to suffer. Like love, sadism is a moment of communion, a moment when the barriers between person and person are broken down. The climax of sadistic joy is loss of the sense of separateness. It is as though the person who is forced to suffer had lost his limits and had melted into the whole universe. At the same moment the self of the sadist dissolves too, and self and universe become one. Heathcliff's relation to Cathy has been fusion with the whole world through her. He feels that he can reverse the process and regain her by assimilating the world, for his sole aim is to "dissolve with" Cathy and be happy at last. Now he proposes to do this by getting control of Wuthering Heights and Thrushcross Grange in order to destroy them both. "I wish," says Heathcliff of his property, "I could annihilate it from the face of the earth." So he gives himself wholeheartedly to acts of sadistic destruction. No other figure in English literature takes so much pleasure in causing pain to others: "I have no pity! I have no pity!" he cries. "The more the worms writhe, the more I yearn to crush out their entrails! It is a moral teething, and I grind with greater energy, in proportion to the increase of pain." In another place he tells Nelly his feelings about his son and the second Cathy: "It's odd what a savage feeling I have to anything that seems afraid of me! Had I been born where laws are less strict, and tastes less dainty, I should treat myself to a slow vivisection of those two, as an evening's amusement."

Heathcliff's effort to regain Cathy through sadistic destruction fails, just as does Augusta's attempt to achieve through sadistic love a fusion with something outside herself, and just as does Cathy's decision to will her own death. Heathcliff's sadism fails because, as things or people are annihilated under the blows of the sadist, he is left with nothing. He reaches only an exacerbated sense of the absence of the longed-for intimacy rather than the intimacy itself. Augusta goes from lover to lover, destroying them one by one because she cannot reach what she wants through them. And Heathcliff finds that his career of sadistic revenge is a way of suffering the loss of Cathy more painfully rather than a way of reaching her again. "It is a poor conclusion, is it not," he asks. "An absurd termination to my violent exertions? I get levers, and mattocks to demolish the two houses, and train myself to be capable of working like Hercules, and when everything is ready, and in my power, I find the will to lift a slate off either roof has vanished! . . . I have lost the faculty of enjoying their destruction . . ."

The reason Heathcliff gives for having lost the will to demolish the two houses is a confirmation of the fact that his relation to everything in the world is a relation to Cathy, and an admission of the defeat of his attempt to regain her by destroying the Grange and the Heights. He says that everything in the universe is a reminder that Cathy has existed and that he does not possess her. Through his destruction of others he has reached, in the wreckage left after his violence, the full realization of her absence: ". . . what is not connected with her to me?" he asks, "and what does not recall her? I cannot look down to this floor, but her features are shaped in the flags! In every cloud, in every tree—filling the air at night, and caught by glimpses in every object, by day I am surrounded with her image! The most ordinary faces of men, and women—my own features mock me with a resemblance. The entire world is a dreadful collection of memoranda that she did exist, and that I have lost her!" The universe is identified not with Cathy, but with the absence of Cathy, and to possess the world through its destructive appropriation is not to possess Cathy, but to confront once more the vacant place where she is not. This is the hell in which Heathcliff lives after her death: "I could *almost* see her, and yet I *could not!* I ought to have sweat blood then, from the anguish of my yearning, from the fervour of my supplications to have but one glimpse! I had not one. She showed herself, as she often was in life, a devil to me! And, since then, sometimes more, and sometimes less, I've been the sport of that intolerable torture!" Heathcliff's sadistic tormenting of others only leads him to be the more tormented, tormented by a Cathy whose strongest weapon is her invisibility.

—J. HILLIS MILLER, "Emily Brontë," *The Disappearance of God: Five Nineteenth-Century Writers* (Cambridge, MA: Harvard University Press, 1963), pp. 194–97

CHRISTOPHER GILLIE

The doubt which must strike the reader is whether the character of Heathcliff is 'credible'. Several answers can be made, and one arises from his ultimate failure to destroy Hareton and Catherine. His son, Linton, a sickly youth for whom he has no feeling except contempt, dies not long after his marriage to the young Catherine; but Hareton resists sheer brutalisation. He is a boor, but he retains dignity, and this for the unexpected reason that, in trying to reduce him into an image of what he has himself been, Heathcliff is not creating a brute. A brutal and brutalized maniac is much what Heathcliff's own persecutor, Hindley, became, but what Heathcliff himself has never been; if he had, he would be incredible on the grounds that he could not have made himself rich during his three years absence from the Heights, and he could not thereafter have completed his plans of vengeance as far as he did. Heathcliff is demonic—and as to the credibility of this, answers have to be made of a different kind—but his passion is not degraded nor degrading, and his ferocity is finely tempered, ruthless when he sees his purpose, but never wasting itself in senseless violence. The result is that instead of loathing and fearing his persecutor, Hareton becomes, as Heathcliff himself says, 'damnably fond' of him, and seeks to emulate him. Catherine Linton, used to the Linton education and refinement, at first despises him, and he feels humiliated by her; but the Earnshaw side is dominant in her, while he is far from being without finer potentialities. So they draw gradually together: 'They lifted their eyes together, to encounter Mr. Heathcliff: perhaps you have never remarked that their eyes are precisely similar, and they are those of Catherine Earnshaw ... I suppose this resemblance disarmed Mr. Heathcliff....' When his enemies look at him with Catherine's eyes, Heathcliff begins to relax his hold on his hatred, and so on life; he begins his strange, haunted, or enchanted, drift towards the only union with her that was ever possible.

A second answer to doubts as to Heathcliff's credibility might be a challenge to the reader's notions of credibility itself. In a novel, we have come to expect a character to be real in terms of social definition, what Lawrence was later to call 'the social ego'. Even our idea of an anti-social man is such a man on social terms: a negative is defined by the positive it denies. Heathcliff, however, is positive; he is the man imbued with natural force, all his life long at war with the social force that excludes—not him, but the human passion which absorbs his titanism. Such a conception is perhaps only possible in the state of society that the novel pictures, and such as existed in the northern England of Emily Brontë's time. She shows us not one world capable of producing one whole way of life, but two, and two more by implication. There is the modern wilderness of the Liverpool slums, where human life is reduced to the level of struggling vermin; there is the immemorial wilderness of the moors in their primitive violence; there is Wuthering Heights, representative of an old human order, already anachronistic in that its daughters will marry into the new order of Thrushcross Grange, with which Jane Austen might have been on visiting terms. Without the desolation of the slums, Heathcliff might never have been transported to the Heights, nor would he have been so alien there; without the liberation and constrictions of Wuthering Heights and the moors, Catherine and he would not have achieved the freedom of each other's souls; without the constraints of Thrushcross Grange, he would not have been thrown into hostile violence. It is not, after all, Heathcliff who is so monstrous, but the worlds about him that are so confining. If Society cannot assimilate a natural force, does this not merely prove that it is unnatural?

—CHRISTOPHER GILLIE, "The Heroine Victim I: Emma Woodhouse of *Emma;* Catherine Earnshaw of *Wuthering Heights," Character in English Literature* (London: Chatto & Windus, 1965), pp. 130–31

INGA-STINA EWBANK

Much modern criticism assumes for *Wuthering Heights* what is applicable to *Agnes Grey:* that everything 'stands for' something else. As it is impossible to make Heathcliff or the Lintons or either Catherine stand for moral categories, and as the forces of nature play such a large part in the novel, the next step is to assume that its people stand for natural, non-moral forces. Hence Emily Brontë becomes morally perplexed or innocent. Even Lord David Cecil's admirable and in many ways epoch-making essay on *Wuthering Heights* tends to make it into a metaphysical allegory, so that, for all that he was the first to bring out many important qualities in the novel, he also helped to squeeze it into a pattern which both oversimplifies and overcomplicates. He reads the novel as a paradigm of what he takes to be Emily Brontë's philosophy: according to him she thinks 'that the whole created cosmos, animate and inanimate, mental and physical alike, is the expression of certain living spiritual principles'. These are the principles of, respectively, storm and calm. Ultimately they are not in conflict but compose parts of a harmony; nor is either inherently destructive: they become so 'only because in the cramped condition of their earthly incarnation these principles are diverted from following the course that their nature dictates'. But, 'when they are free from fleshly bonds they flow unimpeded and unconflicting; and even in this world their discords are transitory'. Hence Emily Brontë does away with 'the ordinary antithesis between good and evil' and also with the antithesis between life and death. Not surprisingly, since most of this philosophy has been derived from the novel, the novel itself then reduces itself neatly into an illustration of these ideas. It shows 'the destruction and re-establishment' of 'cosmic harmony' by playing the children of storm (the Earnshaws and Heathcliff) off against the children of calm (the Lintons): 'unnatural' marriages between Catherine and Edgar and between Heathcliff and Isabella provoke disorder; order is re-established as Heathcliff and the first Catherine are united at last, after death, and Wuthering Heights is left to them as rightful possessors, while Hareton and the second Catherine establish themselves at the Grange.

While the very assurance of such a reading is tempting, it does, I feel, ultimately misrepresent the novel. I feel that the characters in *Wuthering Heights* are, in various ways, presented as moral beings; and, secondly, that they are not used, allegorically, to illustrate a philosophy—one which, in any case, can hardly be substantiated from the poems, the novel, or anything we know about Emily Brontë—but symbolically, to explore the human condition. Support for this belief can be found both in the novel and in the poems of Emily Brontë. To show this, it is natural to turn first to Heathcliff. No one would deny that he is the most compelling and puzzling character in the novel. He is also structurally the protagonist, the only one whose lifetime spans the whole novel. According to Cecil, Heathcliff is *not*

> a wicked man voluntarily yielding to his wicked impulses. Like all Emily Brontë's characters, he is a manifestation of natural forces acting involuntarily under the pressure of his own nature.

He becomes destructive only because his nature was 'frustrated of its true fulfillment—union with its affinity, Catherine Earnshaw'. But he is no more morally responsible for his destructiveness than 'a mountain torrent directed from its channel, which flows out on the surrounding country, laying waste whatever may happen to lie in its way'. Now, Catherine's betrayal, which sends Heathcliff away on the words, 'It would degrade me to marry Heathcliff now', is clearly the decisive moment in Heathcliff's life, but it is hardly a question of his being changed here from a merely 'alien' to an outright 'destructive' force. Before this moment, we have had the gruesome episode of Heathcliff and Hindley fighting over the colts in Chapter IV; we have heard how Heathcliff's idea of bliss is 'painting the house-front with Hindley's blood'; and we have had the impressive passage in Chapter VII— structurally emphasised as Nelly breaks her narrative there for the first time— where Heathcliff is brooding over how to pay Hindley back and Nelly is advising him to leave revenge to the Lord:

> 'No, God won't have the satisfaction that I shall,' he returned. 'I only wish I knew the best way! Let me alone, and I'll plan it out: while I'm thinking of that, I don't feel pain.'

These are hardly the terms of 'a mountain torrent directed from its chan- nel': clearly we are meant to see the destructiveness in Heathcliff here—nearly three years before Catherine chooses Edgar—as a psychological and moral con- sequence of his own mind, hardened under the conflict with Hindley. Nor, as he later pursues his double revenge, against the Lintons (by marrying Isabella and marrying off Linton to the second Catherine, thus 'legally' appropriating the Linton estates) and against Hindley (driving him on to death and acquiring Wuthering Heights), is there anything 'inevitable' or 'involuntary' about what Emily Brontë surely wants us to call his 'wickedness'. His acts of aggression and revenge are laid out clearly and often in painstaking detail, down to his trick of bribing the lawyer away from Edgar Linton's death-bed; they are wilful deeds bound up with moral consequences. That we are to see his course of action as immoral is most obvious in the second half of the novel, where we are more concerned with the conse- quences, rather than the causes, of his acts; and where Edgar Linton's weakness is less emphasized and his kindness and goodness become the channels through which we perceive him. The scene in Chapter XXVII where Heathcliff keeps the second Catherine from her father's death-bed is a very clear (though implicit) placing of Heathcliff against the very standards he is defying; 'Careful and kind,' he sneers, '—that's paternal.' After his return from the three and a half years' absence we only see him (until his death) in scenes where he does harm—mental or physical or both—to other people. The book is full of physical and mental violence, of hurts and pain and people mistreating each other, and we are not asked to suspend our moral judgment in the face of all that violence. 'Terror,' says Lock- wood, describing how he treated the waif ghost in his nightmare, 'made me cruel.' As Lockwood is affected, so the reader is surely expected to be affected, to see the spread of cruelty as evil. Physical violence becomes one measure of evil in the book, as it spreads from Heathcliff outwards. It is he, the 'cuckoo', who brings out the brutality in Hindley; this was initially old Earnshaw's fault for preferring the foundling to his own son, but it culminates in the ghastly fights after Heathcliff's return and in Hindley's death—whether he had 'fair play' or not is left open. It is he who turns Isabella from a silly but innocent creature, via apathy, into something like a bloodthirsty monster, so that she can abet, and even half enjoy, his fight with Hindley. He provokes Edgar Linton's one act of violence in the book, turns Hareton from Nelly Dean's innocent nursling into a swearing little savage and later a coarse lout; he beats up the second Catherine and temporarily kills the human emotions of kindness and pity in her. Significantly, it is Heathcliff's own offspring, Linton, that brings out the cruellest streak in him; and the encounters between them, hinted at in their effects on Linton, rather than described, are the most quietly gruesome passages in the book. The zest of Heathcliff's pleasure in destruction underlines, rather than obscures, its perverseness and immorality:

> 'I have no pity! I have no pity! The more the worms writhe, the more I yearn to crush out their entrails! It is a moral teething; and I grind with greater energy, in proportion to the increase of pain.'

Linton's own form of sadism, both inherited and learnt from Heathcliff, but lacking the vitality of Heathcliff's, is particularly nasty—as Heathcliff himself knows ('He'll undertake to torture any number of cats, if their teeth be drawn and their claws pared'), and as his young bride finds out when Linton draws 'a pleasant picture to Zillah of what he would do if he were as strong as I [Heathcliff]'.

The imagery connected with Heathcliff—whether used by himself or (mainly) by others in reference to him—is uniformly suggestive of savagery and evil. It refers to unyielding, harsh and sterile aspects of nature—'rough as a saw-edge and hard as whinstone;' 'an arid wilderness of furze and whinstone'—or to wild and predatory beasts—he is 'a vicious cur', a 'tiger or venomous serpent', 'a fierce, pitiless, wolfish man', 'a mad dog', has 'basilisk eyes'—or to infernal powers, picturing him as a devil incarnate. This last is much the most frequent type of reference to him. From the moment Old Earnshaw brings to Wuthering Heights the child 'as dark almost as if it came from the devil', to Joseph's triumphant cry, on finding Heathcliff dead, 'Th'divil's harried off his soul', practically every character in the book speaks of him as diabolical. Sometimes this is elaborated into a whole biblical allegory, as in Nelly's worries about Hindley in Heathcliff's claws at the Heights:

> I felt that God had forsaken the stray sheep there to its own wicked wanderings, and an evil beast prowled between it and the fold, waiting his time to spring and destroy;

but mostly it is in a quick reference, like the otherwise mild Edgar Linton's description of Heathcliff to the second Catherine: 'a most diabolical man, delighting to wrong and ruin those he hates'.

Clearly these diabolical references do not suggest the nobly satanic figure of post-Shelley and Byron literature, or the glamorized wickedness of Charlotte Brontë's Angrian Duke Zamorna. Heathcliff has the mysterious origins and the physical appearance—above all the eyes 'full of black fire'—of a Byronic hero; even the untold horrors of the marriage-bed that produced Linton can be paralleled in descriptions of Byron's marriage with Annabella. But it is a Byron with the glamour gone, with cruelty and torture, physical and mental, seen from the point of view of the tortured ones as well, and hence seen for what they are. Mr. Rochester, whom we only see from Jane Eyre's point of view, is forgiven and his moral failings redeemed, where Heathcliff is treated relentlessly. *Wuthering Heights* could, in that respect, be seen as Emily Brontë's 'healthful' reaction to the late-Romantic mode of flirting with glamorised wickedness, to such Byronic heroes in fiction as Bulwer Lytton's Eugene Aram in the very popular novel of that name (1832). The hero and title character of that novel is an infinitely learned and intelligent man, but he has committed a crime and bears with him a burden of guilt, darkly hinted at in the course of the story. He is Faust and Cain and the Wandering Jew thrust into one—'I felt urged on to wander—Cain's curse descends to Cain's children'—and is given every possible excuse for his crime (he was the accomplice in a murder, committed, to be sure, on a worthless, wicked and wretched individual) was executed to enable him to make some great (unspecified) scientific discovery which was to benefit all mankind. He falls in love with a lovely and innocent young girl, whose father is no less pure and innocent; and both father and daughter are allowed to die believing Aram innocent. Throughout the novel, Aram is pictured in an extravagantly elevated fashion; and maybe his greatest moment is when (having been seized on his wedding-day, tried and against denial found guilty, which causes his intended bride to go into a suitable decline and die) he hears his death-sentence passed:

> Aram received his sentence in profound composure. Before he left the bar he drew himself up to his full height and looked slowly around the court with that thrilling and almost sublime unmovedness of aspect which belonged to him alone of all men, and which was rendered yet more impressive by a smile—slight, but eloquent beyond all words—of a soul collected in itself: no forced and convulsive effort vainly masking the terror or the pang; no mockery of self that would mimic contempt for others, but more in majesty than bitterness; rather as daring fate than defying the judgment of others—rather as if he wrapped himself in the independence of a quiet, than the disdain of a despairing, heart.   (Book V, Chapter V)

Aram's letter of confession, written in his last hours, is as noble and lofty—or, to look at it the other way, as morally specious—a statement as can be found in nineteenth-century fiction. Lord Lytton, however, wants to have his cake and eat it too: he wants the maximum of admiration and sympathy for his hero, but he also wants his own authorial moral position to be impeccably orthodox. To achieve this, he has no other resort but to print a footnote to Aram's letter:

> Aram has hitherto been suffered to tell his own tale without comment or interruption.... But here I must pause for one moment to bid the reader remark, that that event which confirmed Aram in the bewildering doctrines of his pernicious fatalism, ought rather to inculcate the divine virtue—the foundation of all virtues, Heathen or Christian—that which Epictetus made clear,

and Christ sacred—FORTITUDE ... I must apologize for this interruption—it seemed to me advisable in this place.

Eugene Aram was read, we know, in the Brontë household, but whether Emily Brontë had read it or not does not matter. What matters is her superiority of control, both moral (in 'placing' Heathcliff) and technical (in not having to resort to footnotes and capital letters to place him) over the author of that novel.

—INGA-STINA EWBANK, "Emily Brontë: The Woman Writer as Poet," *Their Proper Sphere: A Study of the Brontë Sisters as Early-Victorian Female Novelists* (Cambridge, MA: Harvard University Press, 1966), pp. 95–101

Q. D. LEAVIS

I would first like to clear out of the way the *confusions* of the plot and note the different levels on which the novel operates at different times. It seems clear to me that Emily Brontë had some trouble in getting free of a false start—a start which suggests that we are going to have a regional version of the sub-plot of *Lear* (Shakespeare being generally the inspiration for those early nineteenth-century novelists who rejected the eighteenth-century idea of the novel). In fact, the Lear-world of violence, cruelty, unnatural crimes, family disruption and physical horrors remains the world of the household at Wuthering Heights, a characteristic due not to sadism or perversion in the novelist (some of the physical violence is quite unrealized) but to the Shakespearian intention. The troubles of the Earnshaws started when the father brought home the boy Heathcliff (of which he gives an unconvincing explanation and for whom he shows an unaccountable weakness) and forced him on the protesting family; Heathcliff 'the cuckoo' by intrigue soon ousts the legitimate son Hindley and, like Edmund, Gloucester's natural son in *Lear*, his malice brings about the ruin of two families (the Earnshaws and the Lintons, his rival getting the name Edgar by attraction from *Lear*). Clearly, Heathcliff was originally the illegitimate son and Catherine's half-brother, which would explain why, though so attached to him by early associations and natural sympathies, Catherine never really thinks of him as a possible lover either before or after marriage; it also explains why all the children slept in one bed at the Heights till adolescence, we gather (we learn later from Catherine (Chapter XII) that being removed at puberty from this bed became a turning-point in her inner life, and this is only one of the remarkable insights which *Wuthering Heights* adds to the Romantic poets' exploration of childhood experience). The favourite Romantic theme of incest therefore must have been the impulse behind the earliest conception of *Wuthering Heights*. Rejecting this story for a more mature intention, Emily Brontë was left with hopeless inconsistencies on her hands, for while Catherine's feelings about Heathcliff are never sexual (though she feels the bond of sympathy with a brother to be more important to her than her feelings for her young husband), Heathcliff's feelings for her are always those of a lover. As Heathcliff has been written out as a half-brother, Catherine's innocent refusal to see that there is anything in her relation to him incompatible with her position as a wife, becomes preposterous and the impropriety which she refuses to recognize is translated into social terms—Edgar thinks the kitchen the suitable place for Heathcliff's reception by Mrs Linton while she insists on the parlour. Another trace of the immature draft of the novel is the fairy-tale opening of the Earnshaw story, where the father, like the merchant in *Beauty and the Beast,* goes off to the city promising to bring his children back the presents each has commanded: but the fiddle was smashed and the whip lost so the only present he brings for them is the Beast himself, really a 'prince in disguise' (as Nelly tells the boy he should consider himself rightly); Catherine's tragedy then was that she forgot her prince and he was forced to remain the monster, destroying her; invoking this pattern brought in much more from the fairy-tale world of magic, folk-lore and ballads, the oral tradition of the folk, that the Brontë children learnt principally from their nurses and their servant Tabby. This element surges up in Chapter XII, the important scene of Catherine's illness, where the dark superstitions about premonitions of death, about ghosts and primitive beliefs about the soul, come into play so significantly; and again in the excessive attention given to Heathcliff's goblin-characteristics and especially to the prolonged account of his uncanny obsession and death. That this last should have an air of being infected by Hoffmann too is not surprising in a contemporary of Poe's; Emily is likely to have read Hoffmann when studying German at the Brussels boarding-school and certainly read the ghastly supernatural stories by James Hogg and others in the magazines at home. It is a proof of her immaturity at the time of the original conception of *Wuthering Heights* that she should express real psychological insights in such inappropriate forms.

In the novel as we read it Heathcliff's part either as Edmund in *Lear* or as the Prince doomed to Beast's form, is now suspended in boyhood while another influence, very much of the period, is developed, the Romantic image of childhood, with a corresponding change of tone. Heathcliff and Catherine are idyllically and innocently happy together (and see also the end of Chapter V) roaming the countryside as hardy, primitive Wordsworthian children, 'half savage and hardy and free'. Catherine recalls it longingly when she feels she is dying trapped in Thrushcross Grange. (This boy Heathcliff is of course not assimilable with the vicious, scheming and morally heartless—'simply insensible'—boy of Chapter IV who plays Edmund to old Earnshaw's Gloucester.) Catherine's dramatic introduction to the genteel world of Thrushcross Grange—narrated with contempt by Heathcliff who is rejected by it as a ploughboy unfit to associate with Catherine—is the turning-point in her life in *this* form of the novel; her return, got up as a young lady in absurdly unsuitable clothes for a farmhouse life, and 'displaying fingers wonderfully whitened with doing nothing and staying indoors' etc. visibly separates her from the 'natural' life, as her inward succumbing to the temptations of social superiority and riches parts her from Heathcliff. Heathcliff's animus against his social degradation by his new master Hindley is barbed by his being made to suffer (like Pip at the hands of Estella in *Great Expectations*) taunts and insults—mainly from Edgar Linton—

based on class and externals alone. They are suffered again (thus making Emily Brontë's points inescapable) in the second half of the novel by Hindley's son Hareton at the hands of Catherine's and Edgar's daughter Cathy as well as from his other cousin Linton Heathcliff, Isabella's son. And this makes us sympathetic to Heathcliff as later to Hareton; we identify here with Nelly who with her wholesome classlessness and her spontaneous maternal impulses supports Heathcliff morally while he is ill-used (and even tries to persuade Catherine not to let Edgar supplant him in her life)—she retains this generous sympathy for him until she transfers it to her foster-child Hareton when in turn he becomes a victim (of Heathcliff's schemes). Her sympathy for Heathcliff's hard luck, even when she sees that his return is a threat to the Lintons' happiness, is at odds with her loyalty to her new master Edgar, and leads her to consent to some ill-advised interviews between Catherine and the desperate Heathcliff—though she also feels that to consent to help him there is the lesser of two evils (as it probably was), and she has no doubts about her duty to protect Isabella from becoming Heathcliff's victim. ⟨. . .⟩

To hark back to Heathcliff: it follows from this 'social' development to the theme that Heathcliff should go out into the world to make his fortune and come back to avenge himself, 'a cruel hard landlord', 'near, close-handed' and given over to 'avarice, meanness and greed', plotting to secure the property of both Earnshaws and Lintons and also to claim equality with them socially—we are now in the Victorian world of *Great Expectations* where money, as Magwitch the convict learnt, makes a gentleman. Emily Brontë took no trouble to explain the hiatus in Heathcliff's life—irrelevant to her purposes—and in fact it is enough for us to gather that he comes back a professional gambler at cards; a real flaw however is wholly inadequate illustration of the shared life and interests of himself and Catherine that makes it plausible that on his return she should be so absorbed in conversing with him as to cut out immediately and altogether her young husband. After all, we reflect, they couldn't always have been talking about their childhood escapades—that is to say, we recognize a failure in creative interest here in the novelist; nor do we ever hear what they talk about till Catherine attacks him over Isabella and they quarrel, when it becomes clear even to Catherine that he can be only the monster he has been made by his history. This aspect of him is kept before us from now till the end and accounts for his brutalities and violent outbreaks. For various reasons, therefore, after envisaging several alternative conceptions of Heathcliff, Emily Brontë ended by keeping and making use of them all, so that like Dostoievski's Stavrogin he is an enigmatic figure only by reason of his creator's indecision, like Stavrogin in being an unsatisfactory composite with empty places in his history and no continuity of character. [And like Iago and Stavrogin, Heathcliff has been made the object of much misdirected critical industry on the assumption that he is not merely a convenience.] There is nothing enigmatic about either Catherine, we note, and this points to the novelist's distribution of her interest.

—Q. D. LEAVIS, "A Fresh Approach to *Wuthering Heights*," *Lectures in America* by F. R. Leavis and Q. D. Leavis (London: Chatto & Windus, 1969), pp. 88–93, 95–96

DENIS DONOGHUE

Catherine and Heathcliff are allowed to persevere in their natures; they are not forced to conform to the worldly proprieties of Thrushcross Grange. Conformity is reserved for the next generation. But this is too blunt as an account of the later chapters of the book. The juxtaposition of Wuthering Heights and Thrushcross Grange is inescapable, but it is not simple. The values of the Grange are social, political, personal, compatible with the emerging England, the cities, railways, the lapse of the old agricultural verities. Wuthering Heights is, in this relation, primitive, aboriginal, Bohemian; it rejects any pattern of action and relationships already prescribed. Finally, Emily Brontë accepts the dominance of Thrushcross Grange, since the new England requires that victory, but she accepts it with notable reluctance. Wuthering Heights has been presented as, in many respects, a monstrous place, but its violence is the mark of its own spirit, and Emily Brontë is slow to deny it. The entire book may be read as Emily Brontë's progress toward Thrushcross Grange, but only if the reading acknowledges the inordinate force of attraction, for her, in the Heights. We mark this allegiance when we associate the Heights with childhood, the Grange with adult compulsions. The Heights is also the place of soul, the Grange of body. Imagination, the will, the animal life, folk-wisdom, lore, superstition, ghosts: these are at home in the Heights. The Grange houses reason, formality, thinner blood. Much of this opposition is directed upon the question of education. Heathcliff is not a reader, Edgar is despised for his bookishness; but, at the end, the new generation resolves its quarrel in a shared book. I take this to mean that you must learn to read if you want to marry and live in the Grange. The young Cathy teaches Hareton to read, and thus redeems him. Emily Brontë endorses the change, but again with some reluctance, as if the Gutenberg civilization, inevitably successful, meant the death of other values dear to her. The end of the book is an image of concord, but we are meant to register the loss, too. This is implicit in the composition of the book. The fiction is Emily Brontë's composition, her assertion, and in a sense her act of defiance—set against the demonstrable success of fact, time, history, and the public world. At the end, Catherine and Hareton are to marry and, on New Year's Day, to move to the Grange. As for Wuthering Heights, another writer would have burnt it to the ground, but Emily Brontë retains it, in a measure. Joseph will take care of the house, meaning the living rooms, "and perhaps a lad to keep him company." As Mrs. Dean says, "they will live in the kitchen, and the rest will be shut up." The tone of this passage makes it clear that much of Emily Brontë's imagination remains at Wuthering Heights, not as a ghost to haunt it, but as a mind to respect it. It has been argued that we are not to choose between the two houses, but rather to hold them together in the mind. At the end, we choose, as Emily Brontë chose, as Cathy and Hareton chose; but we make the choice with reluctance and with a sense of the values which are inevitably lost. Wuthering Heights is not merely the terrible place of Lockwood's visits, not merely the result of rough manners, bad education, a gnarled landscape. Its chief characteristic is that it exists in its own right, by a natural law formulated, as it were, centuries before the laws of man and society. To that extent, it is closer than Thrushcross Grange to those motives and imperatives which, helplessly, we call Nature. That is its strength. We should not feel embarrassed by the violence of the first part of the book; it is neither melodramatic nor spurious. The energy dramatized there has nothing to sustain it but itself: hence its association with the elements, especially with wind, water, and fire, and with animals, dogs, snow. It is linked also to the landscape, the firs permanently slanted by the wind. "My love for Heathcliff," Catherine says, "resembles the eternal rocks beneath—a source of little visible delight, but necessary." The sentence provides a motto for the entire book, the acknowledgment of quality and character followed by appeal to an older law: necessity.

—DENIS DONOGHUE, "Emily Brontë: On the Latitude of Interpretation," *The Interpretation of Narrative: Theory and Practice,* ed. Morton W. Bloomfield (Harvard English Studies 1) (Cambridge, MA: Harvard University Press, 1970), pp. 131–32

ROBERT KIELY

Though there is general agreement among critics that *Wuthering Heights* is a great work of art, there has never been anything like a consensus about its moral significance. A number of hypotheses have been proposed which tend to collect around two distinct viewpoints. David Cecil and Dorothy Van Ghent, among others, argue that the novel is essentially amoral and point to the fact that Catherine and Heathcliff are treated as natural phenomena, no more subject to moral categories than a mountain or a storm. According to this argument, the presence of conventionally moral characters like Edgar and Nelly Dean only emphasizes Brontë's amorality because these characters are so much less interesting and alive than Heathcliff and Catherine. To those who hold to the opposite view, among them, Arnold Kettle, Brontë makes a firm and clear moral judgment of all her characters. Catherine, like a great many other young women in nineteenth-century novels, betrays her own feelings, marries out of a desire for social respectability, and suffers wretchedly because of it. Heathcliff, like the demonic protagonist of a revenge play, eventually destroys himself with his own passion. And finally, the union of the younger Cathy and Hareton reestablishes a tranquil social order and asserts the civilized value of self-discipline.

Both views have merit, yet if taken to the extreme, both are inadequate. It is difficult, in the face of the cyclical structure of the novel and its ironic last words, to insist upon "conclusive" evidence. There seems little doubt that Brontë sees man as in part a moral being, but it is equally clear that this is not all she sees. One of the reasons the moral elements in the novel are weak is that the will is shown to be effective only when it cooperates with circumstances which it did not create. Catherine and Heathcliff are both "willful" characters, yet there is no evidence that they caused the mysterious bond which develops between them. Catherine appears to want a life with Edgar, but her effort to live happily without Heathcliff is a failure. Heathcliff's attempted revenge on the Earnshaw family is a display of a cruelly strong will, but stronger still is the attraction of Catherine even from beyond the grave.

As Heathcliff's control over the Earnshaws and Lintons increases, his hold on himself diminishes. He speaks of himself more and more frequently in passive terms, and near the end of the narrative confesses to Nelly that the thought of being with Catherine "has devoured my existence—I am swallowed in the anticipation of its fulfillment." The language may remind us of Faust but the situation does not. Heathcliff's demon is not intellectual pride or lust or even love; nor can it be fully characterized by any moral abstraction. His obsession is with a specific human person and it does not yield easily to generalization. To say that he has behaved improperly may be correct without being adequate.

Swinburne once observed flippantly of Catherine and Heathcliff that their manners "are quite other than Belgravian." But, good or bad, neither manners nor morals are the main issue in *Wuthering Heights*. All the characters have them and therefore it would not be appropriate to ignore them altogether. But our most serious attention is attracted by forces which manners cannot conceal or morals control and by the unique reactions of particular individuals to those forces. As Jane Austen so often and so well demonstrated, the writer concerned with "conduct" is concerned with the community and the general principles which apply to its life. There is a community of sorts in *Wuthering Heights*, just as there are morals and manners, but the extraordinary originality and power of the novel come from its presentation of the private life which communal rules cannot touch. In this, Emily Brontë achieved with unmatched success the aim of every romantic novelist.

Heathcliff is not Everyman, and he and Catherine do not, by any means, represent "all young lovers everywhere." Their experience of one another, Brontë appears to be saying, is ultimately unknowable to anyone but themselves. An appropriate observation, then, is not that it defies morality but that it obscures perception and *therefore* makes external moral judgment uncertain. We are, in a curious way, once again facing the problem posed by Ann Radcliffe when she separated Emily St. Aubert from her clear vistas in the dark corridors of Udolpho. In Radcliffe there is always the sense that the traditional moral categories would apply if only the heroines could figure out where they are—as, in each case, they eventually do.

Brontë offers no solution to the sublime. The "secret" of the relationship between Catherine and Heathcliff cannot be divulged, and that may be why we can take it so seriously. Only religion, psychology, and art are able to subsume the paradoxes inherent in a work like *Wuthering Heights* because they too are grounded in the deficiencies of reason. Brontë does not repudiate moral order any more than she does social order, but she sees them as tenuous and fragile constructs in constant need of reshaping and repair in the aftermath of the storm that is over and in preparation for the one that is always coming. To put it another way, it is not the *value* of order that she questions but its durability, its capaciousness, its power. Her own habit of mind is neither syllogistic nor empirical. She does not seek conclusions but rather looks for ways of freeing herself from them in order to be able to ask new questions.

—ROBERT KIELY, *"Wuthering Heights," The Romantic Novel in England* (Cambridge, MA: Harvard University Press, 1972), pp. 249–51

CAROLYN G. HEILBRUN

The androgynous view of the novel is not meant to supplant but to accompany other interpretations of *Wuthering Heights.* Indeed, the androgynous interpretation is simple enough. Catherine and Heathcliff, whose love represents the ultimate, apparently undefined, androgynous ideal, betray that love, or are betrayed by the world into deserting it. Nor is it insignificant that it is Catherine who at the same time articulates her oneness with Heathcliff and is tempted to betray the masculine half of her soul. Catherine refutes heaven, which is not her home: "I broke my heart with weeping to come back to earth," she tells Nelly, "and the angels were so angry that they flung me out, into the middle of the heath on the top of Wuthering Heights, where I woke sobbing for joy. That will do to explain my secret, as well as the other. I've no more business to marry Edgar Linton than I have to be in heaven; and if the wicked man in there had not brought Heathcliff so low, I shouldn't have thought of it. It would degrade me to marry Heathcliff now; so he shall never know how I love him; and that, not because he's handsome, Nelly, but because he's more myself than I am. Whatever our souls are made of, his and mine are the same, and Linton's is as different as a moonbeam from lightning, or frost from fire." Heathcliff, who has overheard her say it would degrade her to marry him, leaves the room and does not hear the final, the true, declaration. Yet whether he had heard it or not, he was correct in assuming that Catherine had betrayed their love because she was seduced by the offers the world makes to women to renounce their selves: adornment, "respect," protection, elegance, and the separation, except in giving birth, from the hardness of life.

Catherine, with such a love, chooses the conventional path, and the androgynous ideal achieves only a ghostly realization. Its only possible home being earth, this pair, who threw away their chance, must haunt the moors in eternal search for the ideal love, each in quest of the other half of himself which has been denied. For it is Cathy's masculine side which she has denied in marrying Linton and moving to Thrushcross Grange. Confined there, she sinks into death. "I'm wearying to escape into that glorious world, and to be always there; not seeing it dimly through tears, and yearning for it through the walls of an aching heart; but really with it, and in it. Nelly, you think you are better and more fortunate than I; in full health and strength. You are sorry for me—very soon that will be altered. I shall be sorry for *you.*" Nelly will still be in "this shattered prison" where Cathy is "tired of being enclosed." She has recognized that she will take Heathcliff with her into death because "he's in my soul."

Heathcliff's temptation, or inevitable fall into the anti-androgynous world, comes after Cathy's death, not before. The betrayal was hers, because of her sex and her background, and Heathcliff tells her so before she dies: "*Why* did you despise me? *Why* did you betray your own heart, Cathy? I have not one word of comfort. You deserve this. You have killed yourself. Yes, you may kiss me, and cry; and wring out my kisses and tears. They'll blight you—they'll damn you. You love me—then what *right* had you to leave me? What right—answer me—for the poor fancy you felt for Linton? Because misery, and degradation, and death, and nothing that God or Satan could inflict would have parted us, *you,* of your own will, did it. I have not broken your heart—*you* have broken it—and in breaking it, you have broken mine. So much the worse for me, that I am strong. Do I want to live? What kind of living will it be when you—oh, God! would *you* like to live with your soul in the grave?"

With his soul in the grave, Heathcliff follows the "masculine" pattern of self-expression. Devoted wholly to his own aggrandizement, whether in desire for revenge or in anger for deprivation, he treats his "wife," Linton's sister, in the manner of a cruel rake; he contrives to cheat and scheme to—as we would say today—make it. He grows rich and powerful. He uses the law to enrich himself, and deprive others. Utterly manly, he despises his "feminine" son, and tries to brutalize young Hareton. Heathcliff has followed the conventional pattern of his sex, into violence, brutality, and the feverish acquisition of wealth as Cathy had followed the conventional pattern of her sex into weakness, passivity, and luxury. They sank into their "proper sexual roles."

—CAROLYN G. HEILBRUN, "The Woman as Hero," *Toward a Recognition of Androgyny* (New York: Knopf, 1973), pp. 80–82

PATRICIA MEYER SPACKS

Passion, that ambiguously valued state of feeling, dictates the plot of *Wuthering Heights,* itself an outpouring of a creative passion with some analogies to the less productive emotion that dominates Catherine and Heathcliff. The plot in its complexities keeps escaping the memory: one recalls the towering figure of Heathcliff, the desperate feelings of Catherine, but easily loses track of the intricacies through which the characters develop. Catherine and her brother Hindley, with their parents and their servants, Joseph and Nelly, inhabit the old house on the moor at Wuthering Heights. After Catherine's father brings home the mysterious foundling Heathcliff, the girl and the waif form an intense, rebellious alliance, weakened when Catherine makes friends with the prosperous and conventional Edgar Linton and his sister Isabella. Heathcliff, neglected and brutalized by Hindley after his father's death, disappears; Catherine marries Edgar; Hindley, whose young wife dies, sinks toward animality. When Heathcliff returns, he encourages Hindley's degradation. Catherine's deep attention still focuses on Heathcliff; Isabella promptly fancies herself in love with him. As part of his elaborate revenge on the Lintons and Hindley,

Heathcliff marries Isabella, who soon flees his brutality but afterwards bears his son, Linton. Catherine dies in childbirth, leaving the infant Cathy, who as she grows becomes devoted to her father. After Isabella's death, Heathcliff reclaims his sickly, petulant son, and tricks Cathy into marrying Linton, imprisoning both at Wuthering Heights. Hindley has died; Edgar Linton soon follows him; Cathy's husband Linton dies shortly after her father, but Cathy remains Heathcliff's victim, as does Hindley's illiterate, degraded son, Hareton. Heathcliff's desire for victims weakens, however, as his obsession with the dead Catherine augments; he dies hoping for union with her, leaving Hareton and Cathy to redeem one another through mature love.

Such bare summary ignores the powerful effects achieved through disjunctive narrative and disparate points of view, particularly through the perspectives of the "outsider" Lockwood—narrator, spectator, and listener—and of self-righteous Nelly Dean. But it suggests the central issues of the novel. The grand passion that determines the fate of Catherine and Heathcliff is intense, diffuse (vaguely involving nature as well as individuals), and sterile. We may believe the lovers in their talk of some mystical union more powerful than death, but no earthly union results from their feeling. Their connection literally produces only destruction. Catherine's incompletely heard confession of her devotion to Heathcliff precipitates his exile, which hardens him into a machine organized for revenge. When Heathcliff returns, his initial appearance causes a quarrel between Catherine and her husband; a subsequent visit produces the painful scene of her articulated contempt for Edgar during which she locks the door and throws the key into the fire; conflict over Heathcliff provokes her desperate illness; his insistence on seeing her eventuates in her death. The side effects of this passion, equally disastrous, include the undoing of Isabella. Linton would never have been born were it not for Heathcliff's plotting; but this fertility contains the seeds of its own frustration. He is born only to be used by others, and to die. The survivors issue not from grand passions but from the union of Edgar and Catherine, Hindley and his socially inferior bride; they point toward the future.

But survival is not the highest of values, nor must the reader judge causes by their effects. Results may be irrelevant; or the truly significant results may be too subtle for evaluation. Catherine is, regardless of her death (perhaps partly *because* of it), a triumphant adolescent, her entire career a glorification of the undisciplined adolescent sensibility. Heathcliff, who looks so much more "manly" than Edgar, is as much as his soul mate an adolescent; more important, he is a projection of adolescent fantasy: give him a black leather jacket and a motorcycle and he'd fit right into many a youthful dream even now. Powerful, manly, mysterious, fully conscious of his own worth, frequently brutal, he remains nonetheless absolutely submissive to the woman he loves—if that is the proper verb. Around her he organizes his life. He provides her the opportunity for vicarious aggression, dominating her husband, tyrannizing over her conventional sister-in-law; when he turns his aggression toward her, though, she can readily master him. A powerful man controlled by a woman's power: when she dies, she draws him to her in death.

Heathcliff is partly a figment of Catherine's imagination as well as Emily Bron-të's. Catherine's fantasies, far more daring than Emma's, are equally vital to her development. She focuses them on Heathcliff: if he were not there, she would have to invent him. In fact, she *does* invent him, directly and indirectly shaping his being. After his boyhood, he instigates no significant action that is not at least indirectly the result of his response to her. Because of her he goes away, returns, marries lovelessly, destroys Hindley, claims his own son as well as Hindley's, arranges Linton's marriage, finally dies. But Catherine is also controlled by her own creation, her important actions issuing from her bond to Heathcliff.

Although Heathcliff dominates the action of *Wuthering Heights,* and the imagination of its author and its other characters, Catherine more clearly exemplifies what the two of them stand for. Not yet nineteen when she dies, she cannot survive into maturity; Heathcliff, who lasts twice as long, matures hardly more. Both are transcendent narcissists. Catherine explains that she loves Heathcliff "because he's more myself than I am. Whatever our souls are made of, his and mine are the same, and [Edgar] Linton's is as different as a moonbeam from lightning, or frost from fire." Her analogies suggest the ground of her exalted self-esteem. She and Heathcliff share a fiery nature—a capacity for intense, dangerous feeling. The intensity and the danger are both criteria of value; by comparison the purity of the moonbeam, the clarity of frost seem negligible, even contemptible. Hot is better than cold: Catherine has no doubt about that. The heat of her sexuality and of her temper attest her superiority to the man she marries and her identity with the man she loves; her sense of self is the ground of all her values.

The theme of justification by feeling permeates the lovers' statements about themselves and one another. Heathcliff remarks of Edgar Linton, "If he loved with all the powers of his puny being, he couldn't love as much in eighty years, as I could in a day. And Catherine has a heart as deep as I have; the sea could be as readily contained in that horse-trough, as her whole affection be monopolized by him." His quantitative assessments of feeling resemble his qualitative ones, as he complains of "that insipid, paltry creature attending her from *duty* and *humanity! From pity* and *charity!* He might as well plant an oak in a flower-pot, and expect it to thrive, as imagine he can restore her to vigour in the soil of his shallow care!" The qualities that Nelly Dean, like most of humanity, would identify as virtues seem vicious to Heathcliff, who, like Catherine, assumes that only passionate feeling is valuable. She is equally intense in her claims for the virtue and the power of her passion, the foundation of her being. "My love for Heathcliff resembles the eternal rocks beneath—a source of little visible delight, but necessary." As she threatens Nelly, and by extension Edgar, with her self-destructive temper tantrums, explosions of feeling so powerful that they issue in that mysterious and devastating Victorian disease of "brain fever," she expresses repeatedly her conviction of uniqueness, that adolescent burden and glory.

—PATRICIA MEYER SPACKS, "The Adolescent as Heroine," *The Female Imagination* (New York: Knopf, 1975), pp. 136–39

AVROM FLEISHMAN

The most ample exposition of the nature of reality in *Wuthering Heights* is provided by the discourses of Catherine Earnshaw Linton. While she supplies the keys to the metaphysics and symbolism of the novel, she is not always a reliable expositor, being an adept who desires a condition she has not yet attained at the time of her death. The Catharist Cathy first sketches a psychology; in answer to Nelly Dean's question, "where is the obstacle" to her marrying Edgar Linton, " '*Here!* and *here!*' replied Catherine, striking one hand on her forehead, and the other on her breast. 'In whichever place the soul lives—in my soul, and in my heart, I'm convinced I'm wrong!' " The physical correlations are perhaps deliberately vague, since the seat of the soul either in the bodily mind or the heart must be a temporary one, at best a matter of indifference, at worst imprisonment. A similar indeterminacy attaches to Cathy's account of the soul's origin and journey: "I was only going to say that heaven did not seem to be my home; and I broke my heart with weeping to come back to earth; and the angels were so angry that they flung me out, into the middle of the heath on the top of Wuthering Heights; where I woke sobbing for joy." More striking than the vivid account of alienation from a heavenly realm is the attribution of demonic agency to "the angels." It is not necessary to identify these with the Archons who rule the orders of the fallen universe to see these angels as instruments of a hostile system at odds with the soul's desires. Yet, curiously, this alienation from heaven is a fortunate fall, for it brings Cathy to "the middle of the heath," where she cries for joy. What sort of heaven and earth can these be, to evoke such reversed feelings?

A hint of an answer is given in the concluding sentence of the same paragraph: "Whatever our souls are made of, [Heathcliff's] and mine are the same, and Linton's is as different as a moonbeam from lightning, or frost from fire." The primary assumption of this proposition is that souls are made of substances akin to material elements. Cathy then goes on to claim that her soul and Heathcliff's are of the same substance—that she is originally of the *earth* and wants to "come back" to it. It is this claim which is shown to be mistaken in the event. The novel will dramatize the more accurate view that Cathy is a creature of *air* who is nevertheless (and inexplicably) not at home in heaven, which in this context means primarily the region of air. She falls (or is pushed) to earth—to the very "middle" of the heath, at the "top" of Wuthering Heights—where she finds herself suddenly happy. She there encounters the manifestation and foremost inhabitant of the earth, whose name derives from the heath itself; and so strong is her affinity that she claims identity with him. But they must each undergo an *askesis* in which their differing natures are transformed, so as to be miscible or permeable to each other.

That Cathy exhibits the well-known fallacy of leaping from similarities to equations is evident not only from the analogy of moonbeam and lightning, frost and fire, with which she discredits her relation to Edgar. She goes on, in the grand finale of her famous speech, to make this precise jump from metaphor to identity: "... my love for Heathcliff resembles the eternal rocks beneath—a source of little visible delight, but necessary. Nelly, I *am* Heathcliff . . ." She is not, of course, but very much wants to be, and the remainder of the fiction is the narrative of Heathcliff's efforts to approximate himself to her, while she hovers in the air and earth about him, till their final union, in which they are distributed in "the soft wind breathing through the grass" as "sleepers in that quiet earth." From this point of view, the novel is metaphysical not only in its landscape—as set out in the definitive essay of Lord David Cecil—or only in its values, encouraging an embrace of death in order to transcend the lesser world of the Lintons, Thrushcross Grange, and ordinary human life. It is metaphysical in its dramatic action, which traces an alchemical transformation of the elements, a creature of earth and one of air transforming themselves so as to realize their union in a substantial medium—not simply by way of death or in some vague beyond-the-grave but in their physical/spiritual existence.

To describe this transformation, it is not necessary to correlate the characters with the *Book on Nymphs, Sylphs, Pygmies, and Salamanders, and on the Other Spirits* by Theophrastus von Hohenheim, called Paracelsus. It is equally unnecessary to specify the chief characters' propensities by reference to the widely shared temperamental psychology of the humors, with their substantial and ethical correlatives: air with sanguine temper and the vices of "Lechery and perhaps Envy," earth with melancholy and avarice. Instead, we may follow the development of character in this novel as we do in most others, by stages and in context, though with an awareness that the general concept of "character" here is less that of modern psychology than that of the humors tradition and its alchemical variants.

Such thinking underwrites the imagery of earth that is consistently used for the hero's characterization; Cathy tells us that "Heathcliff is—an unreclaimed creature, without refinement—without cultivation; an arid wilderness of furze and whinstone." Later, on her deathbed, Cathy goes through a number of dream images which have teased commentators out of thought—the alien, unreturned lapwing, the fairy cave under Penistone Crags, and the black clothespress with its mirror. More decisively, however, it is at this juncture that Cathy enacts her fundamental impulse toward air; before throwing the window open to contract her death, or breath of life, she says: "Oh, if I were but in my own bed in the old house! . . . And that wind sounding in the firs by the lattice. Do let me feel it—it comes straight down the moor—do let me have one breath!" She then expounds the subsequent events of the plot in what seems like delirium: "It's a rough journey, and a sad heart to travel it; and we must pass by Gimmerton Kirk, to go that journey! . . . I'll not lie there by myself; they may bury me twelve feet deep, and throw the church down over me, but I won't rest till you are with me . . . I never will! . . . He's considering . . . he'd rather I'd come to him! Find a way, then! not through that Kirkyard . . . You are slow! Be content, you always followed me!" It is not enough, then, that she go into the earth, or even—as we will learn—that he lie next to her there. The "way" is a transformation, and a technique must be found to make it.

Heathcliff's journey, then, is mapped out for him in material terms, though not in precise operations. It remains for Cathy to prepare his *askesis* with an appropriate doctrine, that of the fallen world and the "other" world: ". . . the thing that irks me most is this shattered prison, after all. I'm tired, tired of being enclosed here. I'm wearying to escape into that glorious world, and to be always there; not seeing it dimly through tears, and yearning for it through the walls of an aching heart; but really with it, and in it." Cathy's spatial designations are crucial; she wants not merely escape from the prison of the world but a relation to the other realm without mediation—neither through the water of tears nor through the bodily forms of the heart. She wants to be *with* it and *in* it, suggesting a compound substance, earth/air. But she also acknowledges that she cannot exist in the other world without uniting first with her lover: "I shall not be at peace" without him, she has just said. The Cathy that Lockwood encounters when he sleeps in her room at Wuthering Heights, at the novel's spectacular opening, is not just a homeless spirit seeking to be "let in" but a creature of air bereft not only of a residing place but of a stable substance.

Heathcliff's task is thus not simply to die but to prepare himself for proper fusion with the lingering departed. First he must locate her; while it is a matter of indifference or confusion to Christians like Nelly Dean whether she is "still on earth or now in Heaven," he must be more precise: "Where is she? Not *there* [indicating the grave]—not in heaven—not perished—where? . . . Be with me always—take any form—drive me mad! only *do* not leave me in this abyss, where I cannot find you!" The abyss is abstractly defined as the place where he cannot find her, not as earth itself. It is through a recognition that his first investigation was too sweepingly negative that Heathcliff will eventually find Cathy—for she is *"there"* in the earth, and in heaven, considered as air, as well.

The major step in Heathcliff's recovery of Cathy is his discovery of the virtues of his own nature, earth. Throughout the novel, the heights above Wuthering Heights—called with a fine orthography not Penniston but "Penistone Craggs"—resonate with a more powerful mana than that of the heath itself. It is the place of Nelly's legendary fairy cave, it is the goal of the second Cathy's pubescent strivings ("Now, am I old enough to go to Penistone Craggs?"), and it is the spot for her meeting with Hareton, foreseeing the eventual rapprochement of the two families and the two houses. The name and its cognates also infiltrate the symbolic diction, as when Cathy declares that her "love for Heathcliff resembles the eternal rocks beneath." And the pictured landscape, in the conversation of Cathy II and Nelly, generates the sense of awe that attaches not merely to mountains but to high and sacred places:

> The abrupt descent of Penistone Craggs particularly attracted her notice, especially when the setting sun shone on it and the topmost Heights, and the whole extent of landscape besides lay in shadow.
> I explained that they were bare masses of stone, with hardly enough earth in their clefts to nourish a stunted tree.
> "And why are they bright so long after it is evening here?" she pursued.

"Because they are a great deal higher up than we are," replied I; "you could not climb them, they are too high and steep...."

"Oh, you have been on them!" she cried, gleefully. "Then I can go, too, when I am a woman."

The sexual power of this place seems inescapable, yet it would be naïve to limit its import to that. It holds the light (and presumably the heat) of the sun longer than other places on earth and, though there is little earth on it, it may be thought of as earth in a particularly pure state. It is these virtues of earth, and his own identity with it, that Heathcliff discovers in his quest.

Only a growth in self-consciousness can account for his learning the limitations of his grotesque technique of material union—removing a slat of Cathy's coffin in order to mingle his body with hers. In contemplation of being buried next to her, he imagines merely corporeal contiguity: "I dreamt I was sleeping the last sleep, by that sleeper, with my heart stopped, and my cheek frozen against hers." But a clue to the actual form of their union comes in the sexton's warning that opening the coffin will change Cathy's composition: "... he said it would change, if the air blew on it, and so I struck one side of the coffin loose—and covered it up ..." The more sophisticated project of "dissolving with her, and being more happy still"—called here "transformation"—requires that both natures change to become a new and conjoint substance. Heathcliff gains an inkling of this chemistry in a subsequent reminiscence of his initial leap at direct contact:

> ... I was on the point of attaining my object [of uncovering the body], when it seemed that I heard a sigh from some one above, close at the edge of the grave, and bending down.—"If I can only get this off," I muttered, "I wish they may shovel in the earth over us both!" and I wrenched at it more desperately still. There was another sigh, close at my ear. I appeared to feel the warm breath of it displacing the sleet-laden wind. I knew no living thing in flesh and blood was by—but as certainly as you perceive the approach to some substantial body in the dark, though it cannot be discerned, so certainly I felt that Cathy was there, not under me, but on the earth.

His awareness of her presence as of a "substantial body" is compounded with a recognition that she cannot be seen; she is of air, a breath "displacing the sleet-laden wind," yet *on* the earth. This distribution of the elements may be appropriate for the desired union.

Heathcliff's highest gnosis is of the symbolic dimension of these physical embodiments. In his final declaration, he proposes a symbolic view of the universe as a set of physical vehicles, the signs of Cathy's presence: "... what is not connected with her to me? and what does not recall her? I cannot look down to this floor, but her features are shaped on the flags! In every cloud, in every tree—filling the air at night, and caught by glimpses in every object by day, I am surrounded with her image!... The entire world is a dreadful collection of memoranda that she did exist, and that I have lost her!" Although pained at perceiving the difference between symbol and reality, Heathcliff is capable of finding the tokens of the soul both in cloud and tree, air and the "objects" of earth. By this awareness of the symbolic properties of his own nature and of Cathy's, he is prepared to merge with her in death—which he readily wills. That this death entails a transformation into a new, fused substance is suggested by their continued presence on and in the heath, as witnessed by "a little boy with a sheep and two lambs," who reports, "They's Heathcliff and a woman, yonder, under t' Nab"—i.e., below the crest of the hill and/or within it.

—AVROM FLEISHMAN, "*Wuthering Heights:* The Love of a Sylph and a Gnome," *Fiction and the Ways of Knowing: Essays on British Novels* (Austin: University of Texas Press, 1978), pp. 44–48

SANDRA M. GILBERT AND SUSAN GUBAR

From the first, Heathcliff has had undeniable monster potential, as many readers have observed. Isabella's questions to Nelly—"Is Mr. Heathcliff a man? If so, is he mad? And if not is he a devil?" (chap. 13)—indicate among other things Emily Brontë's cool awareness of having created an anomalous being, a sort of "Ghoul" or "Afreet," not (as her sister half hoped) "despite" herself but for good reasons. Uniting human and animal traits, the skills of culture with the energies of nature, Heathcliff's character tests the boundaries between human and animal, nature and culture, and in doing so proposes a new definition of the demonic. What is more important for our purposes here, however, is the fact that, despite his outward masculinity, Heathcliff is somehow female in his monstrosity. Besides in a general way suggesting a set of questions about humanness, his existence therefore summarized a number of important points about the relationship between maleness and femaleness as, say, Milton representatively defines it.

To say that Heathcliff is "female" may at first sound mad or absurd. As we noted earlier, his outward masculinity seems to be definitively demonstrated by his athletic build and military carriage, as well as by the Byronic sexual charisma that he has for ladylike Isabella. And though we saw that Edgar is truly patriarchal despite his apparent effeminacy, there is no real reason why Heathcliff should not simply represent an alternative version of masculinity, the maleness of the younger son, that paradigmatic outsider in patriarchy. To some extent, of course, this is true: Heathcliff is clearly just as male in his Satanic outcast way as Edgar in his angelically established way. But at the same time, on a deeper associative level, Heathcliff is "female"—on the level where younger sons and bastards and devils unite with women in rebelling against the tyranny of heaven, the level where orphans are female and heirs are male, where flesh is female and spirit is male, earth female, sky male, monsters female, angels male.

The sons of Urizen were born from heaven, Blake declares, but "his daughters from green herbs and cattle,/From monsters and worms of the pit." He might be describing Heathcliff, the "little dark thing" whose enigmatic ferocity suggests vegetation spirits, hell, pits, night—all the "female" irrationality of nature. Nameless as a woman, the gypsy orphan old Earnshaw brings back from the mysterious bowels of Liver/pool is clearly as illegitimate as daughters are in a patrilineal culture. He speaks, moreover, a kind of animal-like gibberish which, together with his foreign swarthiness, causes sensible Nelly to refer to him at first as an "it," implying (despite his apparent maleness) a deep inability to get his gender straight. His "it-ness" or id-ness emphasizes, too, both his snarling animal qualities—his appetites, his brutality—and his thingness. And the fact that he speaks gibberish suggests the profound alienation of the physical/natural/female realm he represents from language, culture's tool and the glory of "spirits Masculine." In even the most literal way, then, he is what Elaine Showalter calls "a woman's man," a male figure into which a female artist projects in disguised form her own anxieties about her sex and its meaning in her society. Indeed, if Nelly Dean is Milton's cook, Heathcliff incarnates that unregenerate natural world which must be metaphorically cooked or spiritualized, and therefore a raw kind of femaleness that, Brontë shows, has to be exorcised if it cannot be controlled.

In most human societies the great literal and figurative chefs, from Brillat-Savarin to Milton, are males, but as Sherry Ortner has noted, everyday "cooking" (meaning such low-level conversions from nature to culture as child-rearing, pot-making, bread-baking) is done by women, who are in effect charged with the task of policing the realm they represent. This point may help explain how and why Catherine Earnshaw becomes Heathcliff's "soul." After Nelly as archetypal housekeeper finishes nursing him, high-spirited Catherine takes over his education because he meets her needs for power. Their relationship works so well, however, because just as he provides her with an extra body to lessen her female vulnerability, so she fills his need for a soul, a voice, a language with which to address cultured men like Edgar. Together they constitute an autonomous and androgynous (or, more accurately, gynandrous) whole: a woman's man and a woman *for herself* in Sartre's sense, making up one complete woman. So complete do they feel, in fact, that as we have seen they define their home at Wuthering Heights as a heaven, and themselves as a sort of Blakeian angel, as if sketching out the definition of an angel D. H. Lawrence would have Tom Brangwen offer seventy-five years later in *The Rainbow:*

> "If we've got to be Angels, and if there is no such thing as a man nor a woman amongst them, then...a married couple makes one Angel....For...an Angel can't be less than a human being. And if it was only the soul of a man *minus* the man, then it would be less than a human being."

That the world—particularly Lockwood, Edgar, and Isabella—sees the heaven of Wuthering Heights as a "hell" is further evidence of the hellish femaleness that characterizes this gynandrous body and soul. It is early evidence, too, that without his "soul" Heathcliff will become an entirely diabolical brute, a "Ghoul" or "Afreet." Speculating seriocomically that women have souls "only to make them capable of *Damnation*," John Donne articulated the traditional complex of ideas underlying this point even before Milton did. "Why hath the common opinion afforded women souls?" Donne asked. After all, he noted, women's only really "spiritual" quality is their power of speech, "for which they are beholding to their *bodily instruments:* For perchance an *Oxes* heart, or a *Goates,* or a *Foxes,* or a *Serpents* would speak just so, if it were in the *breast,* and could move that *tongue* and *jawes.*" Though speaking of women, he might have been defining the problem Isabella was to articulate for Emily Brontë: "Is Mr. Heathcliff a *man?* Or what is he?"

As we have already seen, when Catherine is first withdrawn from the adolescent Heathcliff, the boy becomes increasingly brutish, as if to foreshadow his eventual soullessness. Returning in her ladylike costume from Thrushcross Grange, Catherine finds her one-time "counterpart" in old clothes covered with "mire and dirt," his face and hands "dismally beclouded" by dirt that suggests his inescapable connection with the filthiness of nature. Similarly, when Catherine is dying Nelly is especially conscious that Heathcliff "gnashed . . . and foamed like a mad dog," so that she does not feel as if he is a creature of her own species (chap. 15). Still later, after his "soul's" death, it seems to her that Heathcliff howls "not like a man, but like a savage beast getting goaded to death with knives and spears" (chap. 16). His subsequent conduct, though not so overtly animal-like, is consistent with such behavior. Bastardly and dastardly, a true son of the bitch goddess Nature, throughout the second half of *Wuthering Heights* Heathcliff pursues a murderous revenge against patriarchy, a revenge most appropriately expressed by *King Lear's* equally outcast Edmund: "Well, then,/Legitimate Edgar, I must have your land." For Brontë's revisionary genius manifests itself especially in her perception of the deep connections among Shakespeare's Edmund, Milton's Satan, Mary Shelley's monster, the demon lover/animal groom figure of innumerable folktales—and Eve, the original rebellious female.

Because he unites characteristics of all these figures in a single body, Heathcliff in one way or another acts like all of them throughout the second half of *Wuthering Heights.* His general aim in this part of the novel is to wreak the revenge of nature upon culture by subverting legitimacy. Thus, like Edmund (and Edmund's female counterparts Goneril and Regan) he literally *takes* the *place* of one legitimate heir after another, supplanting both Hindley and Hareton at the Heights, and— eventually—Edgar at the Grange. Moreover, he not only replaces legitimate culture but in his rage strives like Frankenstein's monster to end it. His attempts at killing Isabella and Hindley, as well as the infanticidal tendencies expressed in his merciless abuse of his own son, indicate his desire not only to alter the ways of his world but literally to dis-continue them, to get at the heart of patriarchy by stifling the line of descent that ultimately gives culture its legitimacy. Lear's "*hysterica passio,*" his sense that he is being smothered by female nature, which has inexplicably risen against all fathers everywhere, is seriously parodied, therefore, by the suffocating womb/ room of death where Heathcliff locks up his sickly son and legitimate Edgar's daughter. Like Satan, whose fall was originally inspired by envy of the celestial legitimacy incarnated in the Son of God, Heathcliff steals or perverts birthrights. Like Eve and her double, Sin, he undertakes such crimes against a Urizenic heaven in order to vindicate his own worth, assert his own energy. And again, like Satan, whose hellish kingdom is a shadowy copy of God's luminous one, or like those suavely unregenerate animal grooms Mr. Fox and Bluebeard, he manages to achieve a great deal because he realizes that in order to subvert legitimacy he must first impersonate it; that is, to kill patriarchy, he must first pretend to be a patriarch.

Put another way, this simply means that Heathcliff's charismatic maleness is at least in part a result of his understanding that he must defeat on its own terms the society that has defeated him. Thus, though he began his original gynandrous life at Wuthering Heights as Catherine's whip, he begins his transformed, soulless or Satanic life there as Isabella's bridal hook. Similarly, throughout the extended maneuvers against Edgar and his daughter which occupy him for the twenty years between Isabella's departure and his own death, he impersonates a "devil daddy," stealing children like Catherine II and Linton from their rightful homes, trying to separate Milton's cook from both her story and her morality, and perverting the innocent Hareton into an artificially blackened copy of himself. His understanding of the inauthenticity of his behavior is consistently shown by his irony. Heathcliff knows perfectly well that he is not really a father in the true (patriarchal) sense of the word, if only because he has himself no *sur*name; he is simply acting like a father, and his bland, amused "I want my children about me to be sure" (chap. 29) comments upon the world he despises by sardonically mimicking it, just as Satan mimics God's logic and Edmund mimics Gloucester's astrologic.

On the one hand, therefore, as Linton's deathly father, Heathcliff, like Satan, is truly the father of death (begotten, however, not upon Sin but upon silliness), but on the other hand he is very consciously a mock father, a male version of the terrible devouring mother, whose blackly comic admonitions to Catherine II ("No more runnings away! . . . I'm come to fetch you home, and I hope you'll be a dutiful daughter, and not encourage my son to further disobedience" [chap. 29]) evoke the black hilarity of hell with their satire of Miltonic righteousness. Given the complexity of all this, it is no wonder Nelly considers his abode at the Heights "an oppression past explaining."

Since Heathcliff's dark energies seem so limitless, why does his vengeful project fail? Ultimately, no doubt, it fails because in stories of the war between nature and culture nature always fails. But that point is of course a tautology. Culture tells the story (that is, the story is a cultural construct) and the story is etiological: how culture triumphed over nature, where parsonages and tea-parties came from, how the lady got her skirts—and her deserts. Thus Edmund, Satan, Frankenstein's monster, Mr. Fox, Bluebeard, Eve, and Heathcliff all must fail in one way or another, if only to explain the status quo. Significantly, however, where Heathcliff's analogs are universally destroyed by forces outside themselves, Heathcliff seems to be killed, as Catherine was, by something within himself. His death from self-starvation makes his function as Catherine's almost identical double definitively clear. Interestingly, though, when we look closely at the events leading up to his death it becomes equally clear that Heathcliff is not just killed by his own despairing desire for his vanished "soul" but at least in part by another one of Catherine's parallels, the new and cultivated Catherine who has been reborn through the intervention of patri-archy in the form of Edgar Linton. It is no accident, certainly, that Catherine II's imprisonment at the Heights and her rapprochement with Hareton coincide with Heathcliff's perception that "there is a strange change approaching," with his vision of the lost Catherine, and with his development of an eating disorder very much akin to Catherine's anorexia nervosa.

    —SANDRA M. GILBERT AND SUSAN GUBAR, "Looking Oppositely: Emily Brontë's
       Bible of Hell," *The Madwoman in the Attic: The Woman Writer and the
       Nineteenth-Century Literary Imagination* (New Haven: Yale University Press,
                                      1979), pp. 293–98

DONALD D. STONE

Whether Emily Brontë intended her hero to be judged from the moral point of view that her sister applied to Rochester in *Jane Eyre* has never been resolved satisfactorily. Charlotte Brontë had no doubt about Heathcliff's "unredeemed" nature, but she suggested in her Preface to *Wuthering Heights* that Emily "did not know what she had done" when she created him, that her sister had acted under the force of a creative inspiration that had rendered her passive during the act of writing. No English novel has inspired such a diversity of interpretations as *Wuthering Heights;* and Heathcliff in particular has been viewed as an anarchic force of nature, a mythic figure thrust into the real world, a Byronic-derived Satanic outcast, a Marxist proletarian-rebel, a representation of the Freudian Id, and a reflection of the heroine's adolescent narcissism. One is tempted to suggest that the novel's popularity is in large part the result of its oblique allusions and its unwritten pas-sages, those dealing, for example, with Heathcliff's origins or motivations, which later readers have interpreted or supplied themselves to suit their own interests. There is much to pity in Heathcliff's youthful deprivation; but as is the case with Bulwer's similarly bereft heroes, there is also something childish about his diabolical antics (such as hanging his wife Isabella's pet dog), something of the smell of Byronic greasepaint about his physiognomy ("A half-civilized ferocity lurked yet in the depressed brows and eyes, full of black fire"). A number of Victorian critics, in consequence, judged Heathcliff and his companions in the novel as representatives of "the brutalizing influence of unchecked passion . . .[,] a commentary on the truth that there is no tyranny in the world like that which thoughts of evil exercise in the daring and reckless breast" (anonymous review in *Britannia*). In this reading, Heath-cliff is analogous to Bertha in *Jane Eyre:* not a hero, but a warning example of the self-destructiveness of the unregulated will. But where Charlotte Brontë deliber-ately put her characters into a moral context, her sister seems to have thought less in terms of conventional morality than of aesthetic logic—of the relations of her characters to literature rather than to life.

    One is tempted to say that *Wuthering Heights* is the Bulwer Lytton novel that Bulwer himself lacked the genius to write. It has many of Bulwer's stocks in trade:

self-willed characters, supernatural occurrences, charged romantic landscapes, a love that transcends death. Within a Bulwer novel the description of Heathcliff's rage following Cathy's death would seem appropriate and properly absurd: "He dashed his head against the knotted trunk; and, lifting his eyes, howled, not like a man, but like a savage beast getting goaded to death with knives and spears." (One recalls the similarly thwarted Castruccio Cesarini's mad fits, in *Ernest Maltrevers,* or the desolation of Falkland after Lady Mandeville's death.) Emily Brontë's triumph was that she went over the same Byronic terrain—"a perfect misanthropist's heaven," as Lockwood describes it—as that followed by Bulwer, and yet avoided making her story seem like the stuff of parody. Bulwer's fiction proves that *Wuthering Heights* is not the great romantic exception among English novels, as was once thought to be the case; yet Emily Brontë had a sense of humor and a conviction that were denied Bulwer. However literary her characters may be in their origins, she believed in them sufficiently to make later readers accept their melodramatic rantings as the echoes of some primal force of reality.

> —DONALD D. STONE, "Introduction" to *The Romantic Impulse in Victorian Fiction* (Cambridge, MA: Harvard University Press, 1980), pp. 42–43

ELIZABETH R. NAPIER

The relationship between Catherine and Heathcliff is the most overt expression of Brontë's sense that character is not determinate, that individuals may achieve a state of radical identification through the breakdown of boundaries of the self. Cathy's confession to Nelly dramatically presents this view:

> ". . . he's more myself than I am. Whatever our souls are made of, his and mine are the same, and Linton's is as different as a moonbeam from lightning or frost from fire. . . ."
> ". . . What were the use of my creation if I were entirely contained here? . . . my great thought in living is himself. If all else perished, and *he* remained, I should still continue to be; and, if all else remained, and he were annihilated, the Universe would turn to a mighty stranger. . . . Nelly, I *am* Heathcliff—he's always, always in my mind—not as a pleasure, any more than I am always a pleasure to myself—but as my own being. . . ."

Heathcliff, in a similar manner, calls Catherine his "life" (p. 132). "Catherine," he says, "you know that I could as soon forget you as my existence!" Heathcliff tells Cathy that in breaking her own heart, she has broken his; and after her death, he cries out to Nelly, "it is unutterable! I *cannot* live without my life! I *cannot* live without my soul!" Such persistent equations between Catherine and Heathcliff suggest an idea of character that is different in fundamental ways from the eighteenth-century notion of the person as a discrete and separate being. It may express, as J. Hillis Miller has argued, a desire of the self to fuse with something outside it in order to achieve a more profound sense of unity. It is, clearly, a view which exposes a strong urge toward fusion (a drive which Miller connects with but does not limit to the relationship of the created soul to God). Brontë's *Wuthering Heights* in part explores the consequences of such a concept of the self.

When Heathcliff speaks of "absorbing" Cathy and "dissolving" with her (when Linton comes to the grave, he says, he will no longer know "which is which"), he is alluding not simply to the all-encompassing quality of his love, but to a procedure of identification and merging which encompasses and annihilates the individual self. A pattern of merging and absorbing repeatedly marks Catherine's later conversations and confrontations with Heathcliff. Life, death, and murder, most particularly, become desires between which Catherine can no longer distinguish. During her fever, a yearning for her own death mingles unhappily with a wish to be loved and a desire for the death of Linton:

> "Oh, I will die," she exclaimed, "since no one cares anything about me. I wish I had not taken that."
> Then a good while after I heard her murmur—
> "No, I'll not die—he'd be glad—he does not love me at all—he would never miss me!" . . .
> "If I were only sure it would kill him," she interrupted, "I'd kill myself directly!"

Cathy's plea for freedom ("Open the window again wide, fasten it open!") becomes, in a similar gesture of paradox, inextricable from her desire for death:

> ". . . Quick, why don't you move?"
> "Because I won't give you your death of cold," I answered.
> "You won't give me a chance of life, you mean," she said sullenly. . . .
> And sliding from the bed before I could hinder her, she crossed the room, walking very uncertainly, threw it back, and bent out, careless of the frosty air that cut about her shoulders as keen as a knife.

In Catherine's last conversation with Heathcliff, the language of love merges with that of murder and death. "I wish I could hold you," Catherine says bitterly, "till we were both dead!" "*Why* did you betray your own heart, Cathy?" Heathcliff returns. "I have not one word of comfort. You deserve this. You have killed yourself." The complex mixture of self-recrimination, accusation, and passion in this scene reveals the extent to which, in the course of the novel, normal categories of thought have become inverted. Death has become equatable with life, love with murder. The destructive confusion is, in part, the natural extension of Catherine's confession to Nelly, "I *am* Heathcliff." In willfully eradicating the boundaries of the self, Heathcliff and Catherine have become involved in a kind of negative unity in which the usual protective barriers of the self no longer operate. Cathy's self-betrayal must thus by definition lead to her own destruction and the destruction of Heathcliff: "I have not broken your heart—" Heathcliff tells her, "—*you* have broken it—and in breaking it, you have broken mine."

Brontë is dealing here not only with the violence of frustrated passion, but with the chaos which emerges when the boundaries of the self break down. Heathcliff is so unable to separate himself from Cathy that he demands haunting and torment over separation: "Be with me always—take any form—drive me mad! only *do* not leave me in this abyss, where I cannot find you! Oh, God! it is unutterable! I *cannot* live without my life! I *cannot* live without my soul!" The exaggerated inability of Catherine and Heathcliff to maintain distance from each other is simultaneously the cause for the intensity of their passion and the destructiveness of that passion. Like *Jane Eyre, Wuthering Heights* gradually evolves into a novel of and advocating distances, Hareton and Cathy "correcting" and at the same time "defusing" the relationship of Heathcliff and Catherine.

—ELIZABETH R. NAPIER, "The Problem of Boundaries in *Wuthering Heights*," *Philological Quarterly* 63, No. I (Winter 1984): 101–3

U. C. KNOEPFLMACHER

Who and *what* is Heathcliff? The question is asked by both Nelly and Isabella. Although Heathcliff is a character in his own right, he is as much the product of animated desire as that nameless sufferer from gender-bifurcations, the Frankenstein Monster. Shelley's creature, fashioned from the tissue of dead men (and women?), is an "it" until converted to male sadism. The boy whom old Earnshaw presents as an "it" is so denominated by Nelly no less than seventeen times until "he" is christened with a dead infant's name that "has served *him* ever since" (ch. 4). "Heathcliff" (the very name, like "Frankenstein," combining openness with hardness) thus exists, I would contend, essentially as part of a relation, first between child/parent and then, more intensely, of boy/girl selves. He is a metaphor made literal, enfleshed. Shaped by a world in which children must grow up and assume rigid identities, he feels betrayed. Only by returning into the metaphoric realm of essences into which Catherine precedes him can he confirm her credo: "I cannot express it," she had told Nelly; "but surely you and everybody have a notion that there is, or should be, an existence beyond you" (ch. 9). It seems hard not to hear Emily Brontë's own accents in this and similar utterances by Catherine and Heathcliff. For *Wuthering Heights* registers, among other things, her disagreement with the two sisters who had come to accept their containment in a reality like Nelly Dean's.

What, then, is Heathcliff/Catherine? Their fusion, separation, and reintegration is cast through the form of kinship most frequently found in this novel of repetitions and redoublings, that of a brother and a sister. There are no less than six brother/sister pairs if we include cousins and foster-siblings:

literal	*metaphoric*	*literal/metaphoric:*
Hindley/Catherine	CATHERINE/HEATHCLIFF	Linton Heathcliff/Cathy
Edgar/Isabella	Nelly/Hindley	HARETON/CATHY

A seventh pair might be added to the other six in the shape of Nelly and Heathcliff. Whether or not these two outsiders are actually Old Earnshaw's illegitimate children is irrelevant. As Hindley's foster-sister and Catherine's foster-brother, the novel's main opponents automatically become each other's foster-siblings.

We have noted that the Hareton/Cathy marriage with which the "Earnshaw Chronicle" ends condenses Catherine's relations to her two "brothers," Heathcliff and Hindley; the union between Nelly's prime nursling and her foster-brother's son also produces a consummation, once removed, between Nelly and Hindley. Edgar and Isabella, that other alienated pair of siblings, can be said to "marry" each other through the brief union of their children, when Cathy becomes Linton Heathcliff's bride, in what can also be considered as still another surrogate espousal between Heathcliff and Catherine. The permutations of this central metaphor of fusing and diffusing brother/sister selves so overwhelm us by their variety that we give our relieved assent to the final contractions of Cathy/Hareton and Catherine/Heathcliff.

If, as I have been suggesting, Emily Brontë's fable of childhood lost and regained stems from her desire to reassert the violated imaginative oneness she once shared with her siblings, it seems unclear at first why she would not have chosen to portray her four children, as her sister Charlotte did in *Jane Eyre,* as three sisters and one brother. In her own tale about a disempowered Cinderella, Charlotte twice situates Jane into a domestic foursome. As a child, Jane is rejected by her Reed cousins, Eliza, Georgiana, and John, the offspring of her mother's brother; as an adult, however she is welcomed by her Rivers cousins, Diana, Mary, and St. John, the children of her father's sister. Both the grotesque John Reed and the handsome St. John are unacceptable as sexual partners. For, unlike Cathy (who finds happiness through Hareton), Jane must wed someone who is not a blood relation. The taint of incest that in some societies still attaches to the marriage of cousins thus can be safely avoided. Charlotte, after all, wants to invest Jane with social, rather than primitive or asocial, powers. Emily, on the other hand, invests Heathcliff's abdication of all power with the same intense pleasure Jane experiences after she gains control over her maimed lover. Jane's erotic passion for Rochester, sanctioned only after his crippling, manifests itself in Emily's novel only when Heathcliff becomes free to make love to a sisterly ghost. In this sense, *Wuthering Heights* and *Jane Eyre* are affirmations of exactly contrary realities.

—U. C. KNOEPFLMACHER, "The Meanings of *Wuthering Heights,*" *Emily Brontë: Wuthering Heights* (Cambridge: Cambridge University Press, 1989), pp. 96–98

LYN PYKETT

For many readers Heathcliff is not only the central male character but also one of the central challenges of this novel. He is the man with no name, the stranger, who is in some ways less a character than a question or series of questions.

'Is Mr. Heathcliff a man? If so, is he mad? And if not, is he a devil?'

'Is he a ghoul, or a vampire?'

Isabella's and Nelly's questions have been echoed by generations of readers and critics, many of whom have seen Heathcliff as the novel's central enigma and the key to its meaning. Graham Holderness offers the most succinct version of this point of view when he asserts,

> Heathcliff is really the central problem of *Wuthering Heights:* our valuation of him determines our sense of what the novel is about.

Terry Eagleton illuminates the nature of the problem in his equally crisp assertion that,

> No mere critical hair-splitting can account for the protracted debate over whether Heathcliff is hero or demon.

In Eagleton's reading Heathcliff is the novel's dominant figure. Heathcliff is also at the centre of Arnold Kettle's account, which presents him as the legitimate rebel against a repressive social order, a 'moral force' who 'wins our sympathy [because] we know he is on the side of humanity', and who retains that sympathy even at his worst because 'we recognize a rough moral justice in what he has done to his oppressors'. Similarly Eagleton sees Heathcliff as a protean figure who stands at the centre of the text and draws all its threads into his person. Heathcliff is at once hero and villain, the oppressed and the oppressor, who is simultaneously the bearer of the novel's progressive forces and the embodiment of its contradictions.

In fact the shifting complexities of Heathcliff's class positions almost defy description. He enters the yeoman-farmer Earnshaw family as a *déclassé* outsider. Old Mr. Earnshaw's attempts to incorporate him into this particular social order are thwarted by Hindley's efforts to 'reduce him to his right place' by withdrawing education, separating him from Catherine, and making him live and work as a servant. Heathcliff's repetition of this process in his own degradation of Hareton makes explicit the systematic brutality and oppression which is implicit in the prevailing social order. During his disappearance from the Heights Heathcliff mysteriously acquires both culture and capital, and when he re-enters the Earnshaw and Linton families the oppressed has become the oppressor. Heathcliff's dynastic and property ambitions do not represent an attempt to become absorbed into the dominant social class, nor do they offer a threat to the existing social structure. He seeks simply to occupy the place of the dominant social class, and to change his own and his heir's position within the existing system of power relations.

> 'I want the triumph of seeing *my* descendant fairly lord of their estates; my child hiring their children to till their fathers' lands for wages.'

Heathcliff's demonic energy is not only associated with social and economic aggression, but also persistently threatens to disrupt the sexual, familial and cultural order. Psychoanalytic critics tend to associate this disruptive energy with 'libidinal desire' (Leo Bersani), or 'libidinal drive' and 'phallic energy' (James Kavanagh). Kavanagh, for example, sees Heathcliff's 'primitive sexual-social energy' as unleashing an 'anarchy of desire', which is the driving force of a narrative whose key events are: Heathcliff's disruption of Earnshaw family stability, and his 'seduction of the daughter' of the family; his disruption of the Linton family, and his 'seduction' of both the wife (Catherine) and daughter/sister (Isabella); his monomaniac plans to acquire the lands and homes of both the Earnshaw and Linton families, and his abduction of the Linton daughter.

Heathcliff's threat to the institution of the family is sometimes seen as a clash between raw natural forces and the cultural order of custom, tradition and form. However, this view of Heathcliff tends to over-simplify the character and the novel, both of which represent multiple contradictions rather than a dualistic struggle of clearly opposed forces. Moreover, although the novel persistently associates Heathcliff with the primitive forces of nature, it also focuses on the way in which he is produced by, and operates within, a specific social and cultural order.

Many of those critics who see Heathcliff as the embodiment of natural or primitive libidinal desire, as a pre-social being, or as a rebel against a decadent and repressive social order, also see him as the novel's sole representative of authenticity and essential humanity. The usual, though by no means inevitable, consequence of this view is the marginalisation of almost every other character in the novel, particularly the two Catherines and Hareton. Eagleton, for example, gives a full and sympathetic account of Heathcliff's struggle with the culture which seeks to contain him, and whose contradictions he embodies, but he is relatively uninterested in the details of Catherine's predicament and what it signifies, particularly the problems of gender politics which it raises. In Eagleton's version Catherine is simply the refuser of the bounty of Heathcliff's proffered gift.

> What Heathcliff offers Cathy is a non- or pre-social relationship, as the only authentic form of living in a world of exploitation and inequality, a world where one must refuse to measure oneself by the criteria of the class-structure.

In the sexual politics of this account Heathcliff is the bearer of meaning and value, while Catherine is the empty vessel which might be filled with the content of Heathcliff's moral and ideological message.

It is perhaps time to remove Heathcliff from his lonely position as the centre of the novel's meaning and value. We need to move beyond viewing this character as the single embodiment of the novel's social and sexual contradictions, and to view him instead as part of a pattern of relationships which figure those contradictions: contradictions which derive not only from class relations but from the social construction of gender and gender relations in a class society. I have tried to make such a move in earlier chapters by focusing attention on the two Catherines and Nelly, on the significance of the novel's narrative patterns and its adaptations of different fictional genres. In particular I have tried to show how *Wuthering Heights* uses its female characters and its generational structure to investigate the contradictory and changing pressures which shape ideas of gender, determine forms of familial and social life, and delimit the horizons of the imaginable.

It is important to reinsert Heathcliff into this complex of fictional relations. It is also useful to see this towering character in the context of a spectrum of male characters, by means of which the novel investigates and explores the social and cultural production of various masculinities. At one end of the spectrum is the motherless Heathcliff, all libidinal desire and phallic energy, the social outsider who is happiest when roaming the moors and who acquires the refinements of the drawing room for purely strategic purposes. At the other end of the spectrum is his son, Linton, whose natural habitat is the drawing room. Brought up exclusively by his mother, Linton Heathcliff is a sickly, enervated youth, the hypersensitive product of an over-refined culture.

Hindley occupies a place at the Heathcliffian end of the spectrum and, like Heathcliff, is both aggressive and competitive, although insecurely so. It is interesting to note that Hindley, like Heathcliff, is only fitfully subject to feminine influences, and that his brief marriage, ostensibly his most social period during which he actively cultivates a genteel domestic existence, is also a period of fierce domestic tyranny which excludes and oppresses Heathcliff and Catherine. Joseph, a dour, ascetic, misogynist is also placed at the Heathcliffian end of the spectrum. He is particularly closely identified with the Heights as masculine domain, and it is significant that he is left as its sole curator at the end of the novel's action.

At the Linton end of the spectrum Edgar is placed next to his nephew as a 'feminised' male, and he shares something of his nephew's nervous emotionalism, peevishness, and passivity. Edgar is, however, a more complex creation than Linton, and it is facile to dismiss him, as many critics have, as a mere milksop who offers Catherine a hollow, sterile gentility in place of the socially subversive authenticity offered by Heathcliff. Edgar is the benevolent face of patriarchy, although the family over which he presides is no less repressive and controlling than the other families in the novel. Edgar is a passive patriarch who exercises power without responsibility. When his authority is challenged he withdraws: when Catherine challenges him over Heathcliff, he withdraws to the library; when Isabella goes away with Heathcliff, he simply relinquishes all responsibility for her. However, he is not entirely selfish, and he has, at least, the virtues of gentleness and tenderness, as is shown in his care of Catherine in the later stages of her illness, in his devotion to his daughter, and in Nelly's commendation of him as a kind master. Edgar's relative virtues are revealed in the novel's comparison of the way in which three of the male characters respond to 'widowhood': Hindley becomes a ferocious drunk who threatens to murder his servant, and who almost kills his own child; Heathcliff succumbs to an excess of passion before steeling himself to his grim, self-appointed task of avenging himself on Catherine's family; Edgar, on the other hand, becomes a devoted—if over-indulgent and over-protective—father, who retreats from society and social duty, relinquishing his office of magistrate for a life of seclusion in his library.

However, it is Hareton who perhaps occupies the most interesting position towards the centre of this spectrum of male characters. Although he is represented with less imaginative power than Heathcliff, Hareton nevertheless occupies a central position in the novel's investigation of the construction of gendered subjects. As with most of the other characters Emily Brontë focuses on the unique set of social and genetic determinants which produce and reproduce Hareton. He is the son of a frail and passive mother of unknown social origin, and a weak but aggressive father whose position in the social and familial hierarchy is persistently threatened. In addition to his natural parents Hareton is also given a range of surrogate parents, who attempt to shape him according to their own needs and desires. In a sense Hareton's upbringing becomes the focus for a battle between contesting masculine and feminine forces. First, Nelly vies with a progressively brutalised Hindley to bring Hareton up according to her perceptions of what is suitable for a child of his social position. Nelly's efforts are systematically undone by Heathcliff, who seeks to reproduce in Hareton his own degradation by Hindley. This attempted reduction of Hareton to a state of crude nature is assisted by Joseph, who also contests, but is unable to resist, Hareton's final reconstruction under the feminine influence of Cathy and Nelly.

If we see Hareton as occupying the central position in the novel's spectrum of masculinities, and if in addition we see his character as the site of a struggle between contending masculine and feminine forces, we begin to move beyond the common view of Hareton as Heathcliff's textual shadow and surrogate, a pale imitation of Heathcliff who lacks his libidinal energy and socially subversive insurgence. Heathcliff claims Hareton as 'a personification of my youth . . . the ghost of my immortal love, my wild endeavor to hold my right, my degradation, my pride, my happiness, and my anguish'. But the novel as a whole offers a view of Hareton as the ghost revivified. The Hareton of the novel's concluding section is not a Heathcliff emasculated, but a Heathcliff socialized and feminised, and hence a Heathcliff whose energies become enabling and operative, rather than repressive and restrictive.

In its male characters, as well as in other aspects of its characterisation and structure, *Wuthering Heights* experimentally separates out and puts into opposition the realms of culture and nature, the socially constructed categories of the masculine and the feminine—and the men and women who inhabit them—and libidinal desire and socialized sexuality. Ultimately, in the figure of Hareton and in his relationship with Cathy, the novel provides a new fusion which partially resolves these oppositions, but it does so only by moving beyond prevailing social norms. As the novel approaches its incomplete closure, the masculine and feminine domains are fused, and nature (whose brutal potentialities have been exposed in the course of the narrative) is accommodated within a feminised culture. However, although socialised, the energies dramatised and explored in the novel do not become fully social. Although Hareton and Cathy establish a relationship of model mutuality which displaces the versions of the patriarchal family found in the first generation story, they will form their household away from the Heights, and indeed removed from the wider social world, in the private domestic enclosure of the Grange.

Wuthering Heights thus moves towards a workable centre, but it does not erase all its other elements in the process. While Heathcliff is not the single key which will unlock the novel's meanings, he nevertheless remains as a crucial strand in its network of relationships. On one level, as Miriam Allott has suggested,

Wuthering Heights rejects Heathcliff, and Hareton is one of the vehicles of his displacement. However, although he is displaced, Heathcliff is not expelled from the text. In Heathcliff's powerful fictional presence, and his persistence in the narrative in spirit form, the novel acknowledges both the force of libidinal desire and its continuing and inevitable challenge to the necessary repressions of civilization. The profoundly ideological nature of its own narrative resolutions, the contradictions embodied and explored in the figure of Heathcliff, as in many other aspects of this complex novel, remain to trouble the momentary equilibrium of narrative closure.

—LYN PYKETT, "The Male Part of the Poem," Emily Brontë (Savage, MD:
Barnes & Noble, 1989), pp. 112–20

CRITICAL ESSAYS

Miriam Allott

THE REJECTION
OF HEATHCLIFF?

I

The influence of Lord David Cecil's analysis of *Wuthering Heights* in *Early Victorian Novelists* (1934) does not necessarily imply a simple approval of the total meaning he ascribes to the book.

Cecil's main contentions about the principles of storm and calm and their relationship to each other in the novel are the following. First, they are 'not conflicting': they are to be thought of either as separate aspects of a pervading spirit or as component parts of a harmony. Second, they are not in themselves destructive. If in life they become so, it is because 'in the cramped condition of their earthly incarnation these principles are diverted from following the course that their nature indicates . . . the calm becomes a source of weakness . . . the storm a source not of fruitful vigour but disturbance . . . even in this world their discords are transitory . . .' Third, the system composed of the balance of these opposites can only be subject to temporary interruptions because it is self-righting. It operates to restore the equilibrium which is momentarily lost. Of the stormy Earnshaws and the Linton 'children of calm', Cecil asserts, 'Together each group, following its own sphere, combines to compose a cosmic harmony. It is the destruction and the re-establishment of this harmony which is the theme of the story.' These are the conclusions drawn by Cecil from his study of the novel. If they are accepted as self-evident, an interpretation of *Wuthering Heights* can be made which does justice to many elements of Emily Brontë's art, but at the same time the pattern of the novel suffers distortion, and much has to be overlooked.

Indeed the whole structure of the novel suggests a deeper and more compulsive concern with the elements of 'storm' than this reading allows for. As everyone has noticed, Emily Brontë extends her themes into the story of a second

From *Emily Brontë:* Wuthering Heights: *A Casebook*, edited by Miriam Allott (London: Macmillan Press, 1970; rev. ed. 1992), pp. 166–80. An earlier version of this essay appeared in *Essays in Criticism* 8, No. 1 (January 1958): 27–47.

generation of Earnshaws and Lintons; Cecil himself comments on the way in which she uses her two generations to illustrate contrasts between 'calm' and 'storm', and to reveal the workings of inherited characteristics. But most remarkable about the second generation story is the effort it makes to modify the 'storm-calm' opposition in such a way as to eliminate the most violent and troubling elements that give the first generation story its peculiar intensity. She substitutes for the violent Cathy-Edgar-Heathcliff relationships of the first part the milder Catherine-Linton-Hareton relationships of the second; and she alters the earlier savage Hindley-Heathcliff relationship (of victimiser and embittered victim) into the more temperate Heathcliff-Hareton relationship (where the tyrant has some feeling for his victim, while the victim himself remains loving and unembittered). Hindley's savage and destructive grief for his wife, Frances, and Heathcliff's frenzy at Cathy's death, reappear as Edgar's deep but quiet grief for the same Cathy, and as Hareton's 'strong grief' for Heathcliff—a grief 'which springs naturally from a generous heart, though it be tough as tempered steel'. Again, while Emily Brontë replaces the wildness of the first generation story by a quality of energy in the second generation which is more normal and human, she also shows us in the second generation a demoralizing extreme of calm. Thus Heathcliff, the epitome of 'storm', fathers Linton, who takes 'Linton' qualities, inherited from Isabella, to their furthest point of lethargic inaction.

Seen in this way, the book describes two nearly symmetrical 'arcs'. The first bears us on through the violence of Catherine's and Heathcliff's obsessional feelings for each other, and through the stress of their relationships with the Lintons, to end in a mood of doubtful equipoise (for the spirits, apparently united and at rest, lie near the bare moors, and in the rain and darkness they still 'walk'). The other 'arc', also passing through stress, ends in the quiet of the valley. The two arcs suggest that the novel is an effort to explore and, *if possible*, to reconcile conflicting 'attractions'. In the story of the first generation the clash of these opposites is worked out in terms of a strong emotional commitment to the values of storm. What does such a commitment in all its furthest implications really entail?—this is the question Emily Brontë, with her unsentimental honesty, seems to ask. The answer is troubling. The second part of the novel examines an alternative commitment and poses another question: if storm-values are dangerous or undesirable, what is the nature of the calm that one must try to accept in the place of storm? For example, are we to accept calm if it implies a universe like Linton's, in which men and women are only 'half alive'?

The book's extraordinary power derives at least in part, then, from an attempt to do justice to the conflicting demands of heart and head. Powerful emotions lie with Heathcliff (or 'storm', or 'earth in its harsher aspects'—whichever of these labels one prefers). But Heathcliff is ultimately a dark and troubling image. Everything suggests that so far from 'union . . . with its affinity' being, as Lord David Cecil suggests, a means to harmony, such a union is, in fact, an ominous conception, generating images of 'darkness' and 'storm' from the first, and gathering increasingly disquieting associations the more it is contemplated. Here one must add that Emily

Brontë would probably have rejected Lord David Cecil's comment that her out-look concerned itself 'not with moral standards, but with those conditioning forces of life in which the naive erections of the human mind that we call moral standards are built up'. They were certainly not 'naive erections' to her. Indeed the second generation story seems to result from a ruthlessly determined effort to supersede Heathcliff and everything identified with the harsher, more destructive aspects of 'storm'—we learn from Charlotte how strong Emily's will could be,[1] and head would have had no success in the conflict of heart and head if her will had been weak or vacillating. I am stressing here that this is the direction in which the second generation story moves, but also that it finds no permanent solution of the conflict. The rights of feeling, however dark and troubling, are safeguarded, for Heathcliff, defeated in one way, is triumphant in another. Even though he can no longer prevent the happiness of Hareton Earnshaw and the younger Catherine, he 'retains' the deserted Earnshaw property that he has usurped, inhabiting Wuthering Heights and the bare moorland with the elder Catherine.

At the end, then, a certain balance has been achieved. But it is not, as Lord David Cecil claims, an inevitable harmony following Heathcliff's posthumous union with his affinity, Catherine, nor the re-establishment of the balance of forces at the beginning of the book when Lintons and Earnshaws existed harmoniously but in separation. It is, in fact, a balance effected by a new combination of Earnshaws and Lintons, with Earnshaw energy modified by Linton calm. Heathcliff obsessions are excluded. Moreover, in order to achieve the new alliance, the Earnshaws at last abandon their old house; the significance of this departure is stressed by Emily Brontë's emphasis on the inscription over the old door, which Lockwood notices early in the first chapter—'among a wilderness of crumbling griffins and shameless little boys, I detected the date "1500", and the name of "Hareton Earnshaw"'—which the dispossessed Hareton is so pleased to be able to read for himself in chapter 24. After three hundred years the Earnshaws withdraw from Wuthering Heights and come down to Thrushcross Grange, bringing to the valley some of their own energy but also in their turn being modified by the values it represents. The situation at the end of the novel, therefore, is vastly different from the situation at its beginning. The management of the narrative suggests how important the establishment of a balanced relationship between Lintons and Earnshaws was for the novel's bringing about at least a partial resolution of opposites. Through Lock-wood's narrative we are brought to the threshold of the first meeting between the two families in chapter 3, we are carried up to this point again in chapter 6, when Nelly Dean speaks portentously of the consequences of the meeting ('there will more come of this business than you reckon on'), and we look back to its effects in the scenes of Catherine's delirium in chapters 11 and 12. Perhaps the one clear assertion is that for the purposes of ordinary life—and given the special Earnshaw nature—Lintons are better for Earnshaws than Heathcliff is. To that extent, Emily Brontë's novel makes a moral judgement; but whether there is a final commitment to the rejection of Heathcliff is another matter.

The reading here suggested is, I believe, forced on us by the book's structure, but the evidence from structure may be strengthened by noting the different texture of the writing in different parts of the novel. The emotional quality of the first part of the book is quite different from that of the second, and to a great extent it is the compulsive nature of the imagery in the first generation story that contributes to this effect. The prevailing images in the first part of the book are sombre and troubling, those of the second part not only carry less disturbing associations, but in many cases they appear to be frankly contrived, though they remain the product of a creative sensibility which still makes them fresh, vivid, genuinely apt.

II

What this sensibility tried to free itself from when seeking an alternative to Heathcliff is suggested by certain recurrent *motifs* that accompany and emphasise the stormy 'Heathcliff feelings' described in the earlier part of the book. These *motifs* appear at moments of great emotional pressure and bring with them over-tones of violence and the supernatural. Heathcliff is inseparably associated with discord and distress from his first arrival. Because Mr. Earnshaw carries the child Heathcliff in his arms all the way from Liverpool, his own children are deprived of the toys he has promised them—Cathy's whip is lost, Hindley's fiddle crushed—and they immediately set up a clamour and turn against the newcomer. The same early chapter (4) gives us other details that underline the discordant elements in Heath-cliff's nature, and it ends with the savage little incident of the two ponies, which drives Heathcliff and Hindley even further apart. Very early in the novel certain images are linked with the farouche figure of Heathcliff. These tend to recur at crucial phases of the story when Catherine's passion for him is most violently felt.

The recurrent image-pattern first appears in chapter 3, where we are still in the 'present' of 1801. Lockwood, lying in the first Catherine's oak-panelled bed at Wuthering Heights—the bed which is itself a part of the pattern—reads her account of the 'awful Sunday' back in 1777, when, as we learn later (on our return from the 'present' of Lockwood to the past of Nelly Dean's narrative in chapter 6), she and Heathcliff, driven out by Hindley, first came into contact with the Lintons. Lockwood falls into a fitful sleep, disturbed by 'the branch of a fir-tree that touched my lattice, as the blast wailed by, and rattled its dry cones against the panes . . .' [ch. 3]. In his dream he is made to recall his surroundings: 'I was lying in the oak closet, and I heard distinctly the gusty wind, and the driving of snow; I heard, also, the fir-bough repeat its tearing sound . . . and, I thought, I rose and endeavoured to unhasp the casement . . .' [ch. 3]. But the hook is 'soldered into the staple' and he has to smash the glass in order to try to reach 'the importunate branch'. As he does so, his fingers close on the fingers of 'a little ice-cold hand!'

> The intense horror of nightmare came over me: I tried to draw back my arm, but the hand clung to it, and a most melancholy voice sobbed, 'let me in—let me in'. 'Who are you?' I asked, struggling meanwhile to disengage myself.

'Catherine Linton,' it replied, shiveringly . . . 'I'm come home: I'd lost my way on the moor!' As it spoke, I discerned, obscurely, a child's face looking through the window. Terror made me cruel; and finding it useless to attempt shaking the creature off, I pulled its wrist on to the broken pane, and rubbed it to and fro till the blood ran down and soaked the bedclothes: still it wailed, 'let me in!' . . .   [ch. 3]

This 'pattern', then, has physical and mental elements: it includes objects such as the oak-panelled bed, the opened window letting in ice-cold wind from the moors, the fir-tree and its tapping cones, but it also includes sensations, feelings and attitudes linked with them—sensations of pain, feelings of savagery and supernatural awe, notions of exile and imprisonment (which are persistent themes of Emily Brontë's poems). The pattern recurs at important moments in the story when 'Heathcliff' feelings are intensified. It is only once associated with the second Catherine—when she escapes from Wuthering Heights and from Heathcliff through her mother's window and with the help of the fir branch (chapter 38). But the first Catherine's connection with the pattern is very different. At the height of her Linton-Heathcliff torment in chapter 12 Catherine lies delirious on the floor at the Grange. She dreams that she is back in her own old bed at Wuthering Heights, and that she is 'enclosed in the oak-panelled bed at home, and my heart ached with some great grief . . . my misery arose from the separation that Hindley had ordered between me and Heathcliff. I was laid alone for the first time . . .' In the dream we are back once more in 1777, the period Lockwood reads about in Catherine's 'diary', and of which Nelly Dean tells him once more in chapter 6. Catherine is remembering the time when she and Heathcliff, already separated by Hindley, are on the point of being driven even further apart by the Lintons. Still dreaming, she tries to push back the panels of the oak bed, only to find herself touching the table and the carpet at the Grange: 'my late anguish was swallowed in a paroxysm of despair. I cannot say why I was so wildly wretched . . .' Her attempted explanation of this despair, beginning '. . . supposing at twelve years' old I had been wrenched from the Heights . . .', with its associations of exile and longing, recalls the dream she has already recounted in chapter 9, where she imagines herself in heaven, breaking her heart 'with weeping to come back to earth'. The feelings are identical. She tries to conjure up the freedom and atmosphere of Wuthering Heights: 'I'm sure I should be myself were I once among the heather in those hills. Open the window wide . . .' Most of this chapter is taken up with the account of Catherine's delirious fantasies—'she alternatively raves and remains in a half-dream', Nelly Dean tells Dr Kenneth—and her dreams are 'appalling': 'I dread sleeping: my dreams appal me,' she declares. With her dreaming is combined an intense desire to hear and feel once more the cutting north-east wind off the moors. Three times we are confronted with such longings:

'Oh, if I were but in my own bed—in the house!' she went on bitterly, wringing her hands. 'Do let me feel it—it comes straight down the moor—do let me have one breath!'

> To pacify her, I held the casement ajar a few seconds. A cold blast rushed through; I closed it and returned to my post. She lay still now, her face bathed in tears. Exhaustion of spirit had entirely subdued her spirit; and fiery Catherine was no better than a wailing child.

The echo of Lockwood's nightmare is unmistakable, particularly in the final phrase. In the third of these passionate outbursts, Catherine not only recalls the earlier appearances of the image-pattern, but also anticipates its final emergence at the end of the book. Struggling to the window to let in the wind once more, she imagines she sees the old house (we are told both here and in chapter 10 that Wuthering Heights is 'not visible' from the Grange):

> 'Look! . . . that's my room with the candle in it, and the trees swaying before it . . . It's a rough journey, and a sad heart to travel it; and we must pass by Gimmerton Kirk, to go that journey! We've braved its ghosts often together, and dared each other to stand among the graves and ask them to come. But Heathcliff, if I dare you now, will you venture? If you do, I'll keep you. I'll not lie there by myself: they may bury me twelve feet deep, and throw the church down over me, but I won't rest till you are with me. I never will!'

And it is because Heathcliff believes that she does indeed 'walk' that he answers her call at last. Years later, exhausted by his self-inflicted fast and spent with watching for her ghost, Heathcliff finally dies in Catherine's oak-panelled bed, where he lay in anguish after Lockwood's dream at the beginning of the novel (which, it should be remembered, refers to a period not long before the date we finally reach at the end of the story). The window is wide open, and it is now his hand, and not that of the wailing child-ghost, that the lattice has grazed: 'his face and throat were washed with rain; the bedclothes dripped, and he was perfectly still. The lattice, flapping to and fro, had grazed the hand that rested on the sill; no blood trickled from the broken skin . . .' [ch. 34].

When we consider the emotional quality of these scenes, and the nature of the obsession which they indicate, it does not seem difficult to understand why, in spite of a tremendous pull the other way, Emily Brontë attempted a final rejection of 'Heathcliff' by constructing a new order from her judicious combination of 'Lintons' and 'Earnshaws'. Passion for sombre earth—which is identified with Heathcliff, and is the same 'earth' for which in her poem, 'I see around me tombstones grey', Emily Brontë declares she will not exchange the brightest heaven—leads ultimately, it would seem, to the wildness and strangeness of an unhallowed afterlife. Obviously no real compromise is possible with this darkly compelling image: its effects are too strong, acting—to use one of the elder Catherine's metaphors—like 'wine in water' and permanently altering the colour of the mind.

The 'wine in water' metaphor occurs in the strange passage leading up to the account of Catherine's dream about heaven in chapter 9. She has just agreed to marry Edgar Linton, but, believing herself to be alone with Nelly Dean and the infant Hareton, she tries to explain her uneasiness about this decision. Nelly Dean, in attempting to elicit from Catherine the real reason for her uneasiness at accepting Linton, says:

> '... you will escape from a disorderly, comfortless home into a wealthy, respectable one; and you love Edgar, and Edgar loves you. All seems smooth and easy: where is the obstacle?'
>
> *'Here and here!'* replied Catherine, striking one hand on her forehead, and the other on her breast: 'in whichever place the soul lives. In my soul and in my heart, I'm convinced I'm wrong!'

The abnormality of Catherine's feelings is stressed by Nelly's comment, 'That's very strange! I can't make it out,' and by Catherine's reply, 'It's my secret,' and her statement that she cannot 'explain' it 'distinctly', but will try to give Nelly 'a feeling of how I feel'. The atmosphere becomes increasingly tense as Catherine, about to recount her dream, grows 'sadder and graver'. Finally, a 'dream' is told—but Catherine's mood has changed . . . 'I was only going to say that heaven did not seem to be my home; and I broke my heart with weeping to come back to earth; and the angels were so angry that they flung me out into the middle of the heath on the top of Wuthering Heights; where I woke sobbing for joy.' The emotional ambiguity is emphasised when Catherine adds: 'That will do to explain my secret as well as the other.' What the 'other' dream was, or even what her 'secret' is, we are never really told. The implication is, of course, that the untold dream is too strange, too terrible or too startling to tell, but one must suppose that the substituted dream gives a real clue to its nature. If this is so, the strangeness and the horror seem to accumulate round the idea of Catherine's becoming aware that she is a predestined being—that the deepest bent of her nature announces her destiny, since she cannot even desire heaven or feel that it is her home. Her secret—with its 'consolation'—is that her destiny cannot be separated from Heathcliff's: she will be doing wrong in marrying Edgar because this is an attempted evasion of what is already determined. Whatever Catherine meant, a range of emotions and fearful imaginings is suggested for which frustrated union with a natural affinity is too simple an explanation. There is at least a kind of cosmic outlawry, and perhaps this explains why Heathcliff should sometimes remind us of Byron's Manfred or Cain.[2]

III

The altered emphasis in the second part of the book is apparent at once from the nature imagery, which is one of Emily Brontë's most important pieces of dramatic apparatus. The predominantly sombre nature imagery expressive of the elder Catherine's love for Heathcliff now gives place to the brighter images of summer landscape and summer heather which surround the younger Catherine.[3] The conflict eventually destroying the first Catherine is presented figuratively in a whole 'series of contrasted alternatives; 'a bleak hilly coal country' or 'a beautiful fertile valley' [ch. 8]; moonbeam or lightning; frost or fire [ch. 9]. Catherine's love for Linton, 'like foliage in the woods: time will change it . . . as winter changes the trees', is set against her love for Heathcliff, which 'resembles the eternal rocks beneath: a source of little visible delight but necessary' [ch. 9]. Again, Heathcliff is 'an unreclaimed creature, without refinement, without cultivation'; and if Isabella Linton marries him it will be like 'putting a little canary into the park on a winter's day' [ch. 10]. The opposition that these contrasts present to us is a direct one between the extremes of 'storm' and 'calm', between 'Earth' in her dark guise and 'Earth' in her fairer aspect and the complication arises because Catherine identifies herself with the darker element while allying herself with the fairer one.

The way in which this opposition is modified in the second generation story is perhaps best illustrated by the account of the younger Catherine's quarrel with Linton in chapter 24. Catherine has fallen in love with her young and sickly cousin, Heathcliff's child by Isabella Linton, and she steals away from the 'valley' and Thrushcross Grange in order to be with him as often as she can. But Linton is peevish, irritable and mortally ill, and their relationship is not harmonious:

> 'One time . . . we were near quarrelling. He said the pleasantest manner of spending a hot July day was lying from morning till evening on the bank of heath in the middle of the moors, with the bees humming dreamily about among the bloom, and the larks singing high up overhead, and the blue sky and bright sun shining steadily and cloudlessly. That was his most perfect idea of heaven's happiness: mine was rocking in a rustling green tree, with a west wind blowing, and bright white clouds flitting rapidly above; and not only larks, but throstles, and blackbirds, and linnets, and cuckoos pouring out music on every side, and the moors seen at a distance, broken into cool dusky dells; but close by great swells of long grass undulating in waves to the breeze; and woods and sounding water, and the whole world awake and wild with joy. He wanted all to lie in an ecstacy of peace; I wanted all to sparkle and dance in a glorious jubilee. I said his heaven would be only half-alive; and he said mine would be drunk: I said I should fall asleep in his; and he said he could not breathe in mine, and began to grow very snappish . . .'

The energetic literary qualities of this passage help to strengthen the point it is trying to make. It is a vivid restatement in fresh terms and with a different emphasis of the conflict expressed in the elder Catherine's dream in chapter 9. Emily Brontë's intention, almost certainly, is that we should recall this dream now when the child of the first Catherine and the child of Heathcliff in their turn discuss ideas of 'heaven's happiness'. It is only one of the many oblique comments that this passage makes on the first generation story that the whole incident should be entirely free from the more troubled feelings that accompany the account of the elder Catherine's dream: the 'quarrel' is a brief one—'and then we kissed each other, and were friends'. More importantly, the passage shows that whereas for the elder Catherine the bare hard moor is 'heaven's happiness', for her daughter that happiness is identified with a bright animated landscape in which the moors are 'seen at a distance'. Moreover, the brilliant sunlit moors in which Linton lies in his 'ecstacy of peace' have nothing to do with the bleak moors in which his father ran wild when he was young. In fact we now find qualities earlier associated with the 'valley' imposed on the Heights, and *vice versa*. Each quality is modified in transit: 'storm' retains its energy but sheds its destructiveness; 'calm', losing its positive qualities, is a delicious but languorous activity (the attitude of the first Lintons to the elder Catherine had involved much more passiveness—'the honeysuckles embracing the thorn' as Nelly Dean says in chapter 10).

In using this passage as part of her commentary on the first generation story, the author also uses her nature imagery to sharpen and contrast the characters of the two Catherines. The younger Catherine's ideal landscape includes larks, thrushes, blackbirds, linnets and cuckoos, all 'pouring out music on every side'. Her mother, the elder Catherine, tears her pillow in a frenzy, and then pulls out the feathers, arranging them in groups and remembering the creatures to whom they once belonged. It is in keeping with the differences in texture in the two parts of the story that the elder Catherine's birds (she mentions lapwings, moorcocks and wild duck) should not only be more identifiable with a northern, moorland countryside but should also bring with them ideas of violence, vanished childhood, winter and death—ideas which are associated with 'Heathcliff' feelings, and have no comparable urgency in the story of the younger Catherine. The younger Catherine's birds, on the contrary, suggest notions of summer and sunshine and happy vitality.

Determination to prognosticate a brighter future for the new Linton-Earnshaws is revealed in the good-weather imagery lavished on the account of the younger Catherine's childhood and adolescence. One of the earliest Gondal poems, 'Will the day be bright or cloudy', is concerned with weather omens presiding over a child's birth: the poem sketches three alternative kinds of destiny, tranquil, troubled or vitally active, according to the omens, and these alternatives more or less anticipate the differences between Linton and the two Catherines. Now, in her novel, Emily Brontë stresses the fact that for the younger Catherine—and also for Hareton, whom she will marry—the weather omens are favourable. Both children are born in fine weather, the one in spring, the other in the hay-making season. They are both children of love, and it is established that Catherine was conceived in the 'calm' period of Edgar's and the first Catherine's 'deep and growing happiness' before Heathcliff's return (the predominant mood of the six months since their marriage is suggested by Nelly Dean in chapter 10 when she tells Lockwood about Heathcliff's sudden return). Though the second Catherine is 'puny' and unwelcome to begin with (her mother dies in giving birth to her), her first morning is 'bright and cheerful out of doors': and this fine weather lasts throughout the week. There is a resurgence of first generation violence in chapter 17, when the first Catherine is buried on the Friday, and so enters her 'glorious world' of the moors: 'That Friday made the last of our fine days for a month ... the wind shifted and brought rain first, and then sleet and snow.' This intervening chapter of storm marks Heathcliff's violent emotional reaction to her death and underlines the supernatural element (explained later, in the 'flashback' of chapter 29, when Heathcliff tells Nelly Dean that he was prevented from opening Catherine's coffin by the sense that her spirit was already standing beside him in the darkness). From the beginning of the next chapter [ch. 18], however, when we are led steadily on into the second generation story, all this violence dies away. Spring and summer images indicate the untroubled years of Catherine's childhood in the valley—her first twelve years are described by Nelly Dean as 'the happiest of my life'. In these years she is almost as secure from the troubling associations of Wuthering Heights as a princess in an enchanted castle, and Penistone Craggs in the distance are 'golden rocks', even though Nelly Dean had to explain 'that they were bare masses of stone, with hardly enough earth in their clefts to nourish a stunted tree' [ch. 18]. Catherine's sixteenth birthday is 'a beautiful spring day', and Nelly Dean describes her vivacity and joy:

> She bounded before me, and returned to my side and was off again like a young greyhound; and, at first, I found plenty of entertainment in listening to the larks singing far and near, and enjoying the sweet warm sunshine; and watching her, my pet, and my delight, with her golden ringlets flying loose behind, and her bright cheek, as soft and pure in its bloom as a wild rose, and her eyes radiant with cloudless pleasure. She was a happy creature, and an angel in those days. It's a pity she could not be content.   [ch. 21]

On other occasions she climbs trees, 'swinging twenty feet above the ground' and 'lying from dinner to tea in her breeze-rocked cradle', singing. (Much of this reminds us of Ellen Nussey's account of the Brontë girls out on the moors.)

The importance of Hareton's birth is stressed by the break in Nelly Dean's narrative at the end of chapter 7, when she takes up the story again at his birthday in 'the summer of 1778, that is nearly twenty-three years ago', and her next words, placed prominently at the opening of chapter 8, suggest the auspiciousness attending the arrival of this latest member of the ancient Earnshaw family:

> On the morning of a fine Sunday, my first bonny nursling, and the last of the Earnshaw stock was born. We were busy with the hay in a far-away field, and the girl that usually brought out breakfasts came running out an hour too soon, across the meadow and up the lane, calling as she ran: 'Oh, such a grand bairn,' she panted out. 'The finest lad that ever breathed . . .'

And in almost all the scenes in which Hareton appears in the second generation story his connection with the fertile earth and gentleness with living things are kept before our eyes. Nelly Dean, seeing him for the first time after his many years with Heathcliff (in ch. 18), detects 'evidence of a wealthy soil, that might yield luxuriant crops under other and favourable circumstances'.

The characters in the second generation story have to contend with Heathcliff's animosity, but their 'dark' scenes of conflict are quite unlike those of the first generation story. In the earlier part of the book storm images establish the prevailing emotional atmosphere. There is no comparable 'stormy' weather in the later story: the 'dark' scenes are not so much different in degree as in kind, their final effect no more sombre than clouds passing over a sunny landscape, an idea suggested more than once by Nelly Dean's descriptions of the second Catherine.

What, then, becomes of the storm-centre, Heathcliff himself, in this second half of the book? Our attention is turned to him once more when he traps Catherine into staying at Wuthering Heights. He inveigles Catherine into the marriage with Linton, he prevents her from joining her dying father, he makes her nurse the mortally sick Linton unaided, he secures her property once Linton is dead, he treats her with systematic harshness. Yet this behaviour seems hardly more sinister than a stage villain's. The strongest emotion Heathcliff arouses throughout the greater part of the later narrative is a kind of angry exasperation at his injustice. He is still capable of making ferocious remarks:

'. . . what a savage feeling I have to anything that seems afraid of me! Had I been born where laws are less strict and tastes less dainty, I should treat myself to a slow vivisection of those two, as an evening's amusement . . .'

but this lacks the resonance of such passionate outbursts as his speech to 'Cathy' before her death:

'. . . You deserve this. You have killed yourself. Yes, you may kiss me, and cry; and ring out my kisses and tears: they'll blight you—they'll damn you. You loved me—then what *right* had you to leave me? What right—answer me— for the poor fancy you felt for Linton? Because misery and degradation, and death, and nothing that God or Satan could inflict would have parted us, *you*, of your own will, did it. I have not broken your heart—*you* have broken it; and in breaking it, you have broken mine. So much the worse for me, that I am strong. Do I want to live? What kind of living will it be when you—oh, God! would *you* like to live with your soul in the grave?'   [ch. 15]

Angry exasperation is an emotion on too small a scale to suit this earlier Heathcliff. On the other hand, the portrayal of Heathcliff still communicates the kind of sympathy which makes the earlier story so remarkable—it is a story, after all, which not only depicts the 'heroine' and 'villain' falling in love with each other, but describes their passion with a sympathetic power so intense that it makes nonsense of the more usual responses to such a situation and upsets conventional value judgements. This sympathy is now partly suggested through Nelly Dean—whose function for Heathcliff is rather more than that of a *confidante*—and partly through such mitigating circumstances as Hareton's persistent love for him, a feeling that is not unreturned (we also remember that Heathcliff saved Hareton's life in ch. 9). Again, the bad effect on us of Heathcliff's callousness to his son is complicated by the fact that Linton is a sorry mixture of peevishness and irritability.

But at the very point where his need for vengeance dies, Heathcliff does in fact fully revive as the powerfully compelling and complex figure of the first part of the story. Hitherto, in the second half of the book, Emily Brontë has concentrated on her 'calm' figures, who represent alternatives to Heathcliff and to everything that he stands for, and as long as she makes him serve as a foil to these figures he is merely their vindictive enemy. But when she turns to look directly and exclusively at him again, we see and feel what we saw and felt earlier. This happens with the monologue she gives him late in the story (in ch. 29), when he tells Nelly Dean about his two attempts to open the first Catherine's coffin—once on the night of her funeral, and a second time, successfully, when—years later—Edgar's grave is being prepared beside hers, and, with the help of the sexton, he at last sees her dead face ('It is hers still'). As he watches the growing alliance between the second Catherine and Hareton (the latter resembling the first Catherine in appearance more and more, 'because his senses were alert, and his mental faculties wakened to unwonted activity'), Heathcliff senses the 'strange change approaching', and in another outburst to Nelly Dean, in chapter 33, he resumes much of the intensity and passion of his earlier appearances:

> '. . . In every cloud, in every tree—filling the air at night, and caught by glimpses in every object by day—I am surrounded with her image! The most ordinary faces of men and women—my own features—mock me with a resemblance. The entire world is a dreadful collection of memoranda that she did exist, and that I have lost her! Well, Hareton's aspect was the ghost of my immortal love; of my wild endeavours to hold my right, my degradation, my pride, my happiness and my anguish—'

Later still, when the tale is nearly at its end and Catherine's ghost seems to walk once more, the old feelings are fully revived, the obsessional pattern of *motifs* reappears, and Nelly Dean, finding Heathcliff lying motionless and soaking wet in the oak bed, his eyes staring, his wrist grazed by the open lattice, cries, 'I could not think him dead', and tries 'to extinguish, if possible, that frightful life-like gaze of exultation'.

It is now that the first of the story's two 'arcs' approaches its final point of rest. It reaches this point, moreover, at the same moment that the second generation story is coming to its own conclusion, and this 'coincidence' draws attention to the ambiguities in the attempted resolution of the conflict. Within the space of a single page, we turn from the phantoms of Heathcliff and the elder Catherine restlessly walking the Heights in rain and thunder, to contemplate those other 'ramblers' on the moors, Hareton and the younger Catherine, who halt on the threshold of the old house to take 'a last look at the moon—or, more correctly, at each other by her light'. The closing passage of the book might suggest to an unwary reader that the final victory is to them. It is possible to mistake this last comment of Lockwood's, indicating 'calm' after 'storm', for a statement of calm's ultimate triumph. But such a reading overlooks the departure of Hareton and the younger Catherine to the valley, and their abandonment of the old house to the spirits of the still restless Heathcliff and the elder Catherine. There is, after all, no escaping the compulsive emotional charge identified with Heathcliff; there can only be an intellectual judgement that for the purposes of ordinary life he will not do. It is the artist's business, Tchekov tells us, to set questions, not to solve them. It is an indication of the urgency of internal conflict that the tones of an authorial voice can be heard even through the controlled 'oblique and indirect view' of Catherine's and Heathcliff's fated alliance. The tones are those of someone aware that conflicting claims remain unreconciled, and that though moral judgement might desire otherwise no ultimate closure is possible.

NOTES

[1] For example, in her letters of September to December 1848 and in her letter to Miss Wooler, 30 January 1846 (*Life and Letters*, II, 76).

[2] And perhaps also why Albert Camus finds it possible to discuss Heathcliff's passion for Catherine in the same context as Ivan Karamazov's 'metaphysical rebellion' in *L'Homme revolté* (1951) ch. 1.

[3] Jacques Blondel also notes in his comments on this part of the essay the importance of Emily Brontë's use of the adjective 'mellow' ('Emily Brontë, récentes explorations', in *Etudes Anglaises*, XI (1958), p. 328 n).

Walter L. Reed

HEATHCLIFF: THE HERO OUT OF TIME

Wuthering Heights has always been regarded as something of a *lusus naturae* in the history of the English novel. While there are anticipations of it in the novels of Sir Walter Scott (*The Black Dwarf* is a demonstrable source) and reverberations from it in D. H. Lawrence, Emily Brontë's novel seems to stand apart from the traditions and conventions of English prose fiction.[1] The only figure close to Heathcliff in his preeminence and passion is Lovelace, but Richardson's character is a villain and an aristocrat, of which Heathcliff is neither. Like the villains of Gothic novels, Lovelace is defined by clear moral categories. Like other Romantic heroes, Heathcliff has gone beyond such conventional good and evil. *Wuthering Heights* is similarly hard to place in the context of Emily Brontë's own development, if only because so little of her development is known. She took part in the family creation of Angria, the literary game run by the older Charlotte and Branwell; then during the ten years prior to the writing of *Wuthering Heights* she and her younger sister Anne collaborated on the saga of Gondal, in prose and poetry, of which only the poetry survives.[2] While the Gondal saga was full of conventional heroic figures— lovers, soldiers, and monarchs—there is little resemblance to the intensity and focus of *Wuthering Heights*.

Yet if the sources of the novel in Brontë's developing literary imagination are obscure, the narrative structure of the finished work is not. It is formally a meditation on the hero; more specifically, it is a joint recounting by two narrators of the life and death of a single heroic figure, who for the first half of the narrative shares the stage with a heroine. The other characters function as foils, impediments, or alternatives to the central heroic conflict. Heathcliff is not a hero of religious faith but a hero of romantic love. His daemon is his possessive passion for Catherine.

To move from Kierkegaard to Emily Brontë is to move from one extreme of Romanticism to the other, from the deeply "sentimental," to use Schiller's term, to the intensely "naïve." Whereas Kierkegaard subjects Romantic themes and forms to

From *Meditations on the Hero: A Study of the Romantic Hero in Nineteenth-Century Fiction* (New Haven: Yale University Press, 1974), pp. 85–119.

a highly reflective irony, Brontë assimilates them into a world of personal myth. There is very little of the literary self-consciousness of *Repetition* and *Fear and Trembling* in *Wuthering Heights*. There are moments of reflexivity, as when Lockwood fancies himself a King Lear in his cursing, or when Heathcliff speaks scornfully of Isabella's "picturing in me a hero of romance and expecting unlimited indulgence from my chivalrous devotion,"[3] but these ironic moments are only occasional foils for the fundamentally unironic presentation of heroic passion. There is little of Kierkegaard's "negative thinker" in Brontë. Kierkegaard subjects the hero to a searching philosophical critique; Brontë invests him with an emotional intensity—an intensity that is sometimes objected to as being in excess of its vehicle.

This is not to say that *Wuthering Heights* and Heathcliff are purely natural and spontaneous creations, owing nothing to literary tradition. This becomes clear once one looks beyond the mainstream of the nineteenth-century novel. As a number of studies of Emily Brontë's sources have shown, there is a good deal of earlier literature being absorbed into *Wuthering Heights*—Shakespearean drama, *Paradise Lost*, Byron, and a number of minor Gothic romances. It is of some interest that these sources are mainly native. Although she had been exposed to French and German literature in her year at the Pension Héger in Belgium, the traces of this foreign influence are slight in comparison.[4] Much more important for the plot of *Wuthering Heights*, along with Scott's *The Black Dwarf*, were an anonymous Gothic romance published in *Blackwood's*, "The Bridegroom of Barma" and a local story of a family near Law Hill whose adopted son's acts of usurpation are strikingly similar to those of Heathcliff's.[5] Of as much interest as the sources themselves is the way in which Brontë uses them. Given enough time and learning, one could write a minor *Road to Xanadu* on the eclectic assimilation by which Brontë's literary memory works. Rather than undertaking the wholesale revival and radical revision to which Kierkegaard subjects his sources, Brontë uses a piecemeal approach in which the original is frequently disguised, perhaps unrecognized by the author herself, and at the same time more organically rooted in the substratum. Since our concern here is with the heroic character of Heathcliff rather than with the various aspects of the plot, I shall give a few examples of the way Brontë unselfconsciously invokes literary support for her hero. Heathcliff is like many other Romantic heroes in reviving earlier, more authoritative examples of heroism, largely from outside the conventions of the novel. The only difference is that in him the revival is less explicit.

There is first the influence on Heathcliff of the Gothic villain, the mysterious figure of evil whose fatal effect is most often felt by the beautiful women he seduces and by the good families whose inheritance he usurps. Besides the villain of *The Black Dwarf*, the figure of the devil in James Hogg's *Confessions of a Justified Sinner* seems a possible prototype.[6] But again, it is important to observe the transvaluation of Gothic values that Brontë brings about. As Lowry Nelson puts it, the universe of *Wuthering Heights* "is almost frighteningly without either God or devil; the God of conventional fiction, even a tyrant God, has effectually disappeared, just as the devil of earlier gothic diabolism has disappeared as the arch-fiend."[7] The same might be said of the social ethics or morals in the novel, as the continuing critical debate over the relative vice and virtue in Heathcliff will attest; they have disappeared as discernible or controlling values.

More important than the Gothic villains as prototypes for Heathcliff, and more truly foreign to the genre of the novel, are the tragic heroes of Shakespeare. The passing allusion to King Lear, mentioned earlier, is largely ironic. However, Catherine's mad scene in chapter 12 echoes Ophelia's madness in *Hamlet*: " 'That's a turkey's,' she murmured to herself; 'and this is a wild duck's; and this is a pigeon's. Ah, they put pigeon's feathers in the pillows—no wonder I couldn't die' " (104). Later Heathcliff echoes Hamlet himself: "If he loved with all the powers of his puny being, he couldn't love as much in eighty years, as I could in a day" (127). As Lew Girdler notes, Heathcliff is not simply a Hamlet figure. He is rather a composite of Shakespeare's tragic heroes—Romeo in his early love for Catherine, Hamlet in his loss of her and in his need for revenge, Richard III in his evil usurpation, Macbeth in his hallucinations, Lear in his isolated rage.[8] As we shall see when we come to *Moby-Dick,* this polymorphous revival of Shakespeare is not unique to *Wuthering Heights;* Brontë is simply more subtle and more sparing in her evocations than Melville.

The presence of Milton's Satan, the archetypal hero of English Romantics such as Blake and Shelley, is also felt in Heathcliff, though less intensely. Catherine makes the identification explicit: "It is as bad as offering Satan a lost soul—Your bliss lies, like his, in inflicting misery . . ." (96). She herself has a Miltonic dream about being cast down from heaven onto Wuthering Heights, and Heathcliff's earlier description of them both looking in on the Linton children in their beautiful, splendid drawing room recalls, in a vague but suggestive way, the passage in Book IV of *Paradise Lost* where Satan looks in on Adam and Eve in Eden. Milton was Mr. Brontë's favorite poet, and he is supposed to have known *Paradise Lost* by heart.[9] The children themselves were probably more versed in Byron, however, and we find here a similar case of an atmosphere that transcends the specificity of allusion. Heathcliff is a composite of Byronic gestures and emotions.

Charlotte Brontë signals the debt to Byron when she says of Heathcliff in her Editor's Preface, "These solitary traits of humanity omitted, we should say he was child neither of Lascar or gypsy, but a man's shape animated by demon life—a Ghoul—an Afreet" (xxxviii). Apparently unconsciously, she is remembering "The Giaour":

> Go—and with Gouls and Afrits rave;
> Till these in horror shrink away
> From Spectre more accursed than they!

What is paramount in Byron's heroes that is generally lacking in Shakespeare's tragic heroes and Milton's Satan is the primary interest in romantic love. Heathcliff's heroism is inseparable from his love for Catherine. Like Heathcliff in the novel, the Giaour has a vision of his dead lover's ghost, and his meditations on her grave may have suggested one of Heathcliff's more macabre schemes for uniting himself with his beloved:

She sleeps beneath the wandering wave—
Ah! had she but an earthly grave,
This breaking heart and throbbing head
Should seek and share her narrow bed.[10]

Another poem of Byron's entitled "The Dream" shows a remarkable similarity in plot outline with *Wuthering Heights*. The dreamer sees two young people, in love as brother and sister. The girl loves another as well, the boy flees and travels in exotic lands, then returns. The girl, now older, is wed to someone she does not love; the boy also marries someone he does not love. The girl goes mad, the boy is left alone in "Hatred and Contention," though eventually he reaches some understanding with "the quick Spirit of the Universe."[11]

What is interesting about this poem is that it is thoroughly autobiographical, dealing with Byron's love for Mary Chaworth and his lack of love for his wife. Emily Brontë, in fact, though probably unintentionally, supplements the plot of this poem by adapting an incident in Moore's *Life of Byron* also involving Mary Chaworth. When Heathcliff overhears Catherine telling Nelly it would degrade her to marry him, missing, of course, her subsequent declaration, he reenacts a situation in which the infatuated Byron overheard Mary saying to her maid, "Do you think I could care for that lame boy?" Byron was deeply hurt, according to Moore, and ran out into the night.[12] Given the interest in Byron, it is also not difficult to see the relations between Heathcliff and Catherine as a purer version of the relationship of Byron and Augusta, as known at the time, or as dramatized in *Manfred*, another Byronic work echoed in *Wuthering Heights*.[13]

In other words, Brontë's use of Byron confirms a cardinal point about Byron's literary reputation, namely, that his life was fully as influential as his works. Although Heathcliff comes trailing clouds of Shakespearean and Miltonic glory, he grows up in the hothouse of Byronic legend. What distinguishes him as a hero from his Byronic predecessors, and from Emily's earlier attempts at Byronic heroes in her Gondal poems, is his emotional presentness. Byron's Giaour and Corsair and even Manfred are interesting because of their distance. The essence of their heroism is their obscurity: "Behold—but who hath seen, or e'er shall see, / Man as himself, the secret spirit free" ("The Corsair," ll. 247–48); "You could not penetrate his soul, but found, / Despite your wonder, to your own he wound" ("Lara," ll. 377–78). Heathcliff's mysterious origins and his three-year rise to eminence are relatively unimportant to his status as hero. Past deeds of glory or of secret sin do not interest us so much as the forceful and assertive presence, what J. Hillis Miller has called the "permanent and unceasing attitude of aggression."[14] There is a force and a substance in Heathcliff that reveals the passivity and hollowness of Byron's heroes by contrast.

Such a comparison is not intended to dismiss the Byronic hero as a sham, but to distinguish his existential nature from Heathcliff's. Byron's heroes are simply more alienated than Heathcliff, more divorced from any immediacy, or, to recall the terms of our previous discussions of the hero, more isolated from any ground of being. A poem of Brontë's written some eight years before *Wuthering Heights*, "The soft unclouded blue of air," expresses this Byronic dilemma explicitly. The speaker reposes in the ground of nature and immortality recalled from early childhood:

> The soft unclouded blue of air;
> The earth as golden-green and fair
> And bright as Eden's used to be;
> That air and earth have rested me.
>
> Laid on the grass I lapsed away;
> Sank back to childhood's day:
> All harsh thoughts perished, memory mild
> Subdued both grief and passion wild.

Beside her, however, sits an anonymous Byronic "iron man." The speaker wonders if this imposing figure retains any connection with the immediacy of nature or childhood:

> But did the sunshine even now
> That bathed his stern and swarthy brow,
> Oh, did it wake—I long to know—
> One whisper, one sweet dream in him,
> One lingering joy that, years ago,
> Had faded—lost in distance dim?
>
> That iron man was born like me,
> And he was once an ardent boy:
> He must have felt, in infancy,
> The glory of a summer sky.[15]

In spite of her desire to connect this hero with the ground she herself feels a part of, the speaker ends with a confession of her failure to do so.

In the light of this earlier effort to give the Romantic hero some support in a mythical realm of nature, Brontë's achievement in *Wuthering Heights* becomes more clear. Heathcliff is an "iron man" successfully provided with a childhood and an intense communion with the landscape. There has been considerable disagreement among critics of *Wuthering Heights* as to the specifically human nature of Heathcliff. Dorothy Van Ghent suspected that "Heathcliff might *really* be a demon," participating, as she saw him, in "the raw, inhuman reality of anonymous natural energies."[16] Other critics emphasize the sympathetic psychological presentation of Heathcliff as a person who suffers and reacts to rejection and abuse.[17] The only one to perceive the complex and shifting relation of self and ground is J. Hillis Miller, and his description of their interdependence is worth quoting at length:

> For Emily Brontë no human being is self-sufficient, and all suffering derives ultimately from isolation. A person is most himself when he participates most

completely in the life of something outside himself. The self outside the self is the substance of a man's being in both the literal and the etymological sense of the word. It is the ultimate stuff of the self, and it is also that which "stands beneath" the self as its foundation and its support. A man's real being is outside himself. . . . The poems and the novel suggest three possible entities with which the self may be fused: nature, God, and another human being.[18]

I would, however, qualify Miller's analysis in two ways. First I would make it more specific: it is only the heroic individual (Heathcliff and to a lesser extent Catherine) who has this outside substance available. It is only the exceptional self that is capable of such participation, it being clearly beyond any other character in the novel. Second, I would rule out the possibility of God as an entity with which the self can fuse. God has not simply disappeared for Brontë in *Wuthering Heights,* He has been replaced by the other two ontological entities that Miller invokes, nature and the object of romantic love.[19] The plentitude of nature and the immediacy of love—together these substances provide the ground for Heathcliff's and Catherine's heroics. Kierkegaard would reject such a naïve resolution of the metaphysical dilemma, but Brontë is neither philosophically nor theologically inclined and adopts the natural super-naturalism of Romantic tradition quite uncritically.

The relationship of Heathcliff to the literary archetypes of the hero (Gothic, Shakespearean, Miltonic, Byronic) in fact resembles the relationship of the heroic figure in the novel to this metaphysical ground. In both cases there is a lack of full differentiation, a tendency of the individual to draw energy and sustenance from a powerful source without achieving full autonomy. Thus Heathcliff echoes Hamlet in the same way that he evokes the moors: as an echo that cannot easily be distinguished from the original sound. The relationship to sources, literary and metaphysical, is almost symbiotic, which is both a strength in the hero and a limitation. As we have seen with Kierkegaard, and as we shall with Lermontov, there are other meditations on the hero where immediate relatedness is notably lacking, where autonomy is fully achieved, but at the expense of strength.

The most heightened invocations of the natural ground in which hero and heroine participate come at the moments of greatest crisis in their relationship. It is when Catherine tells Nelly she is unable to marry Heathcliff and prefers Edgar Linton as a husband that she bursts out with her famous analogy and identification: "My love for Heathcliff resembles the eternal rocks beneath—a source of little visible delight, but necessary. Nelly, I *am* Heathcliff . . ." (70). This moment marks the initial sundering of their romantic identity with one another. There is the equally famous reunion *d'outre-tombe,* where Heathcliff conjures up Catherine's ghost and dies to join it. Lockwood's wondering "how anyone could ever imagine unquiet slumbers, for the sleepers in that quiet earth" (287) misses the point, as usual with him, in that it assumes that their ghosts must be tormented still to walk the moors. Their spirits become *genii loci,* ghosts with a local habitation, rather than Byronic exiles doomed to wander the earth.

This is not to say that Brontë is a literal believer in the popular superstitions of the highlands that she evokes. Her supernaturalism is not a simple animistic belief but the more complex assent that Coleridge called "poetic faith": "My endeavors should be directed to persons and characters supernatural, or at least romantic; yet so as to transfer from our inward nature a human interest and a semblance of truth sufficient to procure for these shadows of imagination that willing suspension of disbelief for the moment, which constitutes poetic faith."[20] Brontë, it seems to me, is dramatizing the supernatural in much this way—as an outward supernaturalism given substance by an inward human interest of a more natural kind. It is not that the supernatural elements can simply be reduced to a more basic human psychology, but that such a psychology is used as an imaginative support.

The central crisis in the love of the hero and heroine makes clear the nature of this supporting psychological interest in *Wuthering Heights:* it is an intense evocation of childhood. Between their initial separation and final reunion Heathcliff and Catherine attempt a reconciliation in the social realm and fail. Catherine is psychically torn between the claims of Linton and the claims of Heathcliff. In the course of the heroine's mental breakdown Nelly Dean observes that "our fiery Catherine was no better than a wailing child" (106). Catherine goes on to validate this rather crude perception:

> Nelly, I'll tell you what I thought, and what has kept recurring and recurring till I feared for my reason—I thought as I lay there, with my head against the table leg, and my eyes dimly discerning the grey square of the window, that I was enclosed in the oak-panelled bed at home; and my heart ached with some great grief which, just waking, I could not recollect—I pondered, and worried myself to discover what it could be; and most strangely, the whole last seven years of my life grew a blank! I did not recall that they had been at all. I was a child; my father was just buried, and my misery arose from the separation that Hindley had ordered between me, and Heathcliff—I was laid alone, for the first time, and, rousing from a dismal doze after a night of weeping—I lifted my hand to push the panels aside, it struck the table top! I swept it along the carpet, and then, memory burst in—my late anguish was swallowed in a paroxysm of despair—I cannot say why I felt so wildly wretched—it must have been temporary derangement for there is scarcely cause—But, supposing at twelve years old, I had been wrenched from the Heights, and every early association, and my all in all, as Heathcliff was at that time, had been converted, at a stroke into Mrs. Linton, the lady of Thrushcross Grange, and the wife of a stranger; and exile, and outcast, thenceforth, from what had been my world—You may fancy a glimpse of the abyss where I grovelled!
>
> (106–07)

Many commentators have noted the regressive qualities in the love of Catherine and Heathcliff, which are simply made explicit at this point. The present crisis in the Grange is interwoven with the past crisis at the Heights in a way that makes it quite difficult to distinguish them in Catherine's speech. The intimations of timelessness in the love of Catherine and Heathcliff are grounded in the nature of the moors, but they are also strongly supported by these recollections of early childhood. Brontë is often interpreted in a Freudian context, but given the general chastity of the relationship of her hero and heroine, she seems closer to Wordsworth.[21] This concern with nature as experienced by the mind of the young child can be seen in the poem quoted above: "He must have felt, in infancy, / The glory of a summer sky."

In fact, it is primarily in association with the emotions of early childhood that nature makes its presence felt in the novel. If one compares Brontë with Hardy, another novelist of the English landscape, one is reminded of how little specific, concrete nature detail is given in *Wuthering Heights.* The winds and the moors provide a general atmospheric background, but very little visual imagery. An exception is the mention of various birds and their nests—for example, Nelly notices a pair of ousels building a nest as she approaches Heathcliff to tell him of Catherine's death—but the symbolism of childhood is obvious; Heathcliff is the cuckoo raised in the nest of another. We are reminded here of Mr. Earnshaw's initial indiscretion with the stray child, even as we are given a natural image of his human childhood. A similar fusion of landscape and early recollection occurs in the description of Heathcliff entering the Grange to take the younger Catherine up to the Heights: "It was the same room into which he had been ushered, as a guest, eighteen years before: the same moon shone through the window; and the same autumn landscape lay outside. . . . Heathcliff advanced to the hearth. Time had little altered his person either. There was the same man . . ." (242). Brontë weaves together the different levels of "sameness" by the repetition of the adjective; the initial memory spreads out quickly to embrace the landscape and the earlier self.

What is remarkable in Brontë's evocation of childhood as the basis of her hero's identity is that it rarely makes one feel that Heathcliff is merely childish. The child is the father of the man, but the man is not therefore to be taken less seriously. What *Wuthering Heights* anticipates, in curious way, is the interpretation of the literary hero given half a century later by Otto Rank in *The Myth of the Birth of the Hero.* Not only does Heathcliff have the requisite mysterious birth and orphanhood described by Rank (unlike all other Romantic heroes treated in this study), but he is also a figure of revolt against an oppressive family structure. "The true hero of the romance, is therefore, the ego, which finds itself in the hero, through its first heroic act, i.e., the revolt against the father." Brontë differs from Rank, however, in the way she uses this psychological insight—as a means of investing the hero with a renewed emotional intensity, instead of as a means of demythologizing the myth.[22]

There is something of the willfulness of the child in the self-assertions of Catherine and Heathcliff. On the one hand their relationship is a romantic identification of lover with loved one; on the other hand it is a partnership in resistance and rebellion against adult authority—an adult authority falsely assumed by Hindley, the older brother. Thus in her mad scene Catherine recalls the traumatic separation from Heathcliff that had been ordered by Hindley. To use a more technical vocabulary, Brontë seems to be dramatizing a particular stage of childhood, the stage described by Erik Erikson as "Early Childhood and the Will to Be Oneself." "This whole stage," Erikson writes, "becomes a *battle for autonomy*.... It becomes decisive for the ratio between loving good will and hateful self-insistence, between co-operation and willfulness, between self-expression and compulsive self-restraint or meek compliance."[23] The struggle is clearer in Catherine than in Heathcliff, perhaps, but Erikson's terms describe quite well the emotional content of many of the acts and expressions of both.

From this psychoanalytic perspective, Heathcliff can be seen as a figure from a "family romance"—as Rank, following Freud, called it—who has been placed within a realistic family history. He is literally a stray child discovered in Liverpool, but in terms of the family chronicle that constitutes so much of *Wuthering Heights,* he is the stranger, the outsider, eventually the usurper. Herein lies his essential difference from Catherine: unlike her he has no legitimate social role within the family—his three years abroad count for nothing when he returns. The focus of the novel is on his asocial, antisocial being rather than on Catherine's social conflict. "If Catherine is the impetus of the story, Heathcliff is its structure," W. A. Craik observes. "Lockwood asks Ellen for his history; he gets exactly and completely what he asked for. Every detail Emily Brontë reveals is present because it is relevant to one or other of Heathcliff's two ruling forces—love and the urge to revenge— whether it is recognized at the time or is merely seen to be so in retrospect."[24] *Wuthering Heights* thus cannot be seen ultimately as a novel of psychosocial or family conflict, however sensitively it probes some of these issues. In its imaginative structure the book belongs to the genre of the meditation on the hero, and it is to the terms of my first chapter that I should like to return here.

Wuthering Heights is a meditation on a hero who exists outside the continuum of social history. We have seen how his heroic action, gesture, and diction incorporate traces of earlier literary heroes, but Heathcliff is not so much a hero of an earlier age is one who belongs, through nature and childhood, to a mythical permanence. In spite of all obvious differences, he is like Kierkegaard's Abraham in this one respect: he is a hero of timelessness trying to enter a world of time. It is important that we first meet Heathcliff as a fully developed figure in Lockwood's introduction to *Wuthering Heights.* Even though we are presented with the story of his childhood by Nelly Dean, we are given little sense of the development of his character after he is introduced into the Earnshaw family. From the first he shows the autonomy, defiance, and general inscrutability that characterize him throughout the novel. It is true, as a number of critics have argued, that his later acts of brutality are shown to grow out of his mistreatment at the hands of various members of the household,[25] but it is significant that Brontë characteristically presents the causal sequence in reverse. For example, we learn of Heathcliff's brutal attack on Hindley from Isabella in chapter 17. Yet the underlying reason for Heathcliff's rage—that he has been trying frantically to communicate with Catherine, corpse and ghost, when he finds the door barred—is only revealed in chapter 29. The genesis of the heroic rage is less important than the expression of it, and we never see the hero in the process of becoming.

Like Abraham, Heathcliff is a hero in the eyes of eternity, but as in Abraham's case also, this eternity is unable to turn its back on time. Kierkegaard would find Heathcliff a hero of the aesthetic, the lower immediacy, rather than of the higher immediacy like Abraham. Yet neither can fully resign himself to living out of the temporal world. Abraham cannot simply accept God's command because he must retain his love for Isaac, in order to realize the paradox of faith. "It is about the temporal, the finite, everything turns in this case." Heathcliff is certainly no Knight of Faith, but neither can he be a Knight of Infinite Resignation. Heathcliff is unable to remain an outsider, ultimately because of his love for Catherine, but also because he has been brought into the family early on. He actively tries to enter into the realm of history, which for Brontë is the genealogical history of the Earnshaws and the Lintons. He was perhaps brought to Wuthering Heights to take the place of a dead son—we never know what moved Mr. Earnshaw to bring him home in the first place—but he is only given that son's first name, not the surname. The name Heathcliff suggests the breadth and height of the natural landscape, but in the social system of family naming it is only half an identity. It is not that Heathcliff actively worked to become Mr. Earnshaw's favorite (although he does become this) or that his desire to marry Catherine is a conscious wish to attain social respectability. But because of the situation he is placed in at the start and is unwilling or unable to resist, he is forced to seek a way of relating to the sequence of generations into which he has been thrust. His love for Catherine is the precipitating crisis. In and of himself, Heathcliff is not a divided self, but as he finds his substance in Catherine ("How can I live without my soul?" he asks on learning of her death), he experiences the alienation that is characteristic of the Romantic hero.

Wuthering Heights is often seen as a novel of the conflict between nature and society, but it seems to me that the conflict can be defined more accurately in terms of temporality. The basic clash is between the values of permanence and the values of change, and though permanence is more commonly associated with natural things, nature can change and social institutions can seem permanent. Thus in her famous declaration of divided loyalties, Catherine identifies her affection for Edgar Linton with a natural image subject to mutability: "My love for Linton is like the foliage in the woods. Time will change it, I'm aware, as winter changes the trees—my love for Heathcliff resembles the eternal rocks beneath . . ." (70). Linton, like Heathcliff, is eventually buried in the quiet earth beside Catherine, but long before his death, Nelly tells us, "Time brought him resignation," a natural healing to which Heathcliff is not privy.[26]

Conversely, in Heathcliff's scheme of revenge, we see a man closely allied with nature skillfully employing the means of society, as Arnold Kettle was the first to point out: "What Heathcliff does is to use against his enemies with complete ruthlessness their own weapons . . . of money and arranged marriages. He gets power over them by the classic methods of the ruling class, expropriation and property deals."[27] What Kettle's Marxist analysis ignores, however is the degree to which Heathcliff is trying to participate in the social milieu of the landlords; he is hardly a proletarian Robin Hood. For a while, at least, Heathcliff is actively trying to enter into the social realm by grafting his scion, young Linton, onto the family tree and by becoming himself the master of the property. At this stage in his career Heathcliff resembles most closely the villain of the Gothic novel, whose villainy often consists in interfering with a legitimate inheritance. "I want the triumph of seeing *my* descendant fairly lord of their estates; my child hiring their children, to till their fathers' land for wages," Heathcliff tells Nelly (177). Though these dynastic ambitions are a product of his desire for revenge, they involve him quite deeply in the realm of society. Yet in Heathcliff's hands the mechanisms of social transference and change become a means of establishing the permanence and finality of his revenge: "I get levers and mattocks to demolish the two houses . . ." (274).

The mythical permanence of the hero is therefore not sufficient unto itself. It needs, for a variety of reasons, to integrate itself with the ongoing processes of social history. If Heathcliff and Catherine could simply *be* one another out on the moors as children, they would be happy, but their inevitable growth brings inevitable socialization. Only in death can they get back out of time, and although this is the ultimate point they reach, it cannot be seized directly. As Blake puts it, eternity is in love with the productions of time. It is not really that Heathcliff wants to get into the stream of history and change, but that he must, because he has mortgaged part of his mythical identity to history by loving Catherine. Even after her death he wants Catherine back, and his revenge is an attempt ultimately to subdue the temporal to the eternal. However, the pursuit of this ultimate goal involves at least a temporary participation in temporality.

The need for myth to enter into history seems to me to lie behind a number of the scenes and motifs in the novel, indeed behind what Bachelard would call its "poetics of space." The motif I am referring to has to do with the attempt of a force to get into a room or house from out of doors, a motif of breaking and entering which has often been noticed in this novel and variously interpreted.[28] The most striking instance of this motif is the incident in Lockwood's much-interpreted dream during his first night at the Heights, when he brutalizes the ghost of the child Catherine Earnshaw trying to get in through the window. While it is possible to read this dream in the light of Lockwood's rejection of the young woman at Bath, or in the light of the brutal treatment he has received as a guest at the house, the forced entry and resistance to it become such a pervasive motif in the novel that they transcend the particularity of Lockwood's character and experience. In fact, what the ending of the novel suggests, with Heathcliff's pursuit of Catherine's ghost and his own death before the same open window, is that Lockwood's dream has been a negative response to a vision that really belongs to Heathcliff. Whereas Lockwood bars the way, Heathcliff has actively solicited the ghost to come in.

To say that the entry of the ghost into the house is an entry of myth into time may seem like special pleading here. But notice how pervasively the houses in the novel are identified with history. Immediately before entering the Heights for the first time Lockwood notices the date over the door: 1500. Some structures are subject to decay, like the chapel; others, like the Grange, are subject to improvement. But all are involved in the movement from one generation to another. It is also significant that Brontë sets her novel some two generations earlier than the time at which she is writing. The house is the focus of the genealogy that is given piecemeal throughout the narrative.

The initial act of extralegal entry is, of course, Heathcliff's arrival at the Heights wrapped in Mr. Earnshaw's greatcoat. "Mrs. Earnshaw was ready to fling it out of doors," we are told (30), but her husband imposes his will on the family and the child remains. There is then the scene where Heathcliff and Catherine look in through the windows of the Linton Grange and are treated harshly as intruders. Both are taken into the house after the dogs attack them, but Heathcliff is thrown out for cursing. Heathcliff is then driven to leave the Heights when he overhears Catherine say it would degrade her to marry him. After three years he attempts another series of entries into the Grange, which become more and more violent. He is able to enter the Heights now, and eventually gains possession of it, but with Catherine's death this becomes a hollow victory. He is master of the property but is still unable to belong to its history.

Chapter 29 is particularly rich in variations on this theme, and the association of the house with the values of temporality is clear. Nelly and the younger Catherine are seated in the library when Heathcliff's approach is announced by a servant, who asks if he should "bar the door in his face" (242). Heathcliff successfully intrudes, however. There follows the passage quoted earlier: "It was the same room into which he had been ushered, as a guest, eighteen years before: the same moon shone through the window; and the same autumn landscape lay outside." But the interior of the room has significantly changed, for the portraits of Catherine and Edgar hang on the wall. Heathcliff is permanent and unchanging ("Time had little altered his person. . . . There was the same man"), but Catherine has been transformed by time—into the artificial image of the portrait, and into the natural image of her daughter. Both these time-bound images Heathcliff has come to claim as his own. As he talks to Nelly, however, he reveals his more avid pursuit of Catherine's ghost, a manifestation of her eternal presence. It is here that he tells about an earlier scene of forced entry:

> Having reached the Heights, I rushed eagerly to the door. It was fastened; and, I remember, that accursed Earnshaw and my wife opposed my entrance. I remember stopping to kick the breath out of him, and then hurrying upstairs to my room, and hers—I looked around impatiently—I felt her by me—I could *almost* see her, and yet I *could not!* I ought to have sweat blood then from the anguish of my yearning, from the fervour of my supplications to have but one glimpse!
> (245–46)

At this point Heathcliff seems to sense the futility of his attempt to break into the family as a revenge for his earlier exclusion. "When I sat in the house with Hareton, it seemed that on going out I should meet her; when I walked on the moors I should meet her coming in. When I went from home, I hastened to return, she *must* be somewhere at the Heights, I was certain" (246). The house no longer contains her spirit, either to love or to take revenge on. In a curious reversal of their positions, Heathcliff is now inside the house, soliciting her to come in and haunt him. Catherine's ghost does not come of its own accord, apparently: Heathcliff must will it to reenter his own temporal existence. Only then, in the logic of the book's double time scheme, can he leave this existence behind. Having entered the world of time on a false basis, the hero must work his way back out, into the communion of the supernatural. The open window Nelly discovers in the room where she finds Heathcliff dead recalls the open window that led to Catherine's death earlier. It is the emblem of a final retreat from the world of time.

Thus Heathcliff never does become "a hero of our time." Just as his blood passes through the genealogy of the Earnshaws and the Lintons without leaving a trace, his entry into the continuum of history never really takes place. He is a hero who tries to force his way into a world of past, present, and future, but his actions, like the narrative itself, only come full circle. In one sense it is Heathcliff's triumph, but in another sense his identity never gains the temporal fullness of humanity. As a figure he gradually reverts back to the ground from which his heroism emerged; this is the way I interpret the softening of his vengeful resolve when he begins to see Catherine's image in every cloud and tree. The culmination of this reversion comes when he is literally buried beneath the quiet earth. Thus as a hero Heathcliff remains archaic and primitive, eternally out of date; *Wuthering Heights* is thus what we have called a retrospective meditation on the hero as gestalt: a figure from the heroic past is considered from the perspective of the unheroic present. The figure of Hareton Earnshaw, however, presents the complementary mode of the hero in development. The revenger's tragedy is succeeded, chronologically, by a miniature Bildungsroman.

Whether the marriage of Hareton and Catherine Linton is an adequate resolution of the conflicts in the novel is open to question. My own feeling is that the marriage works on a thematic level, but that it lacks the imaginative intensity of the love between Heathcliff and the older Catherine. The resolution works thematically because it shows a merging of the natural self and the social context in an organic continuity of time. Hareton is the successor to Heathcliff in his intractableness and unsociability, in his exclusion from social life. Through the natural influence and cultural tutelage of the younger Catherine he is reclaimed for the family, reintegrated into the genealogy of the novel after being dispossessed by Heathcliff. Brontë presents the shift as analogous to the change in Shakespeare's plays from the tragedies to the later romances. There are reminders of *The Tempest* in the relationship of Hareton and Catherine—for example, the "discovery" of them at their lessons, recalling Prospero's revelation of Ferdinand and Miranda playing chess. Hareton appears initially as Caliban but becomes a Ferdinand as upon his nature nurture *is* made to stick.

What is interesting for our discussion of the meditation on the hero is the way Brontë uses the Bildungs-motif as a kind of coda to her meditation on the heroic gestalt of Heathcliff. Although Heathcliff finally abandons his assault on the world of time, his surrogate Hareton is educated into the progression of family history. It is clear, however, that the price that is paid for this resolution is the sacrifice of the heroic substance. Hareton is a Heathcliff only in speech and dress. Vestiges of the willfulness of the older pair remain—Hareton is educated by slaps on the cheek—and, in teaching him to read, Catherine is righting one of the wrongs committed against Heathcliff in the beginning, which was to deny him access to books. But there is no sense that Hareton is thereby developing a potential heroism within himself. The shift in modes provides a thematic resolution of the conflict between permanence and change, but the emotionally charged myth of the hero is replaced by a more stereotyped romance. The story of Hareton runs the story of the adult Heathcliff in reverse, but it fails to be a true mediation between the mythical permanence of the hero himself and the historical progression of "our time." We are left with the problem, in the words of Robert Frost, of what to make of a diminished thing.

The attempt to complement the meditation on a hero of the past with a heroic Bildungsroman was something that we noted in Kierkegaard, of course. *Repetition* complements *Fear and Trembling* in this manner, and within *Fear and Trembling* itself the sketch of the merman complements the meditations on Abraham. I would add another example here of the complementarity of the two modes in Mary Shelley's *Frankenstein*, which is closer to *Wuthering Heights* than are Kierkegaard's two novels and which may even be regarded as an influence.[29]

Frankenstein, in fact, is a Bildungsroman that turns into a revenger's tragedy, the reverse of the sequence we have noted in *Wuthering Heights*. The Bildungs-motif is present in each of the concentric circles of the narrative. Robert Walton briefly sketches his early education in his first letter to his sister, reminding her of the reading in their uncle's library that led him to a conquest of the North Pole. Victor Frankenstein narrates at greater length to Walton the story of his early reading in Cornelius Agrippa, his father's disparagement of such "sad trash," and his rebellious continuation of his studies. From here he proceeds to the university and the fatal specialization of his apprenticeship. Finally, in a more fantastic turn of events than anything the horror movies have envisioned, the monster sits his creator down in a hut on Mont Blanc and narrates the story of *his* education—first his struggles with the rudiments of perception, then his acquisition of language, and finally his formal education: *Paradise Lost*, Plutarch's *Lives*, and *The Sorrows of Young Werther*.

But this series of Bildungsromans leads to a tragic conclusion. Like Heathcliff, the monster tries to break into the world of human society, and also like Heathcliff, he is driven out. He becomes Milton's Satan rather than Milton's Adam (with whom he previously compared himself), just as Frankenstein is transformed from the "Modern Prometheus" of the subtitle to the tyrannical Jupiter of *Prometheus Unbound*. (When it comes to Romantic myth-making Mary Shelley is more sophisticated and more explicit than Emily Brontë.) Neither the monster nor Victor Frankenstein becomes a specifically heroic figure in the sense in which we have defined the hero here, but they become locked in a master-slave relationship that leads to an accelerating tragedy of revenge.

Thus whereas *Wuthering Heights* offers the novel of apprenticeship as a means of resolving the tragically heroic conflict Heathcliff has experienced from the start, *Frankenstein* derives the revenger's tragedy from a novel of education gone awry. The only consolation at the end of Mary Shelley's novel is that Walton, the would-be conqueror of one of nature's secrets, is persuaded to turn back from his quest by Frankenstein's example. Walton is perhaps to be compared with Hareton in *Wuthering Heights,* as a surrogate survivor, but Mary Shelley devotes a good deal less time to Walton's recovery than Brontë does to Hareton's. Unlike the monster and Frankenstein, on the other hand, Heathcliff and Catherine seem to achieve a positive reconciliation in death. One could hardly imagine anything *but* unquiet slumbers for the former pair.

A further similarity between *Frankenstein* and *Wuthering Heights,* again with significant differences, has to do with the narrative structure of the two novels. The tale within the tale within the tale of *Frankenstein* finds a rather precise parallel in the interlocking narratives of Lockwood, Nelly Dean, and, for a brief space, Isabella—a "Chinese puzzle box" of narrators, as Kierkegaard would call it.[30] The major difference here ⟨...⟩ is that Mary Shelley's narrators are telling their own stories, not meditating on a hero. I have reserved for last a discussion of the narrators of *Wuthering Heights* and the relation of the hero to his audience, largely because the narrators in this novel seem to me much more caught up in the existence of the heroic figures than the narrators of Kierkegaard or ⟨...⟩ of Lermontov or Melville. As a hero Heathcliff is a figure who has some difficulty emerging from his ground; at the end of the novel he literally sinks back into it. In a similar way, Lockwood and Nelly are narrators who never fully separate themselves from the hero and heroine they are meditating upon. Since this view runs counter to the views of many commentators on *Wuthering Heights*—the topic of the narrators has been a popular one—I shall have to explain myself at some length.

Most discussions of Lockwood and Nelly Dean are concerned with establishing some kind of moral judgment on them in comparison to the hero and heroine: Nelly is seen either as the "villain" of the book (in the way she is always interfering in the action), or as a shrewd and sane ethical norm against which the failings of Heathcliff and Catherine have to be measured.[31] These conflicting claims can be balanced against one another, as in John Mathison's argument that "Nelly is an admirable woman whose point of view ... the reader must reject."[32] Similar judgments, pro, con, or mixed, are offered on the character of Lockwood. He is "epicoene," as Dorothy Van Ghent sees him, more sinned against than sinning, or like Nelly, a sympathetic guide with some obvious limitations. Such moral judgments are not at all irrelevant to our experience of the novel, but they do not give adequate consideration to the different imaginative level on which, as narrators, Lockwood and Nelly exist. Although Nelly has participated in the story she tells, and this is a question we shall consider shortly, both she and Lockwood are essentially observers of the actions of others, mediating, however complexly, between the strangeness of the hero and heroine and the familiarity of the hypothetical reader's view of human nature. Thomas Vogler is the only critic I am aware of who sees that their modes of perception are fundamentally different from one another. Contrasting the narrators with Heathcliff and Catherine he suggests "the possibility that the novel is about the problem of contrasted vision itself, perhaps even about the impossibility of adopting decisively one or the other mode of vision."[33]

Oddly enough, this is a view I shall want to advance myself in discussing the relation of narrator and hero, Ishmael and Ahab, in *Moby-Dick*. In *Wuthering Heights,* however, it seems to me to go too far in giving the narrators an imaginative autonomy from the hero and heroine. Nelly and Lockwood do not see the world in a radically different way from Catherine and Heathcliff. Although the narrators are tamer, they are quite implicated in the heroic struggle.

A comparison with Kierkegaard may help here. The poet or narrator, says Kierkegaard, cannot do what the hero does. "He is the genius of recollection, can do nothing except call to mind what has been done; he contributes nothing of his own, but is jealous of the intrusted treasure."[34] Is it true that Nelly Dean cannot do what Catherine does, or that Lockwood contributes nothing of his own to his story of Heathcliff? One is inclined to say "yes" until one thinks of the capacity for "doing" that both these superficially passive narrators seem to have. As an observer and reporter Nelly is intimately involved in the action of the plot. It is she who conceals from Catherine that Heathcliff has overheard part of her confession of divided love, it is she who urges Heathcliff "to frame high notions of [his] birth" (48). She is in many ways a literal *tortor heroum,* to use Kierkegaard's figurative phrase from *Fear and Trembling,* though to brand her as "the villain" as James Hafley does is to ignore how pervasive this kind of behavior is among other characters in the novel. Nor is Lockwood immune from such participation in the willfulness and violence of the story, as his dream of rubbing the wrists of the ghost child on the broken win-dowpane shows. Even his rejection of the young lady at Bath, which is often interpreted as a sign of his emotional inadequacy, shows a duality of warmth and coldness which is not unlike that of his hero.

That Lockwood and Nelly share the narrative function in *Wuthering Heights* is a reflection of the fact that Heathcliff shares the stage as hero with Catherine. In fact, Lockwood is presented as a version of Heathcliff, partly parodic but partly also a restatement of the heroic theme in a minor key. Lockwood begins to empathize with Heathcliff upon meeting him, and though most of his speculations are wide of the mark, Brontë does not simply expose him by her irony but allows him to restrain himself: "No, I'm running on too fast—I bestow my own attributes over liberally on him. Mr. Heathcliff may have entirely dissimilar reasons for keeping his hand out of the way, when he meets a would-be acquaintance, to those which actuate me" (3). In his waking experience Lockwood makes several blundering misinterpretations, but in his dream he experiences a vision curiously close to the vision which, we learn at the end of the novel, Heathcliff himself has been pursuing. Indeed, Edgar Shannon has argued convincingly that Lockwood's two dreams dra-matize in capsule form the sequence of isolation, suffering, and desire for revenge that forms the psychological basis of Heathcliff's character.[35] There is certainly a good deal of superciliousness in Lockwood's behavior and conversation, but on a more intuitive level he is not as antithetical to Heathcliff as one might suppose.

A further parallel between the male narrator and the hero is in their similar positions as outsiders. The correspondence between Heathcliff's position and Lockwood's is obvious at the beginning of the novel, when Lockwood tries to gain access to a house where he is quite unwelcome, but it is also emphasized at the end of the book, when Lockwood describes himself in a way that seems unselfconsciously reminiscent of Heathcliff. Lockwood has just overheard and seen the affectionate instruction of Hareton by Catherine: "They came to the door, and from their conversation, I judged they were about to issue out and have a walk on the moors. I supposed I should be condemned in Hareton Earnshaw's heart, if not by his mouth, to the lowest pit of the infernal regions if I showed my unfortunate person in the neighborhood then, and feeling very mean and malignant, I skulked around to seek refuge in the kitchen" (261). Varying the *Paradise Lost* pattern, Adam and Eve move out into nature and Satan is left in the house.

Nelly is Lockwood's opposite, and similar to Catherine is this respect. Like Catherine, she is the insider in family affairs, privy to the secrets of all, including Heathcliff. If Lockwood resembles Heathcliff in his icy reserve, Nelly resembles Catherine in her willfulness and self-assertion. Again, there is much in her character to distinguish her from her mistress, but Brontë is not out to sharpen our powers of judgment and discrimination as she presents the struggles of Catherine and Nelly, each for her own way. "To hear you, people might think *you* were the mistress!" Catherine cries out at her at one point (95). The trouble with Nelly as a narrator is that she is an agent as well as an observer. Her response to Heathcliff is frequently hostile, but she is also capable of sympathizing with him and encouraging him in his rebellion. "Nelly, make me decent, I'm going to be good," Heathcliff confides in her, only to get this support: "You could knock him [Edgar Linton] down in a twinkling; don't you feel that you could?" (47). "Were I in your place," Nelly tells him, "I would frame high notions of my birth" (48). While she deplores Heathcliff's pride, she encourages him in it; while she opposes his schemes, she is often instrumental in furthering them, as when she carries the letter from Heathcliff to Catherine in chapter 14. But in her minor encouragements and betrayals she is not unlike Catherine, whose similarly ambivalent treatment of Heathcliff is so instrumental in his fate.

The function or effect of such a reduplication of the traits of hero and heroine in the persons of the narrators is to implicate the narrative observers in the heroic actions they are witnessing. Although Lockwood and Nelly are to some extent foils for Heathcliff and Catherine, ironic reflections of their mythical substance, the difference is not so much of kind as of degree. Rather than the ironic discrimination that Kierkegaard works so carefully to effect, it is an imaginative fusion at which Brontë seems to aim. There is first of all little attempt to dramatize the potential difference between Lockwood's perceptions and Nelly's, even though they remain clearly distinct as characters. "She is, on the whole, a very fair narrator and I don't think I could improve her style," Lockwood says at one point (132). Secondly, both narrators, the outside observer and the inside informer, participate in the tale in a way that allows for little reflection on the part of the reader. One of the effects of Nelly's "prying," as Heathcliff calls it (247), or "carrying tales" (132), as she calls it herself, is to create a moral ambiguity in the realm of the narrator that helps divert our attention from the moral ambiguity in the realm of the hero. Nelly acts as something of a moral insulator in the way she presents her majority of the narrative.

Nevertheless, since this participation of the narrators in their heroes is based on an active assertion of the will, a will antagonistic to the plans and wishes of others, the narrators of *Wuthering Heights* do, in the final analysis, retain an important degree of autonomy in their meditations. If they were more accepting or devout in their hero worship they would be less effective in keeping Heathcliff and Catherine at the imaginative distance necessary for the hero to maintain *his* autonomy. I would like to insist here on the importance of this distance in the meditative form. If the hero is presented too unquestioningly, too much at heroic face value, he becomes a dogmatic assertion rather than an imaginative possibility. Carlyle's *On Heroes, Hero-Worship, and the Heroic in History,* with its flat, unironic celebration of an unchanging heroic substance, is a case in point. Other instances of the hero threatened by a loss of imaginative otherness can be found in Byron, where the dramatization of various heroic figures is always on the verge of collapsing into thinly veiled autobiography. In a letter to Hobhouse prefacing the Fourth Canto of *Childe Harold's Pilgrimage,* Byron gracefully admits defeat:

> With regard to the conduct of the last canto, there will be found less of the pilgrim than in any of the preceding, and that little slightly, if at all, separated from the author speaking in his own person. The fact is, that I had become weary of drawing a line which everyone seemed determined not to perceive: . . . it was in vain that I asserted, and imagined that I had drawn, a distinction between the author and the pilgrim; and the very anxiety to preserve this difference, and disappointment at finding it unavailing, so far crushed my efforts in the composition, that I decided to abandon it altogether—and have done so.[36]

One could hardly envision such a collapse of the narrative distinction in *Wuthering Heights;* it is only another heroically privileged being who can say "I am Heathcliff." The narrators of *Wuthering Heights* thus preserve the willful autonomy of the heroic presence by a willful antagonism of their own.

A secondary way in which the narrators preserve the heroism of Catherine and Heathcliff is in diverting attention from the so-called structure of the novel. In an essay written in 1926 called "The Structure of *Wuthering Heights,"* C. P. Sanger noted the surprisingly symmetrical genealogies of the Earnshaws and the Lintons, which are mirror images of one another and which merge geometrically in the marriage of Hareton Earnshaw and Catherine Linton.[37] But such a structure is only perceived upon a careful reflection and analysis of the book, as is the exact chronology of events that Sanger also reconstructs. What the accounts of Lockwood and Nelly do is to subsume this structure of plot—who marries whom, who does what next—to a structure of narrative, a structure that focuses attention on the heroic figures. We learned in chapter I that the Romantic hero was often conceived of as too large to be contained by a conventional plot, as were the tragic heroes of Shakespeare in Romantic criticism of his plays. It is significant that Brontë carefully constructs the realistic basis for her story that Sanger has discovered, but it is also significant that she deliberately conceals the realistic groundwork by means of the narrative form of the meditation on the hero.[38]

In the chapter on Kierkegaard we noted the psychological implications of this peculiar narrative form for the author's developing sense of selfhood. For Kierkegaard, the form dramatized a strong existential self virtually inaccessible to its own speculative intelligence. The psychological dimensions of Emily Brontë's use of the meditation on the hero are harder to discern, but no less interesting. Her sister Charlotte was able to present a Romantic hero in a more traditional novelistic mode: Jane Eyre tells her own story in the first person, a story in which Rochester is an important character but by no means such an exclusive focus as Heathcliff in *Wuthering Heights*. A major psychological difference between the two sisters which may explain this difference between the two Brontë novels lies in Emily's obsessive concern with privacy. Charlotte unintentionally but traumatically invaded this privacy on two occasions in her own quest for public recognition. The first crisis came when she discovered by accident the notebook containing Emily's Gondal poems and urged her to publish them, the second when Charlotte revealed Emily's identity as "Ellis Bell" to her publishers. Emily took the protection of her pseudonym much more seriously than either of her sisters.[39]

A possible link between the psychological makeup of the author and the dynamics of the literary form can be forged from Northrop Frye's speculation on the relation of the Byronic hero to Byron: "If we ask how a witty, sociable, extroverted poet came to create such a character, we can see that it must have arisen as what psychologists call a projection of his inner self, that inner self that was so mysterious and inscrutable even to its owner."[40] Brontë was Byron's psychological opposite in this respect, deeply introverted in her withdrawal from public view, even from the view of her family. If Heathcliff is a more vital Byronic hero than Byron's own characters, the reason may lie in this, that the hero for Brontë represents an innermost self that is intimately known but carefully hidden from the eyes of others. In this light the failure of the narrators of *Wuthering Heights* to comprehend their hero and heroine, even as they share some of the latters' traits, takes on a biographical significance.

The absence of evidence about Emily's view of herself makes it difficult to determine the significance of *Wuthering Heights* in her ongoing imaginative development, but it is hard to ignore certain parallels between her life and art. As noted earlier, the writing of *Wuthering Heights,* following the joint publication of the Brontë sisters' *Poems,* represented a dramatic emergence of Emily as author. She moved out of the shared privacy of the Gondal romances, poems and prose into a much more public world. The Gondal world was private; it was also essentially mythic. As J. Hillis Miller puts it, "There is no assertion that the stories have been invented. Rather Emily and Anne speak of their writing as the recording of events which have a prior and objective existence. . . . In one sense the Gondal saga was a sequence of temporally related events like history. In another sense it was a simultaneous existence of all its events in a perpetual present outside of time."[41] In *Wuthering Heights,* as our discussion has emphasized, there is a strong impulse on the part of the mythical hero to enter into history, a history that involves both the experience of passing time and the socialization of a recalcitrant private selfhood. It would seem that the novel enacts a similar impulse on the part of the author herself, a desire to move beyond her accustomed role as family romancer and into a future role as novelist in the company of her sisters.

What happened to Emily after the publication of *Wuthering Heights* is less clear. There is inconclusive evidence that she began a second novel and clearer indications that she wrote more Gondal poetry.[42] But she survived the publication of her novel by only one year. The death of Branwell in September of 1848 plunged her into a psychological withdrawal and a physical decline, which ended in her death on December 18. That there was some connection between Branwell and the figure of Heathcliff is evident, and it seems that Emily increasingly resented Charlotte's attempts to exclude Branwell from the literary ventures of the family.[43] One can only wonder whether in the increasingly autistic privacy of her imagination Emily felt that her only satisfaction lay in joining her brother in a world out of time and family conflict, that her life might well follow the pattern of her art.

NOTES

[1] Winifred Gérin in her recent biography, *Emily Brontë* (Oxford, 1971), pp. 213–14, notes that except for Scott Emily's reading was quite apart from the major English novelists of the nineteenth century. The relevance of the *The Black Dwarf* was established by Florence Dry, *The Sources of* Wuthering Heights (Cambridge, 1937).

[2] Fannie Ratchford attempts to piece together this epic in *Gondal's Queen: A Novel in Verse by Emily Jane Brontë* (Austin, 1955). Her argument that all Emily's poems were part of the Gondal saga is not substantiated.

[3] *Wuthering Heights,* ed. V. S. Pritchett (Cambridge, Mass, 1956), pp. 14, 128. In all further references to the novel page numbers cited parenthetically in text are from this edition.

[4] E. T. A. Hoffmann's story "The Entail" ("Das Majorat") is advanced as an important source by some critics; e.g. Augustin-Lewis Wells, *Les Soeurs Brontë et l'étranger* (Paris, 1937), pp. 149–57; Ruth M. MacKay, "Irish Heaths and German Cliffs: A study of the Foreign Sources of *Wuthering Heights,*" *Brigham Young University Studies* 7 (1965): 28–39. But the most that Brontë could have derived here, aside from some typical Gothic effects used elsewhere, is the device of the narrator's dream as he spends his first night at the castle.

[5] Gérin, *Emily Brontë,* pp. 76–80.

[6] Ibid., p. 217. I am indebted to Gérin for this source, although I would make less of it.

[7] "Night Thoughts on the Gothic Novel," *Yale Review* 52 (1962): 253. One might say of the Gothic villain, however, as Peter Brooks does of the melodramatic mode in general, that the moral values involved are exaggerated precisely because they are no longer felt to be secure; see "The Melodramatic Imagination," *Partisan Review* 39 (1972): 209–11.

[8] Cf. Catherine's mad scene with *Hamlet,* IV, v, 175–78: "There's fennel for you, and columbines; there's rue for you; and here's some for me; we may call it herb of grace o' Sundays; oh, you must wear your rue with a difference." The parallel is also noted by Arnold P. Drew, "Emily Brontë and *Hamlet,*" *Notes & Queries,* n.s. 1 (1954): 81–82, and Lew Girdler, "*Wuthering Heights* and Shakespeare," *Huntington Library Quarterly* 19 (1955–1956): 389–90. Cf. Heathcliff's lines with *Hamlet,* V, i, 257–59: "I loved Ophelia; forty thousand brothers / Could not, with all their quantity of love, / Make up my sum." I am

indebted to Girdler for this parallel. As V. S. Pritchett suggests in his Introduction to *Wuthering Heights* (p. x) Nelly Dean recalls the Nurse in *Romeo and Juliet.*

[9] Gérin, *Emily Brontë,* p. 47. Edgar and Isabella are a parodic Adam and Eve, of course, just as Heathcliff is a Romantically transvalued Satan. Brontë evokes earlier works less by specific verbal echo than by pose and gesture; even in the allusion to Ophelia's speech, where verbal parallels are identifiable, it is the gesture of plucking (flowers, feathers) that carries the burden of the similitude. For an interesting discussion of the "valorization of gesture" in Romantic prose fiction, see Brooks "The Melodramatic Imagination," pp. 207–09.

[10] *The Works of Lord Byron,* ed. E. H. Coleridge (London, 1904), 3:123 (ll. 784–86) and 136 (ll. 1123–26). The reunion in the lady's grave does occur in *The Bridegroom of Barma,* however.

[11] *Works,* 4:40, 41 (ll. 189, 196). This correspondence was discovered by Anne Lapraik Livermore, "Byron and Emily Brontë," *Quarterly Review* 300 (1962): 337–44.

[12] Gérin, *Emily Brontë,* p. 45.

[13] Livermore, "Byron and Emily Brontë," p. 338: "It becomes possible to perceive that probably *Wuthering Heights* was planned as an intertwining of *The Dream* with the facts as then known of Byron's ambiguous love for his half-sister, his marriage to Anne Isabella, and her flight from him." Helen Brown's "The Influence of Byron on Emily Brontë," *Modern Language Review* 34 (1939): 374–81, deals mainly with Byron's influence on the poetry.

[14] *The Disappearance of God* (Cambridge, Mass., 1963), p. 167.

[15] *The Complete Poems of Emily Jane Brontë,* ed. C. W. Hatfield (New York, 1941), pp. 104–06. The speaker of the poem is probably a Gondal character.

[16] *The English Novel: Form and Function* (New York, 1953), pp. 154–57. See also Philip Drew, "Charlotte Brontë as a Critic of *Wuthering Heights,*" *Nineteenth-Century Fiction* 18 (1964): 365–81, who suspects Heathcliff of being a bona fide ghoul or afreet. Thomas Moser uses a more psychological idiom: "Over a century ago Emily Brontë dramatized what Freud subsequently called the id. She discovered and symbolized in Heathcliff . . . that part of us we know so little about. . . ." ("What Is the Matter with Emily Jane? Conflicting Impulses in *Wuthering Heights,*" in *The Victorian Novel,* ed. Ian Watt (Oxford, 1971) p. 183.)

[17] See , e.g., John Hagan, "The Control of Sympathy in *Wuthering Heights,*" *Nineteenth-Century Fiction* 21 (1967): 305–23. Other studies that stress the humanity, moral and psychological, of the hero are W. A. Craik's excellent chapter on *Wuthering Heights* in her *The Brontë Novels* (London, 1968), and F. H. Langman, "*Wuthering Heights,*" *Essays in Criticism* 15 (1965): 294–312.

[18] *The Disappearance of God,* p. 172.

[19] Miller in fact has trouble establishing the relevance of a Christian God to his analysis. He brings Him in by taking seriously the caricature of Methodism in Joseph, and by making too explicit and orthodox a very implicit and displaced Calvinism in Brontë's writing.

[20] *Biographia Literaria,* ed. J. Shawcross (Oxford, 1907), 2:6.

[21] See Thomas Vogler's introduction to his *Twentieth-Century Interpretations of* Wuthering Heights (Englewood Cliffs, N.J., 1968), p. 10 for a perceptive comparison of Brontë with Wordsworth and Blake on the treatment of visionary childhood.

[22] Quote is from *The Myth of the Birth of the Hero,* trans. Robbins and Jelliffe (New York, 1952), p. 81. Cf. ibid., p. 82: "Myths are, therefore, created by adults, by means of retrograde childhood fantasies, the hero being credited with the myth-maker's personal infantile history."

[23] *Identity, Youth and Crisis* (New York, 1968), pp. 108–09. It is tempting to use Erikson further to describe Heathcliff's retentive kind of revenge ("Avarice is growing with him a besetting sin," Catherine says, though this is never really shown [87]). Heathcliff's usurpation of the property and his sudden relinquishing of it are recalled by Erikson's emphasis on "the ability—and doubly felt inability" at this stage "to coordinate a number of highly conflicting action patterns characterized by the tendencies of 'holding on' and 'letting go'" (p. 107). A final intriguing point of similarity between Brontë and Erikson is the emphasis on the social institution of the law as a safeguard for the individual's autonomy at this stage.

[24] Craik, *The Brontë Novels,* p. 22.

[25] See Hagan, "The Control of Sympathy"; Craik, *The Brontë Novels;* and Edgar Shannon, "Lockwood's Dreams and the Exegesis of *Wuthering Heights,*" *Nineteenth-Century Fiction* 14 (1959): 95–109.

[26] Two useful discussions of the temporality of the novel are Robert F. Gleckner's "Time in *Wuthering Heights,*" *Criticism* 1 (1959): 328–38; and Thomas A. Vogler, "Story and History in *Wuthering Heights,*" *Twentieth-Century Interpretations,* pp. 78–99.

[27] *An Introduction to the English Novel* (London, 1951), 1:149–50.

[28] See Van Ghent, *The English Novel;* Moser, "What Is the Matter with Emily Jane?" and the more

sophisticated Ronald E. Fine, "Lockwood's Dreams and the Key to *Wuthering Heights,*" *Nineteenth-Century Fiction* 24 (1969): 16–30.

[29] Although positive evidence is lacking, Gérin thinks that some of Mary Shelley's novels were familiar to Emily Brontë, either through publication or review in *Blackwood's,* which the Brontë children read extensively in back numbers. *Frankenstein* was reviewed, with generous plot summary, in *Blackwood's* of March 1818.

[30] *Either/Or,* trans. David and Lillian Swenson, rev. Howard A. Johnson (Garden City, N.Y., 1959), 1:9.

[31] James Hafley, "The Villain of *Wuthering Heights,*" *Nineteenth-Century Fiction* 13 (1958): 199–215, and John Fraser, "The Name of Action: Nelly Dean and *Wuthering Heights,*" *Nineteenth-Century Fiction* 20 (1965): 223–36, respectively.

[32] "Nelly Dean and the Power of *Wuthering Heights,*" *Nineteenth-Century Fiction* 11 (1956): 106–29. Mathison's synthesis was made before the thesis and antithesis of Hafley and Fraser.

[33] "Introduction," *Twentieth-Century Interpretations,* p. 12. Vogler's essay in this volume, "Story and History in *Wuthering Heights,*" gives sophisticated and wide-ranging support to his suggestion.

[34] Sören Kierkegaard, *Fear and Trembling,* in *Fear and Trembling and the Sickness unto Death,* trans. Walter Lowrie (Garden City, N.Y., 1954), p. 30.

[35] "Lockwood's Dreams," pp. 16–30.

[36] *Works,* 2:323.

[37] Reprinted in *Twentieth-Century Interpretations,* pp. 15–27.

[38] A similar effect was apparently achieved in the Gondal saga, where there was a clearly worked out history and sequence of events in prose alluded to only obscurely in the poems. The poems are chiefly dramatic monologues.

[39] On these two incidents and Emily's reactions, see Gérin, *Emily Brontë* pp. 231–34, 281–83.

[40] "Lord Byron," *Fables of Identity* (New York, 1963), p. 177.

[41] *The Disappearance of God,* pp. 160–61.

[42] See "Emily Brontë's Second Novel," *Transactions of the Brontë Society* 15 (1966): 28–33. Certainly a twenty-five-line revision of a long narrative poem was written; the whole piece may have been written after *Wuthering Heights* (Ratchford, *Gondal's Queen,* pp. 32, 183).

[43] Gérin, *Emily Brontë,* p. 234. My own guess is that Heathcliff reflects Emily's strong sympathy for her brother, the hero's orphanhood being a sign of the brother's exclusion from family affairs by Charlotte, while Hindley, from whose affection Heathcliff wins Catherine initially, reflects the disgust which Branwell's dissipation inspired even in Emily herself.

Ronald B. Hatch

HEATHCLIFF'S "QUEER END" AND SCHOPENHAUER'S DENIAL OF THE WILL

'I wish to be as God made me,' Emily Brontë was wont to reply, leaving her questioners mystified. And her readers to this day have been similarly discomfited by the enigmatic self-sufficiency of *Wuthering Heights.* In her 1964 survey of Brontë scholarship, Mildred G. Christian rightly noted that 'the contradictory judgments on *Wuthering Heights* are the most striking fact in its critical history.'[1] The major reason for the contradictory judgments is that readers have reacted in different ways to Heathcliff and Cathy. While some readers have maintained that Cathy and Heathcliff are invested with positive values, others have seen them representing negative qualities which are exorcized in the end. The two poles can be illustrated by Ruth M. Adams, who maintains that 'Catherine and Heathcliff themselves illustrate the perverse values that prevail in *Wuthering Heights,*'[2] and Edgar F. Shannon, Jr, who advances the antithetical reading when he concludes that the novel 'results in a paradigm of love,'[3] in which Emily Brontë shows that Heathcliff 'is not innately demonic and that hate is subservient to love.'[4] A survey of recent criticism reveals that no consensus has been reached about the novel's ultimate direction. This diversity of opinion of course bears witness to the complexity and greatness of *Wuthering Heights* in its ability to engender different responses. What is needed, however, is an examination of those incidents in the novel which permit opposing interpretations. Since most of the disagreements arise over Heathcliff, I intend to offer a close reading of Heathcliff's actions, especially those near the end of the novel, in order to point out where and why readers diverge in their opinions, and hopefully thereby to clarify some of Emily Brontë's assumptions in the portrayal of her principal characters.

Surprisingly enough, little detailed attention has so far been devoted to a close examination of Heathcliff's death, a curious omission when, as Melvin R. Watson has commented, 'Heathcliff *is* the story.'[5] In part this failure to attend closely to Heathcliff is a result of the emphasis given to the structure of the novel. In his important article 'Nelly Dean and the Power of *Wuthering Heights,*' John K. Mathison showed that the structure of the novel serves the purpose of maintaining the reader's

From *Canadian Review of Comparative Literature* 1, No. 1 (Winter 1974): 49–64.

sympathy with Heathcliff until the end of the book.[6] The reader's desire to over-come the narrative limitations of Nelly and Lockwood permits him to bear with more of Heathcliff's violence than would have been the case had Heathcliff told the story. Yet emphasis on the structure of the novel has at times obscured an im-portant question—what is the reader's final opinion of Heathcliff? While the rhe-torical devices may allow the reader to maintain sympathy with Heathcliff, surely they alone cannot turn Heathcliff into a sympathetic hero.

Readers of *Wuthering Heights* have often been self-conscious and apologetic about their sympathy towards Heathcliff. F. H. Langham, for instance, argues that 'Hindley's brutality, tyranny, and murderous violence far outdo anything of which Heathcliff can be accused on the evidence.'[7] And Langham asserts that the reader continues to sympathize with Heathcliff because of the justice of Heathcliff's desire 'to hold a place in the scheme of things.'[8] Yet Heathcliff's violence obviously troubles Langham, for he remains unwilling to credit Heathcliff with positive values, and his rather lame conclusion is that, 'for all this, in Heathcliff's behaviour there is an excess from which moral sympathy does turn away.'[9] Yet this reading, like so many, ignores the ending of the book, and therefore never entertains the possibility that the narrative method functions to gain enough of the reader's sympathy to keep his attention until the end of the novel when Heathcliff can undergo a re-deeming process.

The phrase 'redeeming process,' it should be noted, has been applied to the character of Heathcliff, and not to the novel as a whole. Elliott Gose, in his inter-esting article, '*Wuthering Heights:* The Heath and the Hearth,'[10] has already shown that the novel embodies 'figurative image and narrative patterns,' whereby the perversion of Heathcliff and Cathy is resolved in the second generation—in Cathy II and Hareton. Gose places the change in the novel's direction near the end when Cathy resists Heathcliff's will in the incident concerning the uprooting of Joseph's mulberry bushes:

> The moral teething is complete; someone has finally resisted tyranny, and Heathcliff, seeing the pattern of his youth repeated, gives up.[11]

But the use of such a phrase as 'Heathcliff ... gives up' indicates that Gose does not believe a positive change occurs in Heathcliff. What I wish to argue is that not only does a positive change occur at this point, but that Heathcliff learns something about himself and embodies this positive change.[12]

The first clear indication of Heathcliff's change in personality occurs near the end of the novel when Heathcliff meets Hareton rushing from the house after the younger Catherine has tormented him into throwing his books in the fire. Sur-prised, Heathcliff lays hold of Hareton's shoulder and asks: 'What's to do now, my lad?'[13] But Hareton refuses to answer, and Heathcliff sighs:

> It will be odd, if I thwart myself! ... But, when I look for his father in his face, I find *her* every day more! How the devil is he so like? I can hardly bear to see him.'
> (ch xxxi p 240)

Such a statement serves both to tease and to appease the reader's expectations. Certainly Heathcliff's sudden change of mind seems to demand an explanation; and in part an explanation is offered when Heathcliff 'explains' that he sees Cathy Earnshaw in Hareton. But why this should deprive him of the will to act remains unclear. The passage seems designed to persuade the reader to accept the change while awaiting further developments. Yet most unexpectedly, at this point when the reader's curiosity about Heathcliff has been fully aroused, the novel's focus shifts abruptly. It will be recalled that Lockwood himself overheard Heathcliff's above-quoted comment while waiting at the Heights to tell him of his intended departure from Thrushcross Grange. Although Lockwood's diary brings the reader to the very point when Heathcliff's change commences, to the point where Lockwood could, if he wished, begin to observe new events for himself, Lockwood himself never witnesses the change. At this point Lockwood returns to London, and breaks off his diary with no evident curiosity about Heathcliff's future. Only when he returns briefly on a chance visit eight months later, in September 1802, does Lockwood hear from Nelly the story of Heathcliff's 'queer end.'

As a result, the nature of Heathcliff's 'queer end' appears as something of an epilogue, and no doubt this is one reason why Heathcliff's death has not received the attention which is its due. Yet to fail to take account of this section is to run the danger of becoming a Lockwood, and to remain unaware of and uninterested in the crucial change towards which the story has been moving.

Although the implications of Heathcliff's death are not spelled out, many clues are given that indicate its seriousness and importance. In her account, Nelly repeatedly emphasizes the changes in Heathcliff's character preceding his death. For instance, Heathcliff brought her to the Heights from Thrushcross Grange because he was becoming 'more and more disinclined to society' (ch xxxii p 246). What this means at the sparsely populated Heights is that Heathcliff does not want to be alone with the younger Catherine. Nelly reports that Heathcliff told her he was 'tired of seeing Catherine' (ch xxxii p 245), that he disliked the way Catherine stared at him with her 'infernal eyes' (ch xxxiii p 251). Heathcliff of course also dislikes Catherine's open defiance. And undoubtedly Gose is correct when he places the change of direction in the novel at the point where Catherine and Hareton uproot Joseph's mulberry bushes for a garden of plants and flowers imported from the Grange. Yet Heathcliff's change is not directly contingent on Catherine's defiance. Actually, the defiance itself arouses his anger, and for a moment, as Heathcliff holds Catherine by the hair, it seems that he may murder her. But as his anger reaches its peak, he suddenly stops:

> his fingers relaxed, he shifted his grasp from her head to her arm, and gazed intently in her face. Then, he drew his hand over his eyes, stood a moment to collect himself apparently, and turning anew to Catherine, said with assumed calmness—
>
> 'You must learn to avoid putting me in a passion, or I shall really murder you, some time!'   (ch xxxiii p 253)

Quite clearly Heathcliff is prevented from hitting Catherine this time because of something he sees in her eyes—the same thing he saw earlier in Hareton's eyes—a resemblance to his own Cathy. Nelly, it will be remembered, comments that Hareton and Catherine Linton have eyes that 'are precisely similar, and they are those of Catherine Earnshaw' (ch. xxxiii p 254).

To the reader interested in understanding Heathcliff's change, the crucial confrontation appears a short time later when Heathcliff finds Hareton and Catherine reading by the fire after he has forbade any further relationship. Nelly first relates how 'they lifted their eyes together, to encounter Mr Heathcliff,' and then makes the above-quoted comment of how similar their eyes are to those of Catherine Earnshaw. Yet the loquacious Nelly has almost nothing to say about Heathcliff's reaction at this important juncture. She merely comments:

> I suppose this resemblance disarmed Mr Heathcliff: he walked to the hearth in evident agitation, but it quickly subsided, as he looked at the young man; or, I should say, altered its character, for it was there yet.   (ch xxxiii p 254)

Unusually vague at this point, Nelly can only 'suppose' that the resemblance disturbed Heathcliff. Thus, curiously enough, Emily Brontë deliberately eschews all overt explanation of Heathcliff's behaviour, leaving it open to the reader's interpretation. This no doubt explains why the novel has generated so many widely varying explanations.

Although the positive reasons for Heathcliff's discomposure may remain mysterious, Emily Brontë takes pains to tell us the reasons that *do not* affect Heathcliff. Heathcliff himself states that he forsakes the chances of revenge neither from pity nor because he has lost the power:

> I could do it [take revenge]; and none could hinder me. But where is the use? I don't care for striking, I can't take the trouble to raise my hand! That sounds as if I had been labouring the whole time, only to exhibit a fine trait of magnanimity. It is far from being the case—I have lost the faculty of enjoying their destruction, and I am too idle to destroy for nothing.'
>
> (ch xxxiii p 255)

Heathcliff's inaction could be construed as altogether unmotivated. But such an 'explanation' requires careful qualification, since Heathcliff himself understands the apparent absurdity of his change of heart, and thus anticipates the reader's possible objection:

> 'It is a poor conclusion, is it not,' he observed, having brooded a while on the scene he had just witnessed. 'An absurd termination to my violent exertions? I get levers and mattocks to demolish the two houses, and train myself to be capable of working like Hercules, and when everything is ready, and in my power, I find the will to lift a slate off either roof has vanished!'
>
> (ch xxxiii pp 254–5)

Although Heathcliff's seeming lack of motivation has led a number of critics to ask whether the novel does not fail artistically in the last section, surely such a reaction misses the point: Emily Brontë recognized that Heathcliff's end was 'queer'; she wanted the reader to puzzle over its meaning.

For the reader to understand Heathcliff's death, the novel demands an intuitive leap from the designedly ambiguous evidence to the ultimate meaning of Heathcliff's change. The very structure of the novel indicates that such a leap is imperative. Since neither Nelly nor Lockwood understands Heathcliff, the reader must overcome the narrators' lack of perception by means of his own insight. Thus the reader finds himself in a position remarkably akin to that described by eighteenth- and early nineteenth-century philosophers where it seemed problematic that man could ever know the 'ultimate reality' (the Kantian Ding-an-sich) when he was limited to his perception of sense data or surface phenomena.[14] Interestingly, Heathcliff at the end of the novel seems to transcend his previous limitations to attain a new mode of perception. The unusual nature of this change is difficult to explain without the context of Romantic metaphysical thought, but is clarified when compared with some strikingly similar examples cited by Schopenhauer in his major work *Die Welt als Wille und Vorstellung* (usually translated as *The World as Will and Idea*).[15] Schopenhauer describes an experience and an attitude to the phenomenal world of which Emily Brontë provides a concrete character example. The one account, while it does not necessarily give rise to the other, helps us to understand it.

Schopenhauer, following Kant, believed that all objects in the material world were but the objectification of another dimension. In Kantian terms this other dimension was called the noumenal world; Schopenhauer preferred to call it 'the Will.' Schopenhauer claimed:

> every individual is transitory only as phenomenon, but as thing-in-itself is timeless, and therefore endless. But it is also only as phenomenon that an individual is distinguished from the other things of the world; as thing-in-itself he is the will which appears in all, and death destroys the illusion which separates his consciousness from that of the rest: this is immortality. His exemption from death, which belongs to him only as thing-in-itself, is for the phenomenon one with the immortality of the rest of the external world.[16]

Steeped in the writings of Plato and Kant, Schopenhauer believed that man could never be happy in this world until he had grasped the basic fact that the phenomenal world which he saw around him, and of which he was a part, was only a shadow of the real world; until he did so, he would continue to pursue unreal ends that would prove transitory. To gain such an understanding, the individual must see through the transitory nature of the world conditioned by the Kantian categories of time and space to the eternal noumenal world where space and time cease to exist.[17] As soon as the individual understood that all phenomena were mere objectifications of the one Will, he would then see the absurdity of striving for transitory and unreal goals, and attempt to realize himself as part of the underlying world Will.

Schopenhauer said that the first step in recognizing that the phenomenal world was only a shadow of the Will would be taken when a man recognized, 'in all beings his own inmost and true self.'[18] What Schopenhauer describes is precisely what happens to Heathcliff. His change commences when he sees the resemblance of the younger Catherine and Hareton to his Cathy, and when he perceives that they are living out the patterns of his own youth. Seeing through exterior appearances, he begins at this point to understand that his life force (Will) is identical with that working in Catherine and Hareton. No longer does he see people merely as phenomena; he is able to see through to their noumenal existence. Of Hareton, he says:

> Five minutes ago, Hareton seemed a personification of my youth, not a human being. I felt to him in such a variety of ways, that it would have been impossible to have accosted him rationally. . . . His startling likeness to Catherine connected him fearfully with her.'   (ch xxxiii p 255)

Heathcliff realizes that Nelly (and possibly the reader as well) will misunderstand him when he says that Hareton resembles Catherine Earnshaw. As Hindley's son, Hareton is Cathy's nephew, and would have the Earnshaw features. But Heathcliff is not referring simply to a family resemblance. He says, 'That, however, which you may suppose the most potent to arrest my imagination, is actually the least, for what is not connected with her to me?' (ch xxxiii p 255). Moreover Heathcliff is beginning to perceive that *all* individuals are mere objectifications of the single world force. Everywhere he looks he finds that 'the most ordinary faces of men and women,' even his own features 'mock [him] with a resemblance' to his Cathy (ch xxxiii p 255). Even objects begin to resemble Cathy: 'I cannot look down to this floor, but her features are shaped on the flags! In every cloud, in every tree—filling the air at night, and caught by glimpses in every object by day, I am surrounded with her image!' (ch xxxiii p 255).

So far what has been described of Heathcliff's change is consonant with Romantic neo-platonism in general. But Schopenhauer's innovation in Kantian thought was his claim that as soon as an individual understood completely that phenomenally different objects were all products of the same world Will, then the individual's volition would cease, since he would see that all differences in the world were only seeming differences. This applies to Heathcliff, since his volition ceases as soon as he sees the spirit of his Cathy in the world around him. His new knowledge of the nature of the world quiets his will.[19]

Interestingly enough, as soon as Heathcliff begins his change, he once again becomes the principal figure of interest. In the middle section of the novel, Heathcliff occupies less of our attention as the stories of the second generation 'people of calm'—Hareton, Catherine, and Linton—are developed at length. That Heathcliff should become a relatively minor figure in the middle section is only natural, since his sole interest at this time is his desire for revenge. Miriam Allott notes: 'At the very point where where his need for vengeance dies, Heathcliff does in fact fully revive *as* Heathcliff, that is to say, as the powerfully compelling and complex figure of the first part of the story.'[20] However, this description is only partly correct. When Heathcliff resumes his place at centre stage, he is not the old Heathcliff, but a changing Heathcliff. Our interest revives because of his change and his 'queer end.'

Heathcliff's death, sometimes described as suicide, has long been a source of confusion, but it becomes less so when seen in relation to Schopenhauer's description. In terms remarkably similar to those of Emily Brontë, Schopenhauer gives a full explanation of the type of 'suicide' which Heathcliff represents:

> There is a species of suicide which seems to be quite distinct from the common kind, though its occurrence has perhaps not yet been fully established. It is starvation, voluntarily chosen on the ground of extreme asceticism. All instances of it, however, have been accompanied and obscured by much religious fanaticism, and even superstition. Yet it seems that the absolute denial of will may reach the point at which the will shall be wanting to take the necessary nourishment for the support of the natural life. This kind of suicide is so far from being the result of the will to live, that such a completely resigned ascetic only ceases to live because he has already altogether ceased to will. No other death than that by starvation is in this case conceivable (unless it were the result of some special superstition); for the intention to cut short the torment would itself be a stage in the assertion of will.[21]

When Schopenhauer says that the reason for this type of death is 'extreme asceticism,' he means that the person becomes so completely absorbed in the attainment of the spiritual life that he neglects the material world. In Heathcliff's case, his 'spiritual reunion' with Cathy so completely overpowers him that he cannot be reached by normal motives. So powerfully does his vision of reunion with Cathy affect him, that he unwittingly starves himself. When Schopenhauer described such starvation cases, he was not speaking entirely theoretically, but attempting to explain a number of historic incidents. He cites several examples, including one which occurred in England in the 1830s, with which Emily Brontë might easily have been acquainted.[22] Certainly Heathcliff's death follows closely Schopenhauer's pattern.

As Schopenhauer explains, a death such as Heathcliff's is actually the opposite of suicide: the person dies, not because he hates the world, but because he has discovered he need not take the world seriously. In fact, such a person cannot be said to 'will' at all. He dies because he has completely lost all will—even the will to eat. The frequently made claim that Heathcliff 'deliberately wills his own death'[23] is a distortion of the text. When Nelly asks Heathcliff whether he has a 'feeling of illness' or whether he is 'afraid of death,' Heathcliff is surprised:

> 'Afraid? No!. . . I have neither a fear, nor a presentiment, nor a hope of death. Why should I? With my hard constitution, and temperate mode of living, and unperilous occupations, I ought to, and probably *shall* remain above ground, till there is scarcely a black hair on my head.'   (ch xxxiii p 256)

To suggest that he deliberately *does* anything is patently absurd; something happens to him over which he has no control.[24]

Indeed, Heathcliff's comments suggest that he is losing all control over his body. He says, 'And yet I cannot continue in this condition! I have to remind myself to breathe—almost to remind my heart to beat!' (ch xxxiii p 256). The passage could be treated as hyperbole, designed to show that Heathcliff is losing all interest in life. However, Schopenhauer discussed this very question of the possibility of a person's losing all interest in willing and so forgetting to breathe. Noting that the question whether breathing belongs to the set of voluntary or involuntary movements is disputed, Schopenhauer concludes that although various people have attempted to explain breathing as a mixed function, it can actually be included in the set of voluntary actions:

> However, we are finally obliged to number it [breathing] with expressions of will which result from motives. For other motives, i.e., mere ideas, can determine the will to check it or accelerate it, and, as is the case with every other voluntary action, it seems to us that we could give up breathing altogether and voluntarily suffocate. And in fact we could do so if any other motive influenced the will sufficiently strongly to overcome the pressing desire for air.[25]

In Heathcliff's case, a motive exists almost strong enough to overcome his desire for air. He exclaims:

> 'I have a single wish, and my whole being and faculties are yearning to attain it. They have yearned towards it so long, and so unwaveringly, that I'm convinced it *will* be reached—and *soon*—because it has devoured my existence. I am swallowed in the anticipation of its fulfilment.' (ch xxxiii p 256)

The 'single wish' is, of course, his desire for reunification with Cathy.

In his discussions of the possibility of an enlightened individual's dying as a result of starvation or suffocation, Schopenhauer generally conceived of the case in terms of the individual's denial of his will. Heathcliff's death, however, may not appear immediately to follow this pattern, since Heathcliff claimed that his will was swallowed up by the single desire of rejoining Cathy. Moreover, the question still remains as to why Heathcliff should become assured of his reunification with Cathy at the moment when he sees in the growing relationship between Catherine and Hareton a reminder of his love for Cathy. Both points are clarified when one recalls what Cathy meant to Heathcliff. Their relationship is not presented as an ordinary love affair, but as the meeting and mingling of two people such that each completes the other. When Cathy explained to Nelly—'I *am* Heathcliff'—she was expressing the feeling that Heathcliff and she were the same substance. It will be recalled that in her dream at the Grange, Cathy found that her 'misery arose from the separation that Hindley had ordered' between Heathcliff and herself (ch xii p 107). She does not mean that they are united sexually, but that they are made of the same 'stuff.' Heathcliff's recognition of his own life patterns in the lives of Hareton and Catherine teaches him that Cathy and he, although phenomenally different, are in essence part of the one Universal Will. This knowledge enables him to understand that he has not lost Cathy, that they are still one. Their bodies are only transitory phenomena; their real nature has never been divided or separated because it partakes of the Universal Will. As a result of this new knowledge, Heathcliff loses all interest in existing as a part of nature, surrenders all volition, and thus delivers himself from any individual existence.[26] He has become conscious that his own nature is identical with the kernel of the world, and thus identical with Catherine's nature.

In the mind of the layman, Schopenhauer's philosophy of the denial of the will has been misconstrued; the belief has arisen that he advocated suicide as a remedy to existence in a world of sorrow. But Schopenhauer always maintained strongly that one could not escape this world merely through death; suicide, he contended, was not a denial of the will, but an assertion of the will. To escape the phenomenal world forever, and so overcome death, one had to attain consciousness of the essential oneness of all objects. Consequently if Heathcliff is to be reunified with Cathy in a noumenal existence, it is not enough that Cathy should have died, but that she should have died eternally to this world.

But is this the case? Although Cathy's death resembles Heathcliff's in a number of important respects, Emily Brontë has chosen to de-emphasize those positive results which arise from Heathcliff's achievement in denying his will. Hints are given that suggest Cathy gives up the world freely for a better world, but the full implications of her death are left to be worked out later in Heathcliff's death. In her comment following Cathy's death, Nelly sums up the reader's puzzled reaction to Cathy:

> To be sure, one might have doubted, after the wayward and impatient existence she had led, whether she merited a haven of peace at last.
>
> (ch xvi pp 137–8)

Yet the sight of Cathy's corpse convinces Nelly that Cathy has achieved peace:

> One might doubt in seasons of cold reflection, but not then, in the presence of her corpse. It asserted its own tranquillity, which seemed a pledge of equal quiet to its former inhabitant.   (ch xvi p 138)

As was the case with Heathcliff, critical opinion has divided over the quality of Cathy's death. The reason for this is that Emily Brontë has again deliberately created an ambiguity. For instance, after the quarrel between Heathcliff and Edgar that causes her fatal illness, Cathy locks herself in her room and asks Nelly to tell Edgar that she is 'in danger of being seriously ill.' Then she adds: 'I wish it may prove true. He has startled and distressed me shockingly! I want to frighten him' (ch xi p 100). These comments seem those of a confused girl, not those of a Schopenhauerian saint. And at this point in the novel, surely Cathy is confused. Although she realizes early that she and Heathcliff are one, she is untrue to this perception when she attempts to compromise with the social world by marrying Edgar. Later, however, when confronted with Heathcliff and her husband, she is forced to choose between them. For a time she tries to blame her plight on Nelly, but soon realizes the failure of her attempted compromise and chooses death as the only solution. When Edgar finally discovers Cathy in her distracted mood, after she has locked herself in her room for three days, she has already made her decision. She tells Edgar:

> 'What you touch at present, you may have; but my soul will be on that hilltop before you lay hands on me again. I don't want you, Edgar; I'm past wanting you.' (ch xii p 109)

This speech might be regarded as another act of petulance on Cathy's part, originating from her irritation at Edgar's failing to come to her immediately, but the following events show this interpretation to be false. As soon as Cathy recognizes that she has no further use for the conventional social world, but requires the freedom represented by the moors, she loses her will. She does not commit suicide. In fact she no longer talks about refusing to eat; she simply acquiesces to all around her.

An important reason for the reader's uncertainty about Cathy's death is that the structure of the novel does not permit him to observe Cathy's crisis. The narrative takes the reader to the beginning of Cathy's change, but then, when the reader is most interested in understanding Cathy's anger and remorse, Emily Brontë interposes the story of Heathcliff's marriage to Isabella. As was noted in the case of Heathcliff's change, the reader remains uninformed of the meaning of the crisis; moreover, with Cathy, the reader is not even permitted to observe the change. Again the novel *forces* him to infer a great deal. After her narration of the events of Heathcliff's marriage, Nelly describes the new Cathy:

> The flash of her eyes had been succeeded by a dreamy and melancholy softness; they no longer gave the impression of looking at the objects around her; they appeared always to gaze beyond, and far beyond—you would have said out of this world. (ch xv p 131)

Thus Emily Brontë again presents us with a *fait accompli*. Although she permits us to observe the beginning of Cathy's change, we are not allowed to witness the process. This type of narrative structure is designed to invite reader-participation and interpretation.

That Cathy near her death understands more about the nature and implications of her relationship with Heathcliff than does Heathcliff is revealed during Heathcliff's last visit to her at the Grange.[27] After the first wild embrace, Heathcliff looks at Cathy, and sees that she is dying. He cries out: 'Oh, Cathy! Oh, my life! how can I bear it?' (ch xv p 132). Cathy, however, perceives at once that Heathcliff is concerned primarily, not with *her* death, but with *his* own coming separation from her. Unafraid of death, Cathy is angered at Heathcliff's own selfish fears; she attempts to help him overcome his egoistic desires, and begs him to help her recapture their original feeling of oneness. When Heathcliff continues resentful, Cathy affirms that the ordinary, perceived world (including the phenomenal aspect of Heathcliff) does not interest her any longer:

'That is not *my* Heathcliff. I shall love mine yet; and take him with me—he's in
my soul. And,' added she, musingly, 'the thing that irks me most is this shattered prison, after all. I'm tired, tired of being enclosed here. I'm wearying to
escape into that glorious world, and to be always there; not seeing it dimly
through tears, and yearning for it through the walls of an aching heart; but
really with it, and in it. Nelly, you think you are better and more fortunate than
I; in full health and strength. You are sorry for me—very soon that will be
altered. I shall be sorry for *you*. I shall be incomparably beyond and above you
all.'   (ch xv p 134)

Whereas Cathy understands that the earthly Heathcliff is not the real Heathcliff, and
that later she will take the real Heathcliff to her 'glorious world,' Heathcliff at this
point still believes that death will separate them forever and does not understand
that he can follow her. This lesson he learns only at the end of the novel. Cathy's
highly mystical statement that the selfish Heathcliff, concerned only with his own
suffering, is not the real Heathcliff, that the real Heathcliff lives in her soul, is clarified
for the reader when Heathcliff, near the time of his death, finally realizes that he is
united to Cathy in essence.

At the time of Cathy's death, however, Heathcliff does not understand how
he can be reunified with Cathy; therefore he believes that in her death he has lost
all chance to satisfy his desires to be one with another person. Again Schopenhauer
is astute in describing what will happen to a man of immense will who finds that all
his longings for the infinite must remain unsatisfied:

If, now, a man is filled with an exceptionally intense pressure of will,—if with
burning eagerness he seeks to accumulate everything to slake the thirst of his
egoism, and thus experiences, as he inevitably must, that all satisfaction is
merely apparent, that the attained end never fulfils the promise of the desired
object, the final appeasing of the fierce pressure of will, but that when fulfilled
the wish only changes its form, and now torments him in a new one; and
indeed that if at last all wishes are exhausted, the pressure of will itself remains
without any conscious motive, and makes itself known to him with fearful pain
as a feeling of terrible desolation and emptiness; if from all this, which in the
case of the ordinary degrees of volition is only felt in a small measure, and only
produces the ordinary degree of melancholy, in the case of him who is a
manifestation of will reaching the point of extraordinary wickedness, there
necessarily springs an excessive inward misery, an eternal unrest, an incurable
pain; he seeks indirectly the alleviation which directly is denied him,—seeks to
mitigate his own suffering by the sight of the suffering of others, which at the
same time he recognises as an expression of his power. The suffering of
others now becomes for him an end in itself, and is a spectacle in which he
delights . . .[28]

Schopenhauer's description helps us to understand Heathcliff's violence; it is the
result of his immense will that cannot find an object.

The extent of Heathcliff's absorption in his own ego causes his violence against other people, especially Linton and Catherine. His violence offers proof that he has not understood the basic identity of his own nature with that of others. Yet he is dimly aware that some sort of reunion with Cathy would be possible if only he could find the means. It will be recalled that at Cathy's death he had cried: 'Not *there*—not in heaven—not perished—where?' (ch xvi p 139). In a vague, intuitive way, Heathcliff understands that Cathy has not been annihilated;[29] yet he cannot understand in what way she still exists. Ironically, all the time Heathcliff implores Cathy to come *in* to him, and he attempts to go *out* to her, he denies such a union by continually asserting his will over other people.

Heathcliff's awareness of his unreadiness to join Catherine is implicit in his much misunderstood explanation for his cruelty to Isabella. He says: 'It is a moral teething, and I grind with greater energy, in proportion to the increase of pain' (ch xiv p 128). Morality is usually associated with actions done for the benefit of others. But Heathcliff does not want to go to the orthodox heaven, and therefore does not attempt to lay up good works. For Heathcliff, to be moral means to realize fully his innermost being, that is, to achieve a state of mind in which he can be unified with Cathy—a state of grace that has no connection with good works. As Schopenhauer comments:

> In the might with which the bad man asserts life, and which exhibits itself to him in the sufferings which he inflicts on others, he measures how far he is from the surrender and denial of that will, the only possible deliverance from the world and its miseries.[30]

His cruelty to others does not, of course, make Heathcliff worthy of Cathy; it simply shows him the distance he has to travel to attain the ideal of willlessness.[31] In a similar way, Baudelaire was to develop his perversities to feel their human significance, to discover in a negative fashion the humanity he was abusing. For a person such as Heathcliff, the greatest danger is to abandon the search for his own higher self in the pursuit of social relations and personal happiness.

This Schopenhauerian account also makes sense of the puzzling dual ending of *Wuthering Heights*. It will be recalled that although Lockwood feels that Cathy, Heathcliff, and Edgar are at peace in the grave under the benign sky, the local people do not agree. The shepherd boy claims to have seen Heathcliff and a woman wandering the moors at night. G. D. Klingopulos has suggested that the ending of the novel is ambiguous, leaving the reader uncertain which interpretation to accept.[32] Indeed, Allan Brick has asserted that Lockwood's statement is merely another instance of his naiveté.[33] Yet there is no reason why these two endings should be contradictory. Both accounts are true. Lockwood is correct if one assumes that as object, Heathcliff and Cathy are dead; their phenomenal existence is completed. But their noumenal existence can never be finished. As people, they were simply the objectification of the universal will which is the eternal force of the universe. Their intrinsic 'other' selves—manifestations of the eternal will—are still alive vitalizing the world.

NOTES

[1] Mildred G. Christian, 'The Brontës' *Victorian Fiction: A Guide to Research*, ed. Lionel Stevenson (Cambridge, Mass. 1964) 244. See also J. H. Miller's statement: '*Wuthering Heights* is ... a work with which no reader has felt altogether at ease.' *The Disappearance of God* (Cambridge, Mass. 1963) 162.

[2] Ruth M. Adams, '*Wuthering Heights:* The Land East of Eden' *Nineteenth-Century Fiction* XIII (June 1958) 6. This belief in the 'perversity' of the novel's values is often presented in a qualified form; Miriam Allott, for example, has suggested that Emily Brontë's piety forced her to reject the qualities Heathcliff represents. Professor Allott, however, concedes that the 'rejection' of Heathcliff is by no means final. See '*Wuthering Heights:* The Rejection of Heathcliff?' *Essays in Criticism* VIII (January 1958) 46.

[3] 'Lockwood's Dreams and the Exegesis of *Wuthering Heights*' *Nineteenth-Century Fiction* XIV (September 1959) 109.

[4] Shannon, *Nineteenth-Century Fiction* XIV 105.

[5] Melvin R. Watson, 'Tempest in the Soul: The Theme and Structure of *Wuthering Heights*' *Nineteenth-Century Fiction* IV (September 1949) 89. The best account to date of Heathcliff's actions in relation to the novel's themes is Frederick T. Flahiff's recent introduction to the Macmillan edition of *Wuthering Heights* (Toronto 1968).

[6] *Nineteenth-Century Fiction* XI (September 1956) 106–29.

[7] F. H. Langham, '*Wuthering Heights*' *Essays in Criticism* XV (July 1965) 310. See also Arnold Kettle, *An Introduction to the English Novel* (London 1951) I 107–22.

[8] F. H. Langham, 310.

[9] Ibid., 311.

[10] Elliott Gose, '*Wuthering Heights:* The Heath and the Hearth' *Nineteenth-Century Fiction* XXI (June 1966). Gose is attempting to refute (quite successfully, I believe) the arguments of Richard Chase and Wade Thompson that the central characters are portrayed as perverse. See Richard Chase, 'The Brontës: A Centennial Observance' *Kenyon Review* IX (Autumn 1947) 487–506; Wade Thompson, 'Infanticide and Sadism in *Wuthering Heights*' *PMLA* LXXVIII (March 1963) 69–74.

[11] Elliott Gose, 18.

[12] Richard Chase, in the article cited in n 10, alleges that no such learning process takes place, but he has offered no evidence for this belief.

[13] *Wuthering Heights*, ed. William M. Sale Jr, Norton Critical Edition (New York 1963) 239 (ch xxxi). All future page references are to this edition and are indicated parenthetically.

[14] See Allan R. Brick, '*Wuthering Heights:* Narrators, Audience, and Message' *College English* XXI (November 1959) 83–4.

[15] It is impossible to argue that Emily Brontë had actually read any of the works of Schopenhauer, since the extent of her reading is unknown. However, Charlotte Brontë's characterization of Emily as an immature genius, secluded from the world, and relying entirely on her own imagination is no longer acceptable (Charlotte's preface to the 1850 edition of *Wuthering Heights*). Even if it were not that Charlotte herself, in another passage, describes the extreme dependence of the entire family on books and study, Emily's period as a schoolteacher at Law Hill, Halifax, and her period abroad studying at the Hégers' in Brussels indicate that she had more opportunity to read and study than Charlotte revealed. By the time they left Brussels, Emily and Charlotte both read French fairly fluently, and Charlotte mentions her sister's rapid progress in learning German (letter to Ellen Nussey, July 1842), but the extent of Emily's knowledge of German literature remains uncertain. However in the 1830s and 1840s it was unnecessary to read German in the original to learn something of German philosophy. The Brontës' favourite journal, *Blackwood's*, reviewed and commented on a great deal of German literature and philosophy. Moreover, Emily Brontë's period in Brussels was 'at a time when romanticism was in flood in the French-speaking countries,' and she would surely receive some account of the major figures in the home of Madame Héger (see John Hewish, *Emily Brontë: A Critical and Biographical Study* [New York 1969] 34).

[16] Arthur Schopenhauer, *The World as Will and Idea*, trans. R. B. Haldane and J. Kemp, 11th impr. (London 1964) I 364 (bk IV sec 54). The first edition appeared late in 1818 (with the date 1819). The second edition appeared in 1844 in two volumes. The first volume was a slightly altered reprint of the first edition; the second volume consisted of a commentary on the first edition. The first English translation appeared in 1883.

[17] Although it is unwise to place undue emphasis on Emily Brontë's short French *devoirs* which she wrote in Brussels for M. Héger, one cannot help noting their similarity to some of Schopenhauer's ideas. In 'The Butterfly,' Emily Brontë writes: 'Nature is an inexplicable puzzle, life exists on a principle of

destruction; every creature must be the relentless instrument of death to the others, or himself cease to live.' This vision of a universe without meaning is transformed, however, when she recognizes that man's soul can escape into a 'new heaven' at death. Compare also her essay on King Harold where she describes him transformed on the field of battle, ready to yield to Death, whose touch will strike 'off his chains.' See *Five Essays Written in French,* trans. L. W. Nagel (Austin, Texas 1948).

[18] *The World as Will and Idea* I 489 (bk IV sec 68)

[19] In a curious, but extremely insightful essay on 'affinities' between Lord Byron and Emily Brontë, Margiad Evans pointed out that the clue to Emily Brontë's writing was her 'pacifism towards death.' 'Byron and Emily Brontë: An Essay' *Life and Letters* LVII (June 1948) 203.

[20] *Essays in Criticism* VIII 45.

[21] *The World as Will and Idea* I 518 (bk IV sec 69).

[22] Schopenhauer notes: 'Old examples of this may be found in the "Breslauer Sammlung von Natur- und Medicin-Geschichten," September 1799, p 363; in Bayle's "Nouvelles de la république des lettres," February 1685, p 189; in Zimmermann, "Ueber die Einsamkeit," vol. I p 182; in the "Histoire de l'Académie des Sciences" for 1764, an account by Houttuyn, which is quoted in the "Sammlung für praktische Aerzte," vol. I p 69. More recent accounts may be found in Hufeland's "Journal für praktische Heilkunde," vol. X p 181, and vol. XLVIII p 95; also in Nasse's "Zeitschrift für psychische Aerzte," 1819, part III p 460; and in the "Edinburgh Medical and Surgical Journal," 1809, vol. V p 319. In the year 1833 all the papers announced that the English historian, Dr Lingard, had died in January at Dover of voluntary starvation; according to later accounts, it was not he himself, but a relation of his who died.' *The World as Will and Idea* I 518–19 (bk IV sec 69)

[23] Wade Thompson, *PMLA* LXXVIII 73.

[24] That Heathcliff knows something is happening to him is evinced by his statement to Nelly: 'There is a strange change approaching' (ch xxxiii p 255), but clearly he has no idea what shape this change will take.

[25] *The World as Will and Idea* I 151 (bk II sec 23).

[26] D. H. Lawrence in his insistence that what man sees as the universe and as himself is 'not much more than a mannerism' and that the 'one glorious activity of man' is 'the getting himself into a new relationship with a new heaven and a new earth,' is the British novelist whose position most closely resembles that of Emily Brontë. See 'The Crown' *Phoenix II,* ed. W. Roberts and H. T. Moore (New York 1968) 415.

[27] Frederick Flahiff has recently suggested the possibility that Cathy has been aware of the 'substantial identification' existing between herself and Heathcliff from the time she was a little girl. See introduction to the Macmillan edition of *Wuthering Heights* (1968) xxxiii. While I agree with Flahiff that Heathcliff becomes aware of his unity with Cathy only at the end of the novel, I find that Emily Brontë's depiction of Cathy is much more complex than Flahiff concedes. Cathy, it seems to me, is quite capable of making mistakes in her assessment of what is important to her; clearly one such mistake is her marriage to Edgar in order to obtain conventional happiness.

[28] *The World as Will and Idea* I 470 (bk IV sec 65)

[29] Compare Heathcliff's threat to Nelly: 'You shall prove, practically, that the dead are not annihilated!' (ch xxxiv p 263).

[30] *The World as Will and Idea* I 474 (bk IV sec 65)

[31] The crucial point is that Heathcliff comes *to understand* his own life force in relation to the world order. The novel does not show, as J. H. Miller contends, 'that the suffering sin brings will be sufficient expiation for that sin' and will allow the sinner 'to escape to heaven' (*The Disappearance of God,* 200). For Emily Brontë, suffering does not create expiation; it may, however, be the precursor to an individual's awareness of his proper relation to the noumenal world, which would then show the individual the way to achieve his intrinsic immortality.

[32] 'The Novel as Dramatic Poem (II): *Wuthering Heights' Scrutiny* XIV (1946–7) 85.

[33] *College English* XXI 226.

John Beversluis

LOVE AND SELF-KNOWLEDGE: A STUDY OF *WUTHERING HEIGHTS*

The Catherine-Heathcliff relationship has traditionally been defined in terms of reciprocal love, a love not merely sexual or romantic, but metaphysical, in character: an 'affinity' arising from a shared moral response to the world. Clifford Collins, for example, asserts that the love of Catherine for Heathcliff '... is the opposite of love conceived as social and conventional acceptance, the love Catherine has for Edgar which has only her conscious approval. What she feels for Heathcliff is a powerful undercurrent, an acceptance of identity below the level of consciousness. . . . It is an extension of the deepest layers of the self into another. . . .'[1] Similarly, Lord David Cecil holds that the deeper feelings of Emily Brontë's characters are '. . . only roused for someone for whom they feel a sense of affinity, that comes from the fact that they are both expressions of the same spiritual principle. Catherine does not "like" Heathcliff, but she loves him with all the strength of her being. For he, like she, is a child of the storm; and this make a bond between them, which interweaves itself with the very nature of their existence.'[2]

In this paper I wish to question the traditional interpretation of *Wuthering Heights*. More particularly, I wish to re-examine the relationship of Catherine to Heathcliff in order to determine whether the claim regarding an alleged 'affinity' between them is a plausible claim.

All such readings of *Wuthering Heights* rely heavily upon the following well-known passage:

> 'It would degrade me to marry Heathcliff now; so he shall never know how I love him; and that, not because he's handsome, Nelly, but because he's more myself than I am. Whatever our souls are made of, his and mine are the same, and Linton's is as different as a moonbeam from lightning, or frost from fire. . . . I cannot express it; but surely you and everybody have a notion that there is, or ought to be, an existence of yours beyond you. What were the use of my creation if I were entirely contained here? My great miseries in this

From *English* No. 120 (Autumn 1975): 77–82.

world have been Heathcliff's miseries, and I watched and felt each from the beginning; my great thought in living is himself. If all else perished, and *he* remained, I should still continue to be; and, if all else remained, and he were annihilated, the Universe would turn to a mighty stranger. I should not seem a part of it. My love for Linton is like the foliage in the woods. Time will change it, I'm well aware, as winter changes the trees. My love for Heathcliff resembles the eternal rocks beneath—a source of little visible delight, but necessary. Nelly, I *am* Heathcliff—he's always, always in my mind—not as a pleasure, any more than I am always a pleasure to myself—but as my own being. . . .'[3]

It is, of course, true that this passage, the so-called 'I *am* Heathcliff' speech, must be central to any plausible interpretation of Catherine's relationship to Heathcliff. It is not the fact, but the kind, of centrality ascribed to this passage by the traditional interpretation that I question. Mary Visick provides a clear and representative statement of the traditional thesis. 'In the great scene with Nelly,' she writes, 'in which [Catherine] weighs up her love for the two young men and talks, for the first and only time, of her real feelings for Heathcliff as 'more myself than I am,' the usually hidden self looks out, and we know what she really is. . . .'[4]

It seems to me, on the contrary, that an examination of Catherine's behaviour toward Heathcliff yields results which are quite incompatible with such talk about her 'hidden', but none the less 'real', self. As I read *Wuthering Heights,* this passage can serve neither as the criterion for revealing to us the real Catherine nor for determining the character of her actual relationship to Heathcliff. I shall argue that it serves, rather, as a clear instance of her self-deception, of the false way she has of picturing herself to herself.

In this paper, then, I put fourth an interpretation of *Wuthering Heights* which constitutes a reversal of the traditional one. I will try to show that the passage I have quoted cannot bear the weight that the traditional interpretation demands that it carry. Catherine's impassioned avowals regarding Heathcliff must not be examined and assessed in isolation; rather, they must be examined in conjunction with her *total* behaviour toward him. If they are examined in this way, her behaviour is seen as contrasting significantly with her avowals, not as consistent with them. And it is her total behaviour, not simply her avowals, which defines her psychologically decisive response to Heathcliff.

In making the 'I *am* Heathcliff' speech, Catherine believes herself to be torn merely between which of two men she ought to marry. Her existential conflict is, of course, more fundamental than this. Indeed, her momentary indecision is only a symptom of this more radical conflict, a conflict involving the necessity of choosing between two very different ways of life. For, clearly, Edgar and Heathcliff do not share a common world.

The surface of this obvious fact does not, to be sure, escape Catherine's attention. But she fails utterly to grasp its full significance. We can go further. She fails even to perceive the full content of this fact. One of the chief reasons for these failures in her pre-occupation (one might almost say her obsession) with a certain picture of herself; she sees herself as powerfully, even irresistibly, attracted to Heathcliff. The traditional interpretation accepts this picture as authentically descriptive of her actual relationship to Heathcliff; I do not. In what follows I will attempt to show why.

I begin with a disclaimer. Surely such an attraction is in evidence during their early years at Wuthering Heights. As children, both reject and mock authority and the attempts on the part of authority to control them. They are wild, intractable children, who flourish in their role as 'rude savages'. They are always together. Their favourite form of amusement is to run off and spend the entire day on the moors. Their forthcoming punishment 'became a thing to laugh at'; they forgot it the minute they were reunited. As a child, Catherine's worst punishment is to be kept from Heathcliff. When her father dies, it is to Heathcliff that she turns for consolation. There is, then, throughout their childhood, a powerful bond between them.

What is not sufficiently recognized, however, is that it is a bond of a fundamentally negative character: they identify with one another in the face of a common enemy, they rebel against a particular way of life which both find intolerable. It is not enough, however, simply to reject a particular way of life; one cannot define oneself wholly in terms of what he despises. One must carve out for oneself an alternative which is more than a systematic repudiation of what he hates. A positive commitment is also necessary. The chief contrast between Catherine and Heathcliff consists in the fact that he is able to make such a commitment (together with everything it entails) while she is not. And, when the full measure of their characters has been taken, this marks them as radically dissimilar from one another, whatever their temporary 'affinities' appear to be. It requires only time for this radical dissimilarity to become explicit.

Their visit to Thrushcross Grange provides a dramatic anticipation of the change which is soon to come about in their relationship. The Lintons examine Heathcliff and ridicule him. To our surprise, Catherine participates in the ridicule. This quite unexpected behaviour on her part proves to be an ominous forecast of the quality of their subsequent relationship. After five weeks have elapsed, Catherine returns to Wuthering Heights, 'her ankle thoroughly cured, and her manners much improved'. But a more important change is immediately apparent. Heathcliff discovers that the girl who returns is no longer the 'dirty, wild counterpart of himself', but a 'lady' who has 'taken readily to fine clothes and flattery'. She finds him 'black and cross', 'funny and grim' in comparison to Edgar and Isabella. She avoids touching him, fearing that her clothing had 'gained no embellishment from its contact with his'. When he finally dashes from the room in humiliation, her response is that of the perfected conventional specimen: she cannot comprehend how her remarks could have produced such an exhibition of 'bad temper'. Bad temper! Such a description—an infallible index of the fully respectable, but unperceiving, sensibility—is concerned only with the socially unacceptable behaviour. What a 'scene' he's making! She fails totally to grasp his inner anxiety, his humiliation, the fact that she has violated him. She has become in her own person a paradigm of the very respectability, empty and loveless, against which they both had formerly rebelled, and she fails to perceive it. One might be inclined to say that after this incident Heathcliff loses her little by little. It would be more accurate to say that he gradually comes to the realization that she was never his at all.

But this incident is significant in a second way. Not only does it mark a turning-point in Catherine's relationship to Heathcliff; it signals a change in her behaviour *in general.* From now on her rebellion becomes remarkably moderate. Whereas earlier she was 'never so happy as when everyone was scolding her at once', defying them with her 'bold, saucy look, and her ready words', she now adopts a different strategy. She discovers silence to be an excellent tactic in that its employment enables one to make one's compromises almost without detection. Almost. Nelly Dean tells us (an unusually perceptive comment from her) that Catherine began to develop 'a double character without exactly intending to deceive anyone'. When Edgar calls Heathcliff 'a vulgar, young ruffian', or describes him as being 'worse than a brute', Catherine does not rise to his defence. Indeed, she makes no protest whatever; instead, she takes care not to act like him in the presence of his cultured detractors. Long before they marry, she dares not treat Edgar's sentiments with indifference, 'as if depreciation of her playmate were of scarcely any consequence to her'. She and Heathcliff spend increasingly less time together. When he touchingly produces a calendar showing how much more time she has spent with the Lintons than with him, she rebuffs him most insensitively. She calls him 'foolish' for noticing such things. And she adds that she gets 'no good' from seeing him, that he might as well be 'dumb or a baby' for all he says to amuse her, and that it is 'no company at all when people know nothing and say nothing.'

Where, one wants to ask, is the 'affinity' of which she speaks? The real Heathcliff is now intolerable to her. More and more she seeks out the society of the Lintons. Yet, when Edgar proposes marriage, she is in some sense torn, indecisive. She vacillates. It is while in this state of mind that her famous 'I *am* Heathcliff' speech occurs. In the light of her total behaviour toward him, how is this passage to be interpreted? Does it, as so many readers have supposed, exhibit the 'real' Catherine, the Catherine who still belongs, and who will always belong, to Heathcliff? I believe the answer to be, No. The passage is psychologically revealing, but not in *that* way. Her avowals regarding Heathcliff, I observed earlier, must be examined in conjunction with, and in the light of, her total behaviour toward him.

We discover who the real Catherine is in much the same manner in which we discover who anyone really is. We observe. We do not, that is to say, wish to be present only when a person is on the brink of making a resolution, or intending to turn over a new leaf. Nor are we unduly impressed with mere talk. We have hope at such times; but we neither exaggerate their importance nor (after a while) take them at face value, dissociating them from past performances and disconnecting them from future ones. So with Catherine Earnshaw. Her 'I *am* Heathcliff' speech would, perhaps, be tolerable as an acknowledgement of her past indifference toward him; as an expression of her past and present 'affinity' for him, it is not tolerable. In fact, it is outrageous. Nelly Dean is unimpressed by it; and no one, not even Nelly Dean, is an infallibly wrong judge of character. While the fact that she did not tell Catherine of Heathcliff's presence can never be condoned, her response to Catherine's speech is singularly appropriate. 'I was,' she says, 'out of patience with her folly.' Folly! It is exactly the right word. Catherine has persuaded herself that there is still some affinity on her part toward Heathcliff. But she has deceived herself. This is merely the picture of herself of which she is enamoured: Catherine and Heathcliff together on the moors as in the past. They are, however, no longer children tormenting the adults and running away for the afternoon. Catherine's participation in Heathcliff's life has by this time become imaginative rather than real. His reality pulls her up short; he is intolerable in his concreteness. In her moments of lucidity she realizes that Heathcliff's way of life exacts a price, and that she is neither willing nor able to pay it. Yet, the idealization of that way of life continues to exercise an intermittent hold upon her imagination. It is part of her double character: the wanting of two fully romanticized worlds—Edgar's and Heathcliff's—coupled with the inability of making a genuine commitment to either of them as they are.

But it is also only a picture of Heathcliff of which she is enamoured. For all her alleged 'affinity' for him, Catherine does not comprehend that his way of life is no longer to be assessed as a prolonged tantrum directed at life and its obstacles. Heathcliff has self-consciously chosen his way of life, decided what he shall become. Catherine, on the other hand, never outgrows her own tantrums, never chooses what she is to be. Although both she and Heathcliff are capable of violent action, their violence springs from different sources. Hers is emotional, arbitrary, prompted by and directed to what is immediate; his is willed, principled, teleological. Hers is grounded in irritation and self-pity; his is motivated by the desire to destroy one world and create a new one. And Catherine, by virtue of her marriage to Edgar, identifies herself with the world Heathcliff wants destroyed. She is seduced by the surface of that world, thereby showing her lack of commitment to Heathcliff and the values his way of life embodies. But she marries Edgar still hoping in some bizarre sense not to lose Heathcliff, thereby showing her lack of commitment to Edgar.

Critics ponder her chief motive for marrying Edgar. Was it his good looks? His money? The status such a marriage would enable her to achieve? Her desire to help Heathcliff? It seems to me that she has no clear motive. She simply drifts into the marriage unreflectively. And she acts in bad faith to everyone concerned.

In marrying Edgar, however, she does not betray her deepest self, for she has no self recognizable enough to betray. Nor, strictly speaking, does she betray Heathcliff, for her adult relationship to him is never defined unambiguously enough so as to constitute the condition under which an act of betrayal could *significantly* occur. Indeed, Catherine's defining characteristic appears to be her incapacity for significant action. She has preferences, does this rather than that, is found here and not there; but, because of her inability to choose, she does not act in the full, agonizing sense of the word. Her 'I *am* Heathcliff' speech, then, taken in conjunction with her total behaviour, does not reveal her love and lasting 'affinity' for him; on the contrary, it reveals her inability to love or to commit herself to anyone.

In short, Heathcliff is desirable to her only as an imaginative possibility, not as a person. Instead of abandoning the conception for the reality, she marries Edgar (another imaginative possibility) only to reject him because he is not Heathcliff. And so, in a curious sense, her imagination wins out over both. It is little wonder, therefore, that she becomes wholly incapable of living in the present, and that the specific form which her illness takes is that of a regression to the symbols and experiences of her childhood. Since the present has become unbearable, she opts for a new ideal. This time it is not Heathcliff as such, but the past, a time when her self was still undivided. What she fails to understand is that it was undivided then only because there were no choices to be made, no consequences to be endured. Nothing was unalterable. All that was needed in order for the world to come back into focus was a noisy tantrum and a day on the moors. But it was a world that can never be again. And there was room for Heathcliff in it only because it was not a world at all.

A retreat into the past conjoined with a projection of her own flaws upon others characterizes Catherine's last days on earth. She is not, however, a tragic figure; she is merely a pathetic one. She suffers, but her suffering is self-inflicted. She is not even capable of meaningful remorse; the form of her suffering is almost wholly that of self-pity, whining. It is not that her 'wrong' is a violation of her nature, and that she cannot right it. It is, rather, that she can bear the weight of no reality whatever, neither Edgar's nor Heathcliff's.

And so, never content with what is, she becomes an incurable dreamer, a dreamer obsessed with what might have been and with what (she believes) once was. She becomes given to contrasting the actual with the ideal, and to employing the latter as the basis (and the justification) for her rejection of the former. The world of her daily experience is now intolerable to her when compared to the past and what she has persuaded herself to believe was her 'real' life, her 'real' identity. She cannot see that the past was not as she now envisions it. Again she is the victim of a picture. She fails to comprehend that the past was as intolerable then as the present now appears to be. Indeed, it was so intolerable that she rejected it for the sake of her (now intolerable) present. Hence, grasping at everything, she attains nothing. And the responsibility for this she confidently assigns to others. She has been 'abominably treated'. Self-deception is no longer a mere tendency; it has become a vocation.

That this is so may be seen by noticing her settled responses to both Edgar and Heathcliff. During one of Edgar's visits prior to their marriage she, supposing that he is not observing her, pinches Nelly for alleged insubordination, then denies that she did so, and, when trapped in her lie, proceeds to slap them both. Edgar, somewhat disquieted by this spectacle, prepares to leave. Catherine, however, prevents him from doing so; she prevails upon him by employing her usual strategy: 'Well, go, if you please—get away. And now I'll cry—I'll cry myself sick.' Edgar is manipulated. He stays. He is 'a soft thing'. 'He's doomed', says Nelly Dean, 'and flies to his fate'. Again, she is right.

Catherine's treatment of Edgar after their marriage, however, is equally outrageous. She continues to see Heathcliff despite Edgar's protests; then, later, she belittles him for not having had the courage to put a stop to these visits, assuring him that Heathcliff would 'as soon lift a finger against him as the king would march his army against a colony of mice'. Edgar, however, remains with her, toward the end caring for her as devotedly as any mother would have nursed an only child, 'enduring all the annoyances that irritable nerves and a shaken reason could inflict', sacrificing his own health and knowing no limits of joy when she is once again out of danger. Yet, for Catherine, Edgar is 'one of those things that are ever found when they are least wanted. . . .' 'Return to your books,' she tells him. 'I'm glad you have a consolation, for all you had in me is gone.' Edgar has pity for her; better, he has compassion and commitment. And she loathes him for it.

Where Edgar is gentle and forbearing, Heathcliff is hard. 'I have no pity! I have no pity! The more the worms writhe, the more I yearn to crush out their entrails. It is a moral teething, and I grind with greater energy, in proportion to the increase of pain.' Earlier he had told her: 'I want you to be aware that I *know* you have treated me infernally—infernally! Do you hear? And if you think that I don't perceive it, you are a fool; and if you think that I can be consoled by sweet words you are an idiot.' Shortly before her death he reaffirms this. She has told him that he and Edgar have broken her heart, that they have killed her. For the last time he reveals her to herself. It is she who is cruel and false. '*Why,*' he asks her, 'did you despise me? *Why* did you betray your own heart . . . ? I have not one word of comfort. You deserve this. You have killed yourself. Yes, you may kiss me and cry; and wring out my kisses and tears. They'll blight you—they'll damn you. . . . Because misery, and degradation, and death, and nothing that God or Satan could inflict would have parted us, *you,* of your own will, did it. . . . I have not broken your heart—*you* have broken it. . . . It is hard to forgive, and to look at those eyes, and feel those wasted hands. . . . I love my murderer—but *yours!* How can I?'

Indeed, how can he? It is impossible. And yet, of course, he does. He loves her despite the fact that her great miseries have not lately been his. But he remembers or thinks he does. Was there not a time? Surely she could not have forgotten? Hence, his rage, his violent protest, his accusations. He is reminding her.

This, too, is part of his 'moral teething'. But how, we ask, can such apparently brutal tactics count as moral? The answer to this question can only be formulated in terms of Heathcliff's earlier choices and his commitment to their consequences. The moral quality of which he speaks attaches not to his actions, but to his person. Whatever we may say of his hardness, his cruelty, his revenge, it is not mere hardness, mere cruelty, mere revenge. It is, rather, the behavioural manifestation of his own values, of a self undivided by fantasy and unmoved by tears and tantrums. Heathcliff sees that Catherine, because of her inability to choose, has negated the possibility of achieving an identity, and with it, negated her capacity to act, to hope, to love. He sees and despairs. But not simply because Catherine does not know the truth about herself. For part of what Heathcliff knows is that knowledge is not the issue. Not even self-knowledge, unless self-knowledge means the capacity to *acknowledge,* to acknowledge, who (and what) one is—in terms of one's actions—and to forgo the evasive, and essentially uncostly, policy of appealing to one's inner states, one's 'hidden' self. The real person is not, in this sense, hidden from us. On the contrary, it lies open for all who have eyes to see. The difficulty is not one of insufficient or ambiguous evidence; it is, rather, one of a capacity for discernment. And so Heathcliff's outburst, while perhaps deplorable as an isolated incident, is none the less intelligible as a teleological assault upon Catherine's carefully nurtured myth of having been abominably treated. His hardness is kinder than the softness of Edgar: it is therapeutic in intention. For Edgar desires only Catherine's physical recovery, whereas Heathcliff desires her inner purification, her moral cleansing. When the sickness is 'unto death', the kindness of silence is not kindness at all; it is an acquiescence in the destruction of the self.

Immanuel Kant began the *Critique of Pure Reason* with the words: 'Human reason has this peculiar fate that in one species of its knowledge it is burdened by questions which, as prescribed by the very nature of reason itself, it is not able to ignore, but which, as transcending all its powers, it is also not able to answer.' This phenomenon occurs not only in man's cognitive life, but in his affectional life as well. That is, not only are there questions which cannot be answered; there are also desires that cannot be satisfied. And, like the questions, those desires are the deepest, the most recurring, the most definitive of human needs. Yet they remain desires for illusory objects. Nothing objectively real or achievable answers to them. And if it is perilous to ignore them, it is much more perilous to act for the sake of them, to allow their pursuit to become constitutive of one's way of life. They must be exposed, unmasked. Catherine's inability to risk such self-exposure is precisely what renders her permanently inaccessible to Heathcliff. Heathcliff sees this. Catherine does not. This is why Heathcliff despairs.

NOTES

1 'Theme and Conventions in *Wuthering Heights*', *The Critic* (Autumn, 1947), 43–5.
2 *Early Victorian Novelists* (New York, 1935), p. 56.
3 *Wuthering Heights* (New York, 1963), pp. 72–4.
4 *The Genesis of* Wuthering Heights (Hong Kong, 1958), p. 45.

Walter E. Anderson

THE LYRICAL FORM
OF *WUTHERING HEIGHTS*

> ... heaven did not seem to be my home; and I broke my heart with
> weeping to come back to earth; and the angels were so angry that they
> flung me out, into the middle of the heath on the top of Wuthering
> Heights; where I woke sobbing for joy.

In *Wuthering Heights* death—or rather, life in death—is the supreme value. By understanding this we can understand that Brontë's central aim is to express the reality of Heathcliff's and Catherine's life and love continuing on the moors, as they attain immortal union with the living earth itself. Properly considered, this fact allows us to explain such unresolved critical questions about the book as the function of the second-generation characters and of Heathcliff's hatred of both them and life in this world. Brontë achieves in *Wuthering Heights* a singular power which most of her critics have felt. The crucial issue remains one of integrating all the novel's parts and meanings by a hypothesis adequate to its form and effect as a whole. The fundamental paradox of death against life cannot be resolved by synthesizing such concepts as storm and calm, or the house of the valley and the house of the moors, or the civilized family and the wild family inhabiting them. Nor finally are we to suppose, I shall argue, that the tempest of passion emerging in the course of the story is quelled or the issues resolved by the Hareton-Cathy relationship in a harmonious combination of Earnshaw energy and Linton calm. Brontë works within the conventional constraints of ordinary themes and a quasi-realistic plot structure, but her accomplishment lies in transcending them. She creates a radically new form, through which she endues Catherine's and Heathcliff's existences after death with living force. She shifts the planes of reality to such a degree that ordinary life gradually comes to seem less vital than death. The book induces in us not simply a belief, but the vivid sense that Catherine and Heathcliff's union is fulfilled after death upon the literally living earth. Heathcliff's conviction, when he

From *University of Toronto Quarterly* 47, No. 2 (Winter 1977–78): 112–34.

reopens Catherine's grave, that she is not there, 'not under me, but on the earth,' parallels the reader's final impression that these lovers do not rest quietly in the grave but walk together as spirits on the Heights.

I

Catherine and Heathcliff's love is from the beginning a *donnée*. The formal sufficiency of the story is determined, therefore, not by a representation of the gradual emergence of their love, but by the need to define its transcendent nature and express its peculiar power. In *Wuthering Heights* we have, in place of a logical structure and a realistic plot, a symbolic action progressing towards 'lyric' revelation[1] and shaped according to a probability and necessity with other-worldly implications. Change and fluctuation in this action are subsumed finally under the realization of a timeless, permanent world, as constant as Catherine and Heathcliff's love and as enduring as the moors.

Brontë invites us to release her principal subject from ordinary limits and values and to focus on a transcendental vision. The book belongs to Catherine and Heathcliff, but they do not belong to this world. They draw away from all earthly hopes, yielding completely to another expectation. By concentrating on their love for each other, by causing them to deny a lasting affection with any other person, Brontë sufficiently expresses a love and a life which even death cannot sunder or alter. As she lies dying, Catherine says to Heathcliff: 'Will you forget me—will you be happy, when I am in the earth? Will you say twenty years hence, "That's the grave of Catherine Earnshaw. I loved her long ago, and was wretched to lose her; but it is past. I've loved many others since—my children are dearer to me than she was, and, at death, I shall not rejoice that I am going to her, I shall be sorry that I must leave them!" Will you say so, Heathcliff?'[2] Of course, he does not. By raising the issue Brontë points to the meaning and formal nature of her novel. Catherine defines the arc Heathcliff's career will eventually complete. Once she is dead he refers to life not as living but as remaining above ground, suspended in an abyss. He endures those twenty years of separation, and hates their children, to rejoice all the more in attaining his real life out of this world. When these lovers approach their ends, their eyes glitter with keen perception, but not of the objects around them: 'they appeared always to gaze beyond, and far beyond—you would have said out of this world' (p 131; cf pp 260–4). We are meant to focus on the peculiar reality of their life in death, not on the relatively common existences of those they leave behind.

Through Catherine and Heathcliff's uncompromising love, which admits no resolution short of total union with the earth, Brontë overcomes the isolation from each other and from nature we inevitably feel in life. She denies her lovers a marriage in this world to sustain their yearning for an eternal consummation. Catherine and Heathcliff defeat death by expecting to live completely only in death—not in any heavenly spiritual realm, but by means of the total commingling of their dust and therewith their souls. When Catherine reveals her dream of having gone to heaven and how unhappy she was there, Nelly says: 'All sinners would be miserable in heaven.' Catherine takes this chance to explain: 'it was not that.' Rather, it 'did not seem to be my home . . . and the angels were so angry that they flung me out, into the middle of the heath on the top of Wuthering Heights; where I woke sobbing for joy' (p 72). Catherine's and Heathcliff's wildness, even their wickedness, stresses their repudiation of a union in this world or in heaven for one with tumultuous nature.

In the well-known passage in which Catherine declares 'I *am* Heathcliff!" she says: 'I cannot express it, but surely you and everybody have a notion that there is, or should be an existence of yours beyond you. What were the use of my creation if I were entirely contained here? . . . my great thought in living is himself . . . he's always, always in my mind . . . as my own being—so, don't talk of our separation' (pp 73–4). We have here no ordinary intimation of immortality. Catherine refuses to accept an existence confined within her personal self, separate not from God or heaven, but from the beloved *in* whom she would live (cf pp 107, 133). Catherine reaches beyond the limitation of self towards 'Heathcliff' who *is* herself in the other—an existence of *yours* beyond *you*. Heathcliff also speaks of her as his soul, his life (p 139), in a literal, not figurative, sense. To be perfect soul mates, they must become death mates. From the windows of their prisons they see the graveyard near the moors, which promises them triumph, not defeat. To speak of their love as tragic or destructive—even self-destructive—is nothing to the purpose.

The love story will appear perplexing if we try to interpret its moral, psychological, and emotional involutions in terms appropriate either to the normal social world or to any orthodox Christian belief about the next. Whereas the Christian God and heaven are wholly distinct and other, these two lovers, possessing the same soul or being, become each other's 'all in all' (p 107) by uniting in the middle of the heath, on top of Wuthering Heights. Upon Catherine's death, Nelly believes her spirit is 'at home with God' (p 137), but Heathcliff demands to know where she is: 'Not *there*—not in heaven—not perished—where?' (p 139). In this novel, to go to heaven is really to perish. Heathcliff may pray 'like a Methodist,' but the 'deity' he implores is Catherine (p 144). And Heathcliff is Catherine's source of life: 'my great thought in living is himself. If all else perished, and *he* remained, I should still continue to be, and, if all else remained, and he were annihilated, the Universe would turn to a mighty stranger. I should not seem a part of it' (p 74). As a demiurgic, primordial force of raw energy, Heathcliff is like the moor itself; and his fiendishness better comprehends the violent aspect of the living world than does any pantheistic conception. Heathcliff is, in Catherine's words, 'a fierce, pitiless, wolfish man,' 'an arid wilderness of furze and whinstone,' which conceals no subterranean 'depths of benevolence' (pp 89–90). Their furious passion is like a tempest on the moors (p 76). When Catherine expresses her feeling for Heathcliff with the ideas that she *is* Heathcliff and that *he* is as 'necessary as the rocks,' we understand, finally, the novel's expression of a life at one with the *heath* and the *cliffs.*

Critics have questioned whether Heathcliff and Catherine's relationship is sexual, non-sexual, perversely sexual, asexual, or pure. The riddle is not to be solved by any one of these terms, for in some senses their love is both sexually dynamic and chaste. Their violent confrontations convey their passionate desire, but its force must not be spent in this world. Catherine's death determines that these lovers reach each other only through the grave. Heathcliff's desire throughout the entire action is shown in his straining towards the dead Catherine 'as a tight-stretched cord vibrates—a strong thrilling, rather than trembling' (p 258). After Catherine and Heathcliff become adults only one can be left physically alive to prevent their coming together in the flesh. After a single passionate embrace with Heathcliff, Catherine must die, keeping them apart until they meet in dust. Brontë paradoxically reverses the traditional metaphoric comparison of the sexual act with death by switching vehicle and tenor. The lovers embrace really to die, and, in dying, they live forever with the intensity of a sexual embrace in a chaste fusion with the animated earth.

Catherine says she will marry Edgar Linton because 'it would degrade me to marry Heathcliff now' (p 72), that is, now that she has tasted life at Thrushcross Grange. But Catherine never really changes. Her language, like her character, must be taken not primarily in its conventional, literal sense but for its general, symbolic function. Despite her apparently divided character, she actually exhibits an underlying singlemindedness equal to Heathcliff's. We might say, with Nelly, that Catherine adopts 'a double character without exactly intending to deceive anyone' (p 62). The question is, why does Brontë move her in two directions at once? In the first place, Catherine's marriage to Linton obviates a union between her and Heathcliff. Second, her and Edgar's marriage demonstrates the meaninglessness of their socially conventional union: existing only for the present, it discloses how much she and Heathcliff can dispense with. Catherine and Linton's temporal association is the inverse measure of what Catherine and Heathcliff come to possess in their eternal union. After she accepts Edgar's proposal, Catherine avows she loves Heathcliff and cannot love Edgar, except superficially, and only for 'the present' (p 71): 'My love for Linton is like the foliage in the woods. Time will change it, I'm well aware, as winter changes the trees. My love for Heathcliff resembles the eternal rocks beneath—a source of little visible delight, but necessary' (p 74). Catherine knows that she has 'no more business to marry Edgar Linton,' than 'to be in heaven' (p 72). Yet Brontë has her marry the decent, humane man and move to Thrushcross Grange, the home of beauty and social grace, to demonstrate ultimately her profound dedication to another kind of life altogether. Catherine repeatedly expresses her rejection of both Edgar and the Grange, just as she rejected a conventionally pleasant vision of heaven. Married to 'a stranger' and exiled from what had been 'her world,' Catherine feels at Thrushcross Grange like an outcast in an abyss (p 107). The story leaps over three years of Catherine's married life to resume with Heathcliff's sudden return (p 81). Catherine then renews her struggle towards Heathcliff, affirming, prior to her death, how much she loves him. From an overview of the novel's goal, we see that a union in this world between her and

Heathcliff would be a degradation. Brontë focuses not on what they forfeit on the earth, but on what they realize in it.

To think that these lovers destroy their love and themselves through mismatches is to neglect the formal reasoning which overrides the apparent bearing of events. Both Edgar and Catherine's this-worldly marriage and Heathcliff and Isabella's terminate at the same time (in successive chapters, 16 and 17), leaving Heathcliff and Catherine's to come. 'What you touch at present, you may have,' Catherine tells Edgar a short time before she dies, 'but my soul will be on that hilltop before you lay hands on me again. I don't want you Edgar; I'm past wanting you. Return to your books, I'm glad you possess a consolation, for all you had in me is gone' (p 109). Edgar will find further consolation in their daughter Cathy, who takes possession of his heart after Catherine's death. And as the two men who have loved Catherine in such different ways approach their own deaths, Heathcliff rejoices whereas Edgar begins 'to shrink and fear it' (p 205).

The word *affinity* has often been used to describe Heathcliff and Catherine's attraction for each other, but *identity* is more accurate.[3] 'Whatever our souls are made of,' Catherine says, 'his and mine are the same' (p 72). Neither character is an incomplete half—merely masculine or feminine—seeking ordinary wholeness through love. As persons, both Heathcliff and Catherine are complete in themselves, being incomplete only in their separation. When her death is near, Heathcliff rages at her: 'Do I want to live? What kind of living will it be when you—oh, God! would *you* like to live with your soul in the grave?' (p 135). Heathcliff arranges for the sexton to remove the facing sides of his and Catherine's coffins when they are both dead so that 'by the time Linton gets to us, he'll not know which is which' (pp 228–9). Both lovers are opposed to the meek and patient Edgar, who is excluded from the eternal marriage bed where Catherine's and Heathcliff's two selves merge into a single identity through fusion with the living earth. Their graves are located 'on a green slope, in a corner of the kirkyard, where the wall is so low that heath and bilberry plants have climbed over it from the moor' (p 140; cf p 266).

Heathcliff and Catherine's love appropriately takes on a paradoxical mode of expression whenever they compare the life they look forward to with the life they are living. The central idea is clearly communicated to the reader when Catherine eagerly contemplates her death:

> 'Oh, you see, Nelly! he would not relent a moment to keep me out of the grave! *That* is how I'm loved! Well, never mind! That is not *my* Heathcliff. I shall love mine yet; and take him with me—he's in my soul. And,' she added, musingly, 'the thing that irks me most is this shattered prison, after all. I'm tired, tired of being enclosed here. I'm wearying to escape into that glorious world, and to be always there; not seeing it dimly through tears, and yearning for it through the walls of an aching heart, but really with it, and in it. Nelly, you think you are better and more fortunate than I; in full health and strength. You are sorry for me—very soon that will be altered. I shall be sorry for *you*. I shall be incomparably beyond and above you all. I *wonder* he won't be near me!'
>
> (P 134)

The opening sentences of this passage are more ironic than first appears, for *that*, in a sense, is how Heathcliff loves Catherine. She wonder whether he will be near her, but we do not. We have already seen (in the third chapter) his tearful yearning for her. They need only wait twenty years, one generation—a short time within the perspective of eternity—before meeting in and on the moors whose wind is 'so full of life, that it seemed whoever respired it, though dying, might revive' (p 211). Catherine's exultation here over a complacent Nelly is not bravado; it anticipates her triumph in death.

In an earlier passage, when Heathcliff is present only in her imagination, Catherine foresees and accepts the conditions of their love:

> 'It's a rough journey, and a sad heart to travel it; and we must pass by Gimmerton Kirk, to go that journey! We've braved its ghosts often together, and dared each other to stand among the graves and ask them to come. But Heathcliff, if I dare you now, will you venture [that is, into the grave to seek her]? If you do, I'll keep you. I'll not lie there by myself; they may bury me twelve feet deep, and throw the church down over me, but I won't rest till you are with me. I never will!'
>
> She paused, and resumed with a strange smile, 'He's considering—he'd rather I'd come to him! Find a way, then! not through the Kirkyard. You are slow! Be content, you always followed me!'   (P 108)

Prior to this moment, Nelly would not open the window to Catherine's room lest she catch her death of cold. For Catherine, however, death provides 'a chance of life,' and she opens it herself. She seeks a way through the kirkyard, knowing that Heathcliff will eventually follow. He will find no better way to life.

Before dying Catherine wishes to hold Heathcliff 'till [they] were both dead,' and he embraces her so intensely it seems doubtful she will emerge alive (pp 133–4). In a sense she does not, for she dies that night in childbirth. Seeing them together, Nelly tells Lockwood, she felt that she was not 'in the company of a creature of [her] own species' (p 134), and she is right. Catherine and Heathcliff become strangers to everyone alive because they exist only in their dedication to each other and to death. Before Heathcliff retreats to his room to die, his last exchange is with Cathy (Linton) Heathcliff: 'Will *you* come, chuck? I'll not hurt you. No! to you, I've made myself worse than the devil. Well, there is *one* who won't shrink from my company! By God! she's relentless' (p 263). And as he contemplates his imminent union with Catherine, Heathcliff ecstatically proclaims: 'I'm too happy, and yet I'm not happy enough. My soul's bliss kills my body, but does not satisfy it' (p 262). His body will be satiated only with its dissolution along with hers. 'Strange happiness!' Nelly says; to be sure, but this is the essential strangeness at the heart of the book.

The idea of this novel's form and meaning which I have been forwarding will explain the highly restricted function of both Heathcliff's hate and the symmetrical replication of the first-generation characters in the second. Because critics of *Wuthering Heights* generally have taken the ostensible plot of revenge involving Hareton Earnshaw, Cathy Linton, and Linton Heathcliff as an independent development in its own right rather than as a screen for fully projecting the central love story, many problems of interpretation have arisen. Perhaps the most important of these involves the supposed incongruities in the novel, given the apparent shift from a story of grand passion to one of sordid revenge after Catherine's death midway in the action (chap 16). But instead of losing control of her subject in the second half of her novel, Brontë ingeniously manages to augment its power by substituting the second generation for the first, once Catherine is present only as a memory or a ghost. As I shall attempt to show in the next two sections, the logical extension of the plot with a revenge motive constitutes only an apparent complication; the story continues to express its single concern, though in a different mode. The structure is peculiar because the subject is fundamentally paradoxical. Although the later action grows out of the earlier, it does not introduce new consequences and goals of its own, but points back to the affairs of the first half. Because her action has much to do with hate and love, but nothing to do with the accomplishment of revenge, Brontë abruptly terminates Heathcliff's seeming struggle to destroy his enemies before the novel closes. Her purpose in the literal action is not to complete Heathcliff's revenge but through his desire for revenge, to express his hatred of the world and, correlatively, his love of Catherine. The idea of revenge permits full dramatization of Heathcliff's rejection of all those ordinary human values the other characters represent. Renunciation would not be emotionally powerful enough, and hate is more nearly the mirror image of love than mere rejection or indifference. After serving as echoes of the first-generation characters, the members of the second either die or fade into the dim background of the normal world as Catherine and Heathcliff come forward to assume their immortal life.

The story, like Heathcliff himself, is monomaniacal, having at its centre only 'one absorbing subject' (p 230; cf p 256). One common focus connects the apparently different parts as Brontë converts the hate/revenge motif to an expression of the principal subject, centring in Heathcliff's love of Catherine. The strange happiness Heathcliff enjoys at the close is the happiness of a soul outstripping the body, just as the book's strange power evolves from a form outstripping its literal action. Brontë did not shrink from her 'mad' vision, but held it in her mind's eye until she had found the complex form to give it nearly perfect expression.

II

Given her conception of Catherine and Heathcliff's love, why did Brontë choose to make her hero a fiend? The question touches the book's morality, a subject which has aroused its critics as much as any other. *Wuthering Heights* has been judged moral, immoral, amoral, and even pre-moral, but, as with the question of sexuality, this one admits no simple either/or solution. Although we acknowledge Heathcliff's diabolism, we cannot deny him our primary sympathy. The problem disappears once we grasp the connection between his savagery and his love, and between our feelings towards him and the way Brontë renders her material.

Despite Heathcliff's viciousness, he retains our sympathy to the end, for our feelings are never as convinced of his cruelty as is our reason. We believe in his ferocious power, but we do not fear him. Brontë never represents Heathcliff's malevolence without extenuation, and the harm he perpetrates does not live after him. That the reader is meant to acquit him of wrongdoing is reflected, though in a curiously indirect manner, by those critics who have attempted to fix the blame for all the mayhem on one of the other characters. Even the inoffensive Nelly Dean and the innocuous Lockwood have been charged and convicted. There is good reason, at least, for our feeling ambivalent towards Heathcliff. Just when destruction of those he hates is within his grasp, he arbitrarily restrains his hand. And although he takes the trouble to prevent Edgar Linton from protecting Cathy by modifying his will, he never bothers to make one of his own: 'How to leave my property, I cannot determine,' he says (p 262)—a curious indifference for a man bent on destruction. Also, Heathcliff despises his son Linton enough to wish him dead, yet he carefully preserves the sickly youth far longer than he might otherwise have lived. The 'father's selfishness' is made to contribute to Linton's comfort (p 171). Heathcliff's motive is revenge, since he gains Cathy's property after she marries Linton Heathcliff and he dies. Yet Cathy ultimately comes into possession of her estate and forms a happy alliance with Hareton, who is restored to his rights. I would suggest that Brontë has arranged matters in this way to limit the consequences of Heathcliff's diabolical machinations. In this section, then, I shall argue that Heathcliff's hatefulness, not his actual cruelty, is the subject expressed, and in the next, that his power to achieve revenge, not its accomplishment, is the matter represented.

In the first and second chapters we witness Heathcliff's savagery, and in the third we learn that its cause is love. These are the two major poles of the book. Consequently we see all his fiendishness in light of his misery over being separated from Catherine. Brontë communicates the nature of Heathcliff's love in association with his rejection of the world and all earthly affections. Had he not loved Catherine so well, he could not hate all others as he does; did Brontë not have him renounce the world so completely, she could not fully represent his longing for death. She did not allow Heathcliff and Catherine to die at the same time, but continued the story with a second set of characters to express the intensity of Heathcliff's torment and longing.

Very soon after the book opens, Lockwood's nightmare occasions the scene which reveals Heathcliff's ferocity to be but a corollary of his love:

> He got on to the bed and wrenched open the lattice, bursting, as he pulled at it, into an uncontrollable passion of tears.
> 'Come in! come in!' he sobbed, 'Cathy, do come. Oh, do—*once* more! Oh! my heart's darling, hear me *this* time—Catherine, at last!'
> There was such anguish in the gush of grief that accompanied this raving, that my compassion made me overlook its folly. (P 33)[4]

What is folly to Lockwood makes sense to us. To deny Heathcliff's assurance of Catherine's presence is to deny the novel. His love, as fresh and vital as it was when she died eighteen years before, continually intimates that its consummation is still to come. Aware from the book's start that Catherine is dead and yet somehow still alive, we can accept the termination of the worldly portion of their affair. From the beginning Brontë endows their love with eternality by presenting the past within the present as well as by Heathcliff's confident expectation of future fulfilment.

At strategic moments during the novel's second half, Brontë reminds us of the lovers' closeness by Heathcliff's continual wandering on the moors and at the Heights in search of Catherine. Only when he feels her spirit nearby, is he 'un-speakably consoled' (p 230). Twice he uncovers her coffin, the better to contemplate the ultimate transformation, 'of dissolving with her, and being more happy still!' (pp 228–9). For these reasons, Heathcliff's words near the end of the novel provide an apt commentary on its form: 'it is by compulsion that I notice anything alive, or dead, which is not associated with one universal idea' (p 256). His violent outbursts towards others give the impression of temporary distraction, having no permanent effect. All the objects of his hate function as 'an aggravation of the constant torment' he suffers (p 255). Of his son Linton, he says, I 'hate him for the memories he revives' (p 170). Likewise we are often reminded of Heathcliff's sense of Catherine through Cathy: 'He looked up, seized with a sort of surprise at her boldness, or, possibly, reminded by her voice and glance of the person from whom she inherited it' (p 215). But, unlike Edgar, he must not feel too much of Catherine in Cathy for he is not to compromise his love of the mother by loving the daughter. Instead, he insists, 'I don't love you!' (p. 218). 'Keep your eft's finger off; and move, or I'll kick you!... How the devil can you dream of fawning on me? I *detest* you!' (p 219). Recognizing the underlying cause of Heathcliff's hate, we adjust the surface action to the reality of his undeviating love for Catherine, the subject represented on nearly every page of the work. His 'entire world is a dreadful collection of memoranda that she did exist, and that [he has] lost her!' (p 255). Thus, his 'monomania on the subject of his departed idol' (p 256) provokes his rage but at the same time continually interrupts his intention to destroy and allays our concern for his would-be victims.

It remains to demonstrate how Brontë shapes her material to evoke the desired response in the reader. I think it is safe to say that we feel more indignant towards Alec d'Urberville during his first carriage ride with Tess in *Tess of the d'Urbervilles* than we ever feel towards Heathcliff. Compared with Thomas Hardy, Brontë is a great spendthrift of malice and violent passions, but always to avoid isolating Heathcliff's malignity for moral reprobation. She makes us so familiar with fiendishness that she diffuses the disgust while she sustains the terrific. The effect Hardy achieves with Alec depends on his comparative parsimony in the distribution of evil. Brontë's purpose is quite different.[5] For contrast we need only imagine the effect had Heathcliff possessed the only violent temper or appalling hatred in the world of this novel. Or suppose that Isabella Linton had been as amiable as Tess, with Heathcliff seducing her against her will. Instead Brontë has Isabella rush head-long into her miserable marriage against all that advice and observation can do to dissuade her.

Brontë enlists our sympathy for Heathcliff by telling the story of his childhood conflicts with Hindley Earnshaw and Edgar Linton, thereby raising our antipathy against those who inspire his lust for revenge. When Heathcliff throws hot apple-sauce into young Edgar's face, Nelly Dean's reaction directs our own. She 'rather spitefully' scrubs Edgar, 'affirming it served him right for meddling' (p 55). Nelly is there later to condemn the wretched Linton Heathcliff for the same want of spirit she observed in his uncle. She discovers him to be 'the worst-tempered bit of a sickly slip that ever struggled into its teens! Happily, as Mr. Heathcliff conjectured, he'll not win twenty!' (p 195). And earlier, Nelly 'began to dislike, more than to compassionate, Linton, and to excuse his father, in some measure, for holding him cheap' (p 179). Strong resemblances are drawn between the ineffectual Edgar and the abject, ill-natured Linton—who emphatically 'does not resemble his father (p 205; cf pp 206, 211). 'Where is *my* share in thee, puling chicken?' Heathcliff asks (p 169). Our favour turns to Heathcliff and Catherine, to whom all vital qualities rebound, qualities which define the norms of the novel, as Edgar's conventional values and vapid gentility do not. By stressing the opposition between Heathcliff's and Catherine's potency and Linton's and Edgar's weakness, Brontë forcefully imparts the idea that these lovers have not exhausted their vitality in living. In our imaginations, they bear more strength into the grave than the others possess in life.

Although we never lose a sense of Heathcliff's potential for evil, he elicits our sympathy when exercising his passion against Edgar, Isabella, Hindley, or Linton. Even though we appreciate the mutuality of Hindley and Heathcliff's hatred, Brontë consistently turns our feelings against the former. Heathcliff delights in Hindley's destruction, but his role in it is, on consideration, negligible. He instigates nothing. Hindley's self-ruination is well underway before Heathcliff returns to the Heights, and he ends by drinking himself to death. Like Heathcliff, Hindley idolizes his beloved, and after she dies he also curses and defies both God and man (pp 60–1). But unlike Heathcliff, Hindley 'gave himself up to reckless dissipation.' His self-destruction distinctly contrasts with Heathcliff's course. Although both men are notable for savage sullenness and ferocity, Hindley degrades himself 'past redemption' (p 61). With Frances dead, he is lost. Before terminating Hindley's perverse career, Brontë devotes more of the action to his destructive intentions towards Heathcliff than the reverse, as one of the major confrontations between them shows.

For many days following Catherine's death, Heathcliff is away from the Heights mourning at her grave. When he returns home one night during a snowstorm—anticipating, we learn later, the presence of Catherine's ghost in her room—he discovers that Hindley and Isabella have conspired to bar his entrance. Hindley holds a gun and a knife, intending to assassinate Heathcliff, who breaks in and disarms him. The gun discharges, causing the knife to recoil and slash the would-be murderer's arm. Heathcliff proceeds to thrash the villain, but only with one free hand, be it noted, since he holds Isabella with the other. Sometime later, Heathcliff tells Nelly that he then rushed directly to Catherine's bedroom, but that is not what Isabella recounts in her detailed narration of events. Instead, Heathcliff carries Hindley to the settle, binds up his wound, and advises him to sleep off his drunkenness. Of course Joseph supposes Heathcliff to be the devil in the mischief, and Isabella has to labour 'to satisfy the old man that Heathcliff was not the aggressor' (p 148). Here, as usual, Brontë realizes as much violence as possible consistent with exonerating Heathcliff. She seeks a maximum of blood and malice with a minimum of harm and blame, as is epitomized in one phrase in particular. Heathcliff 'bound up [Hindley's] wound with brutal roughness' (p 147). Rough though he is, he binds the wound.

In this episode Heathcliff's hate and revenge motive are, as always, subordinated to the love which is their cause. The next morning Heathcliff stands at the fireplace oblivious of Hindley, despite the latter's murderous assault the night before. 'His basilisk eyes were nearly quenched by sleeplessness, and weeping,' Isabella tells Nelly, 'his lips devoid of their ferocious sneer and sealed in an expression of unspeakable sadness' (p 148). Our attention is then diverted to Isabella's vindictiveness: 'I couldn't miss this chance of sticking in a dart,' she says. 'Fie, fie, Miss,' Nelly interrupted, 'one might suppose you had never opened a Bible in your life.'

The entire pattern of this seventeenth chapter establishes a frame for many episodes to follow. Brontë consistently embeds Heathcliff's savagery within a larger scheme of others' malice or disagreeableness and of his overriding love for Catherine. Only thus qualified does she permit a savage eruption, which is quelled when Heathcliff's thoughts turn to 'the subject of his departed idol.' Isabella experiences 'pleasure in being able to exasperate' Heathcliff, whom she taunts for mourning over what she supposes to be 'senseless dust and ashes': 'Heathcliff, if I were you, I'd go stretch myself over her grave and die like a faithful dog. The world is surely not worth living in now, is it?' (p 146). Indeed it is not; and there is nothing Heathcliff would prefer to doing as she says. No plot requirement delays him, for he is in a similar posture in the thirty-third chapter, the third, the seventeenth, and many others. The formal requirement is expressionistic—a full and powerful revelation of the novel's spiritual core. Isabella complains about that 'monster' Heathcliff, wondering how Catherine could have loved him, for she better than anyone knew his true nature. The reader understands these lovers' mutual obsession: their alienation from others only emphasizes the harmony prevailing between them.

Cathy Linton later taunts Heathcliff as Isabella did. When Linton Heathcliff spitefully tells Cathy that her mother hated her father and loved his, she calls him a liar (p 192). Yet her confrontations with Heathcliff deflect the reader's attention from his harshness towards her to his love for Catherine: 'I don't hate you, I'm not angry that you struck me. Have you never loved *anybody*, in all your life, uncle? *never?*' (p 219). Unwittingly, she evokes the true state of affairs by connecting Heathcliff's cruelty with its cause: 'Mr. Heathcliff, *you* have *nobody* to love you; and, however miserable you make us, we shall still have the revenge of thinking that your cruelty rises from your greater misery! You *are* miserable, are you not? Lonely, like the devil, and envious like him? *Nobody* loves you—' (p 228). By such means Brontë continually directs the reader to an ever fresh apprehension of the central subject.

Cathy is not crushed by Heathcliff's contempt. She pities him more than she hates him, and retains her boldness in the face of his savage outbursts. Brontë employs similar devices in delineating Heathcliff's and Hareton's dispositions towards each other. When Heathcliff dies, only Hareton mourns him. If we consider Hareton rationally as he kisses the dead savage face and bitterly weeps, we may be perplexed, as Nelly is, that 'the most wronged' should feel such grief upon the death of his persecutor (p 264). But we never completely convinced that Heathcliff has wronged him. Brontë's treatment of Heathcliff's and Hareton's relationship further discloses her double-dealing technique both in portraying the fiend/no-fiend Heathcliff and in representing a revenge/no-revenge plot. In Heathcliff's supposed revenge on Hindley through Hareton, Brontë reveals his violent will, but simultaneously acquits him of wrongdoing. 'If he were the devil, it didn't signify,' Hareton tells Cathy, and Brontë tells the reader.

When we meet Hareton as a little boy during one of Nelly's rare visits to the Heights (chap 11), we find that his brutalization is well underway as a consequence of Hindleys' sottish neglect. Hareton's chief lesson, he tells Nelly, has been to avoid 'Devil daddy,' who he knows cannot abide him. Heathcliff encourages the alienation, to be sure, but at the same time he becomes the boy's protector; 'he pays Dad back what he gies to me—he curses Daddy for cursing me' (p 95). Through dissipation Hindley not only wastes his son's heritage, but nearly kills him. Once, attempting to escape from his father's drunken clutches, Hareton falls from an upper story and would at least have been maimed had Heathcliff not caught him (pp 68–9). Heathcliff diabolically regrets having saved the lad, yet those who witness 'his salvation' rejoice nonetheless. We might say that he preserves Hareton's life with 'brutal roughness.' In accord with the patterns already traced, Nelly immediately turns her wrath upon Hindley for abusing his son: 'He hates you—they all hate you,' she exclaims. 'Have mercy on this unfortunate boy' (p 68). Hindley responds by drinking a tumbler of brandy and discharging a series of curses too blasphemous to record. By comparison with Hindley, Heathcliff commits mostly sins of omission against Hareton.

While Heathcliff rants, after Hindley's death, about making one tree grow as crooked as another, Hareton lovingly strokes his cheek, a gesture which resembles Cathy's snuggling up to him after he viciously slaps her face (pp 154, 219). Ironically, we recognize the 'gold' in Hareton because Heathcliff virtually loves the lad in spite of himself (p 178). Charlotte Brontë felt that the single link connecting Heathcliff with humanity is 'his rudely confessed regard' for Hareton.[6] She was wrong to conclude, however, that he had ruined the young man. When the time is ripe for aborting the putative revenge plot, Cathy promptly falls in love with Hareton, who renews himself by virtue of his noble spirit (p 254). The boy happily never had more than 'a dim notion of his inferiority' (p 177), a fact which mitigates the effect of Heathcliff's malevolence. Perhaps the most remarkable instance of Brontë's calculated ambiguity is Heathcliff's triumphant boast of surpassing the cruelty of Hindley's persecution of him by making his victim love him (p 178). All victims should have so rare an oppressor.

III

Cathy Linton, Hareton Earnshaw, and Linton Heathcliff are not very memorable characters, and I am not surprised to learn that, like myself, other readers remember distinctly only Catherine and Heathcliff shortly after reading *Wuthering Heights*. 'Great as the novel is,' E. M. Forster writes, 'one cannot afterwards remember anything in it but Heathcliff and the elder Catherine.'[7] Even if this reaction is typical, it ought not to reflect disparagingly on Emily Brontë's conduct of the story, as Forster's reservation does. Much of her art goes to securing just that effect. Her masterful control becomes apparent once we realize that she creates chains of associated ideas which cut loose from the present occurrence and reach to something deeper and, for her, more real. What is momentarily present is nothing but an occasion for releasing again the framing situation which precedes and overrides those events involving the second generation.[8] The latter half of the novel appears more accidental, less probable, poorer in effect than the first only if we take the revenge plot too literally. Critics who do so become dissatisfied when later developments fail to produce the effects their premises logically dictate. Actually, the improbabilities and forced plotting in the novel serve Brontë's positive intention. Even the demise of several characters immediately after they outlive their usefulness assists in denying the literal action more than a slight natural probability. It is just possible, as it were, and no more than half-real. In the words of an early reviewer, Brontë achieves a 'nice provision of the possible even in the highest effects of the supernatural.'[9] We reserve our fullest belief for the realm in which Catherine and Heathcliff ultimately abide.

The second-generation characters' importance formally depends not on their existences in their own right but on their reprojection of the original principals—Catherine, Edgar, and the young Heathcliff. The children amplify, by repetition, the original sets of events. Consequently their traits detach from them as individuals to reflect their generic source. At the same time, the paleness of the reflection shows us how little of what matters in Brontë's world *could* be mirrored in these relatively ordinary creatures. Several critics have noticed the symmetrical pedigree of the generations, but we must go further. Brontë purposely denies the children distinctive traits of their own because she wishes them to fade away, leaving only Catherine and Heathcliff. The second generation dimly personifies the first, recreating the structure of the original relationships. The plot does not progress for the sake of logical complications, but for symbolic revelation. The revenge plot is a red herring. Intentionally so. Brontë sustains it only superficially to abort it after exhausting its restricted functions. Before the novel closes, the idea of Heathcliff's hatred and revenge also fades from our memory, leaving only the image of his living love for Catherine. Everyone eventually gives way to these two lovers, as life in this world gives place to life in death.

By the end of the book only four of the chief actors remain: Catherine and Heathcliff, perfectly united as ghostly lovers in the grave and on the moors; and Cathy and Hareton, happily restored to everything they almost lost. But the living pair resolve nothing. They recede into relative insignificance, whereas the dead pair come forward into greater life. The shift in the planes of reality is given sharp focus in Nelly and Lockwood's final exchange. Nelly duly believes that 'the dead are at peace,' but, she says, reports persist that Catherine's and Heathcliff's ghosts wander on the moors and near the Heights. Just then Nelly and Lockwood see Cathy and Hareton returning from a ramble. Lockwood says, '*they* are afraid of nothing . . . Together they would brave Satan and all his legions' (pp 265–6). The words have some applicability to Cathy and Hareton but much more to Catherine and Heathcliff. We automatically shift from the lesser to the greater: we know who feared nothing, not even death itself, and who outbraved both heaven and hell. Cathy and Hareton lend an aura of corporeality to the spiritual pair. Towards the domesticated lovers at Thrushcross Grange, we, like Heathcliff, become comparatively 'regardless' how they go on together and 'can give them no attention any more' (p 255).

As substitutes, Cathy, Hareton, and Linton image the young Catherine, Heathcliff, and Edgar. Brontë introduces the idea of substitution early in the novel when Isabella tells Nelly that Heathcliff looked upon her as 'Edgar's proxy in suffering, till he could get a hold of him' (p 123). Heathcliff's getting a hold of Edgar does not signify; only his declaration of the desire counts. But to sustain the original situation, Edgar must be present in principle once communication between him and Heathcliff almost ceases after Catherine's death. Isabella's son Linton now provides the perfect proxy. When Heathcliff looks at Linton, he affirms the boy's resemblance to Edgar; and Edgar was convinced 'that as his nephew resembled him in person he would resemble him in mind' (pp 205–6, 211).

The fullest and most explicit statement of the idea that the second generation is absorbed into the first comes near the close, when Heathcliff tells Nelly his feelings towards Cathy and Hareton. The passage evinces Brontë's own reasoning about her formal intentions:

> 'Five minutes ago, Hareton seemed a personification of my youth, not a human being. I felt to him in such a variety of ways, that it would have been impossible to have accosted him rationally.
>
> 'In the first place, his startling likeness to Catherine connected him fearfully with her. That, however, which you may suppose the most potent to arrest my imagination, is actually the least, for what is not connected with her to me? and what does not recall her? . . . I am surrounded with her image! The most ordinary faces of men and women—my own features—mock me with a resemblance. The entire world is a dreadful collection of memoranda that she did exist, and that I have lost her!
>
> 'Well, Hareton's aspect was the ghost of my immortal love, of my wild endeavours to hold my right, my degradation, my pride, my happiness, and my anguish—'   (P 255)

This passage clearly indicates that Brontë deprived the second generation of a fully independent existence because she meant it to mirror the past, not to introduce an extended action posing new consequences and goals. Hareton is, by substitution, the 'ghost' of Heathcliff's earlier self. His struggling towards Cathy revives the idea of Heathcliff's original struggle towards her mother. Cathy and Hareton serve as a sympathetic reminder of Heathcliff's love and loss, even his unappeasable pride. Remembering his own life, Heathcliff admires Hareton and would set him against Linton, as he himself opposed Edgar: 'twenty times a day, I covet Hareton, with all his degradation[.] I'd love the lad had he been some one else. But I think he's safe from *her* [Cathy's] love. I'll pit him against that paltry creature [Linton] unless it bestir itself briskly' (p 176; cf pp 99–100). Of Hareton, he says; 'When I look for his father in his face, I find *her* every day more! How the devil is he so like? I can hardly bear to see him' (p 240). Thus does Brontë sustain, in an immediate way, Heathcliff's aspiring love for Catherine.

The Cathy-Linton relationship also excites Heathcliff remembering conscious-ness, indelibly fixed on the fact that Catherine belongs to him, not to Edgar. Cathy and Linton's marriage repeats Catherine and Edgar's, proving again how thoroughly null and void it was and is. Cathy's feelings for Linton are as contradictory as Catherine's were for Edgar: 'You're not much, are you, Linton?" she says to him after one of his peevish fits (p 193). Her courage before Heathcliff starkly contrasts with Linton's timidity, as when she abjures the weeping wretch: 'Rise, and don't degrade yourself into an abject reptile' (p 212). We recall Edgar Linton's 'nervous trembling' before the threatening Heathcliff, which prompted Catherine in revul-sion to call him 'a suckling leveret' (p 100). Cathy's discovery that she is not like Linton (p 168) echoes Catherine's acknowldgment that her soul and Edgar were 'as different as a moonbeam from lightning, or frost from fire' (p 72). Still, Cathy, insisting she loves Linton, marries him. But like her mother's marriage, Cathy's has been invalidated before it occurs. After she and Linton marry, we see him in his usual enfeebled state, sucking a piece of candy. Brontë exhibits him at his spiteful worst before mercifully allowing him to die; and his timely death prevents our feeling the marriage had been consummated. Everything we know about Linton betrays his impotence. 'No—don't kiss me,' he says to Cathy during their courtship. 'It takes my breath—dear me!' (p 190). He can 'contribute to her entertainment' even less than Edgar could to Catherine's (cf pp 208, 86). Upon Linton's death, Cathy turns to Hareton in life as Catherine turned to Heathcliff in death.

Soon after Hareton ventures towards 'higher pursuits,' Heathcliff gazes after him admiringly and sighs: 'It will be odd, if I thwart myself!' (p 240). The real trend of events in the second part of *Wuthering Heights* leads to Heathcliff's baffling, not accomplishing, his great revenge. He does not bother to do his worst because he has but one objective, and in that he is not thwarted. By extending Heathcliff's life twenty years beyond Catherine's, Brontë validates his unalterable commitment. She makes this intention almost explicit when Heathcliff unseals his thoughts to Nelly by gelling her what occurred on the night that he thrashed Hindley: 'I looked round impatiently—I felt her by me—I could *almost* see her, and yet I *could not!* . . . And, since, then sometimes more, and sometimes less, I've been the sport of that intolerable torture! Infernal—keeping my nerves at such a stretch, that, if they had not resembled catgut, they would, long ago, have relaxed to the feebleness of Linton's (p 230). After producing her full effect Brontë bring Heathcliff to a 'strange change' (p 255). He rather arbitrarily decides to hold his hand and strike at nothing, even though 'now would be the precise time,' he realizes, to revenge himself completely on 'the representatives' of his old enemies (p 255). This final attenuation of the revenge plot has been well prepared for and does not jar with the peculiar system of probability informing the world of this novel.

Heathcliff's decision not to revenge himself appears, he says, to be 'an absurd termination to my violent exertions' (p 254); it 'sounds as if I had been labouring the whole time, only to exhibit a fine trait of magnanimity' (p 255). Brontë seems here to reflect upon the form she has created, upon the point of her own labour. Those critics who sense a certain clumsiness in this episode try to explain it either by penetrating what they suppose to be its moral and psychological implications or by concluding that the novel splits into incongruous halves, with the second marred by improbabilities and irresolution. Heathcliff's change seems too sudden and in-adequately motivated by the rationalization he provides: 'I don't care for striking, I can't take the trouble to raise my hands! . . . I have lost the faculty of enjoying their destruction, and I am too idle to destroy for nothing' (p 255). Quibbling over his motives is, I would suggest, beside the point. The revenge plot has been stretched on a cord which snaps, hurtling Heathcliff towards Catherine.

Although the revenge plot abruptly snaps, in doing so it loses none of its qualitative significance, for its impact is transferred from a worldly to an other-worldly terminus. The symbolic action firmly establishes Heathcliff's control over fate. He makes his will felt in a series of successes which ultimately imply that he brings to his real goal the same success and control. Heathcliff, who begins as an unwanted, sometimes persecuted waif, in time becomes sole master over Wuther-ing Heights, Thrushcross Grange, and their inhabitants. As a young man he went away for three years, to return rich and independent, the image of a man who has dominated circumstances. Heathcliff proceeds to win control of the Heights from Hindley, who had hoped to master him and whose rage and hatred come to nothing, as if to underscore his comparative ineffectuality. Heathcliff's power and control are reaffirmed continually throughout the action, but at the very moment he might exercise his accumulated strength in destruction, he holds his hand, for there is to be no mere worldly stop to his energetic forward movement. Quali-tatively his power seems augmented by its suspension, confirming his ability to guide fortune where he chooses, to achieve the single goal for which he cares. That he will fulfil the strange fate Brontë has imagined for him is, in short, given full credibility by the pattern of power which he displays throughout. Brontë must at this point hasten towards her conclusion to that the reader does not lose the impression of this symbolic pattern, but transmutes it to a conviction that Heathcliff reaches Catherine in spirit.

By the thirty-third chapter, all mediation through resemblances, memoranda, personification, and associations may be discarded as Brontë drives Heathcliff, far from spent or altered, *directly* towards his source. All his thoughts turn exclusively towards Catherine, whom he sees before him as if she were in the same room. Heathcliff now thinks solely of his single wish, convinced that 'it *will*, be reached—and *soon*—because it has devoured my existence' (p 256). The book is devoured by the same goal. The line disappears in the circle.

Heathcliff dies, not exhausted and will-less, but at the height of his strength and passion, a fact Brontë emphasizes by keeping him in perfect health until his self-willed end. He takes his life into the grave. Not surprisingly, Dr Kennedy was 'perplexed to pronounce of what disorder the master died.' His fast, Nelly is persuaded, 'was the consequence of his strange illness, not the cause' (p 264). During his last days Heathcliff's grimly smiling countenance communicated 'both pleasure and pain, in exquisite extremes' (p 261), an image fitting perfectly the book's formal polarity. The 'joyful glitter in his eyes' remains in the 'life-like gaze of exultation' on the face of the corpse (p 264). Yet it is also 'sarcastic, savage,' expressing both his fearless anticipation of death ('he looks grinning at death,' says Joseph) and his contempt for this world (his eyes 'would not shut; they seemed to sneer at my attempts,' says Nelly). Heathcliff's anguish is quieted as he attains his 'soul's bliss.'

IV

Most of the events in *Wuthering Heights* are *faits accomplis*. What has happened cannot be changed and therefore induces acceptance and belief. The complicated narrative view frequently shifts from the present to the past and the future perfect; the world of Wuthering Heights alternately seems close and remote, as we are assaulted with savage action or lulled with quiet summary. The most concrete, natural, immediate events support the most visionary, giving the whole a quality of reality. Throughout the novel, life lends reality to death. The shifting temporal perspective evokes a sense of omnitemporality, which contributes to our belief in the eternity of Heathcliff's love for Catherine. These two are released from the time boundary which consumes the lives of all the other characters.[10] We view the action through a narrative casement ranging from single to quadruple thickness: events touch Lockwood more or less closely as he experiences them first-hand or through Nelly, at one, two, or three removes. The function and effect of the peculiar narrative technique of this novel, as it specifically involves Nelly Dean as narrator to Lockwood, remain to be considered.

I have already touched on Nelly's function in diverting, at crucial points, the moral onus from Heathcliff onto one of the other characters. She frequently sides with Heathcliff against Edgar, Isabella, and Linton, yet she feels more at home with the platitudinous Lintons. Although her commonsense humanity often promotes our charitable view of Heathcliff as he interacts with the other characters, on one point she consistently opposes him: his love for Catherine after she marries Edgar. Nelly's commitment to the normal social world naturally makes her a stranger to Catherine's and Heathcliff's passion. She listens, but does not learn; knows the whole story, but fails to apprehend its implications. Her view is not only inadequate, but ultimately irrelevant to the significance of their love.[11] Her good-natured, commonplace sense of things does, however, make an inestimable contribution to Brontë's mode of expressing the central love story and its goal.

Nelly's view of human nature is almost always reliable whenever she judges normal relationships. Her attitude towards Edgar and Catherine's marriage, for example, is as reasonable as Edgar's own; and when Catherine confesses her feelings towards Edgar, Nelly finds no sense in her 'nonsense' except that she is ignorant of the duties she undertakes in marrying (p 74). She is equally uncomprehending when she opposes Heathcliff after he returns from his three-year exile. Because illness had altered Catherine, Nelly imagines that anyone compelled to be her companion 'will only sustain his affection hereafter by the remembrance of what she once was, by common humanity, and a sense of duty!' (p 125). Heathcliff scorns the idea of leaving Catherine to Edgar's *'duty* and *humanity,'* as he tries to impress upon her the distinction between their feelings. She makes no pretence of understanding him. To her his talk is insane, as Catherine's is delirious. When Heathcliff tells her that he exhumed Catherine's body, Nelly quite naturally exclaims: 'you were very wicked, Mr. Heathcliff! were you not ashamed to disturb the Dead?' (p 229). In contrast, Edgar's response to Catherine's death strikes her as proper: 'he was too good to be thoroughly unhappy long. *He* didn't pray for Catherine's soul to haunt him. Time brought resignation, and a melancholy sweeter than common joy. He recalled her memory with ardent, tender love, and hopeful aspiring to the better world, where, he doubted not, she was gone' (p 151). Edgar had, in addition, 'earthly consolation and affections' to divert him, Nelly approvingly notes, in his daughter Cathy, who soon 'wielded a despot's sceptre in his heart' (p 152). In another book these might have been the norms for judgment, but in *Wuthering Heights* they are not. Paradoxically the values rest, instead, in Heathcliff's hating the children and denying Catherine any rest until he joins her. Nelly neither comprehends nor sympathizes with such passions.

By continually raising, through Nelly, the social, moral perspective, Brontë precludes the reader's judging events according to any conventional sense of the world. Because we see that Nelly's judgments of Heathcliff and Catherine, as well as any advice or remedy she offers them, are irrelevant, we give ourselves wholly up to an appreciation of that love for the extraordinary thing it is. What we perceive as impertinent in Nelly's position, we understand to be inappropriate in ourselves. Thus near the end of the book, when Heathcliff rapturously declares his anticipation of shortly joining Catherine and Nelly feels called on to 'offer some advice' which would make him 'happier' (p 262), we can only smile at their irreconcilable notions of happiness. Her advice has no more to do with these lovers than they have to do with shame or fear.

Brontë does not, I would suggest, construct her indirect narration, then, because the reader would become passive and not exercise his own perception and judgment if the story were approached directly.[12] The direct method of, say, Jane Austen or Thomas Hardy exacts the most active kind of moral awareness and discrimination from the reader. Brontë's indirect narration functions, instead, to make us morally passive but imaginatively flexible. A shift of view is called for because Catherine and Heathcliff fulfil their love outside this world, a transcendence which becomes the ground for evaluation and appreciation. The nature of their love places it beyond all conventional standards. The reader, therefore, adopts a view not morally superior to Nelly's, but completely different in sensibility—as different as Heathcliff's love is from Edgar's.

The effete Lockwood, who foolishly imagines himself another Heathcliff (see chaps I and 2), is even less capable than Nelly of judging or appreciating these lovers' experience. He is a *poseur,* both as misanthrope and as lover, leading us to appreciate Heathcliff's authenticity, however savage its expression. Lockwood learns the story of these lovers while idly passing time in the sick room or casually moving in and out of the world of the Heights. Brontë never intended that either he or Nelly should be instructed in her lover's grand passion, but she did not wish to obscure it for her readers.

Just as Nelly embodies the ordinary moral perspective, the old servant Joseph voices the full rigour of divine law, which we also feel to be irrelevant—if not irreverent. Nelly articulates our response to him adequately: 'He was, and is yet, most likely,' she informs Lockwood, 'the wearisomest, self-righteous pharisee that ever ransacked a Bible to rake the promises to himself, and fling the curses on his neighbours' (p 42). Yet Nelly, like Joseph, reviles Heathcliff for his unchristian life, warning him as he approaches his end, how unfit he is for heaven. But we share Heathcliff's attitude, not hers: 'No minister need come; nor need anything be said over me. I tell you. I have nearly attained *my* heaven; and that of others is altogether unvalued and uncoveted by me!' Heathcliff requires only that the sexton heed his special instructions 'concerning the two coffins' so that his and Catherine's meeting will not be spoiled (p 263; cf pp 228–9). Nelly may be shocked by his 'godless indifference,' but we find it harmonious with both the strange happiness Brontë has prepared for him and the strange power she has devised for us.

Everyone else in *Wuthering Heights* is given a place in the world as we know it; only Catherine and Heathcliff belong to another. It is their experience which we carry away from the book, leaving all the rest behind, as they themselves do. Nelly's idea of happiness is realized in Cathy and Hareton's union; but their love is only the afterglow of the conflagration we have witnessed. At the close of the story, Lockwood visits Catherine's and Heathcliff's graves and notices that 'decay had made progress' upon the church walls. How much more quickly does flesh decay. We are reminded of the dissolution Heathcliff long desired as the perfect consummation of his 'immortal love.' Lockwood wonders 'how any one could ever imagine unquiet slumbers for the sleepers in that quiet earth' (p 266), but we do not. Within the story we accede to the conviction that ghosts 'can, and do exist, among us' (p 229), that 'the dead are not annihilated' (p 263). The wind blowing on the boldly swelling health is the respiration of a living world.[13]

NOTES

[1] I adopt the world *lyrical* as a general descriptive term to point up the radical formal difference between *Wuthering Heights* and those novels—Fielding's, Austen's, and Hardy's, for example—shaped by a

principle of logically progressive plots. In discussing similar forms in 'Novelists as Storytellers,' Sheldon Sacks formulates the concept of 'a *plot* of "lyric" revelation' (*Modern Philology*, 73 [May 1976], 109). Sacks borrows the phrase 'fluctuating stasis' from Leonard M. Meyer's general description of such forms: in the imaginative world of such a work, progress as normally conceived is absent, since 'the distinction among past, present, and future becomes obscured, is static' (see *Music, the Arts, and Ideas* [Chicago: University of Chicago Press 1967], p 169).

In the course of formulating my conclusions about Brontë's technique, I was influenced by Erich Auerbach's analysis of Virginia Woolf and Marcel Proust, 'The Brown Stocking,' in *Mimesis: The Representation of Reality in Western Literature*, trans Willard R. Trask (Princeton: Princeton University Press 1953), pp 525–53. Brontë should be placed in the tradition of the novel which leads to Woolf and Proust rather than to Conrad and Lawrence through Hardy. Brontë in some ways anticipates the technical goals of stream-of-consciousness narrative, but whereas a writer like Woolf may oppose exterior events directly to the representation of the processes of consciousness itself, Brontë discloses the remembering consciousness of Heathcliff by playing events off against each other in parallel fashion—the Edgar/Heathcliff, Linton/Hareton conflicts and the Catherine/Edgar, Cathy/Linton marriages—as well as through parallel characters—Catherine/Cathy, Edgar/Linton, and Heathcliff/Hareton. She adapted the methods of realistic, logical plot-action novels to her own peculiar ends, as I hope to show.

[2] *Wuthering Heights: An Authoritative Text with Essays in Criticism*, ed William M. Sale, Jr (New York: Norton 1963), p 133. Page references to the novel are given in the text.

[3] See Cecil W. Davies's fruitful pursuit of this idea in 'A Reading of *Wuthering Heights*,' *Essays in Criticism*, 19 (July 1969), 254–72.

[4] Compare Heathcliff's anguish here with his rage immediately after Catherine dies. Nelly observes that he 'dashed his head against the knotted trunk; and, lifting up his eyes, howled, not like a man, but like a savage beast getting goaded to death with knives and spears' (p 139). The exaggeration of Heathcliff's passions symbolically expresses an extra-ordinary existence. As Virginia Woolf has observed, 'it is as if she [Brontë] could tear up all we know human beings by, and fill these unrecognizable transparencies with such a gust of life that they transcend reality': 'Jane Eyre and Wuthering Heights,' in *The Common Reader* (New York: Harcourt, Brace 1925), p 165.

[5] A early reviewer of *Wuthering Heights* intuited an effect Brontë intended, but he thought it disclosed an intrinsic flaw: 'like all spendthrifts of malice and profanity, however, he ['Ellis Bell'] overdoes the business. Though he scatters oaths as plentifully as sentimental writers do interjections, the comparative parsimony of the great novelists in this respect is productive of infinitely more effect': *The North American Review*, October 1848, rpt in *The English Novel: Background Readings*, ed Lynn C. Bartlett and William R. Sherwood (Philadelphia: Lippincott 1967), pp 197–8.

[6] 'Editor's Preface to the New Edition of *Wuthering Heights* [1850],' in Sale, ed, pp 11–12.

[7] *Aspects of the Novel* (New York: Harcourt, Brace 1927), pp 209–10.

[8] In the preceding two sentences I adopt some of Auerbach's phrasing from his analysis of *To the Lighthouse* to suggest the relationship between Brontë's and Woolf's techniques. These authors radically differ, of course, in their general thematic intentions. *Wuthering Heights* does not, for example, breathe 'an air of vague and hopeless sadness'; and if it is 'hostile to reality,' it is so in a very different sense from Woolf's novel (see Auerbach, p 551). Brontë is as certain of her transcendent reality as Austen is of her social reality.

[9] Sidney Dobell in the *Palladium*, September 1850, in Sale, ed, p 280.

[10] Compare Thomas A. Vogler's provocative treatment of time and point of view in *Wuthering Heights*, 'Story and History in *Wuthering Heights*,' in *Twentieth-Century Interpretations of* Wuthering Heights, ed. T. A. Vogler (Englewood Cliffs, NJ: Prentice-Hall 1968), pp 85ff.

[11] John K. Mathison provides a valuable analysis of Nelly Dean's role and the reader's response to it in 'Nelly Dean and the Power of *Wuthering Heights*,' *Nineteenth-Century Fiction*, 11 (September 1956), 106–29. Mathison argues that we are released from Nelly's point of view, because of its inadequacy, to become sympathetically involved with 'conventionally despicable' characters (p 118). But for him our gain is exclusively a more 'genuine insight into human emotion' (p 127), specifically of 'the tortured, emotionally distraught person' (p 109).

[12] Cf Mathison, p 109.

[13] I wish to thank Professor Ralph Wilson Rader, who read the original version of this essay and generously suggested ways to draw out more fully the implications of its argument.

Mary Burgan

IDENTITY AND THE CYCLE OF GENERATIONS IN *WUTHERING HEIGHTS*

In her preface to *Wuthering Heights* (1850), Charlotte Brontë offered an apologia for her sister's novel that acknowledged a division between the "realism" of the work and its power as the expression of the myth of the hero who is not defined or limited by mere "reality." Recognizing a threat to social order in the depiction of Heathcliff's passionate alienation, Charlotte also insisted upon the domestic pragmatism of her sister's novel. The narrative, she asserted, is rooted in the facts of Yorkshire life: Emily understood the people around her; she "knew their ways, their language, their family histories: she could hear of them with interest, and talk of them with detail, minute, graphic, and accurate. . . ."[1] In thus attempting to balance the mimetic acuity of *Wuthering Heights* against its dramatization of Romantic rebellion, Charlotte Brontë defined a task which continues to challenge critics of the novel.

In this essay I want to second Charlotte Brontë's emphasis upon the realism of *Wuthering Heights* by investigating the social and psychological context of the love story of Cathy and Heathcliff, for I believe that Emily Brontë's power as an observer is most impressive in her insistence upon placing her lovers within a detailed and consciously emphasized history of the generations that preceded and follow them. To be sure, they stand in the middle, inheritors of an abuse of parental authority which they can deflect only by clinging to one another in defiance of all convention. But if they are shown as victims, they are also shown as victimizers whose rebellion threatens their children. While Emily Brontë portrays the dimensions of their passion with a sympathy verging on endorsement, she never forgets its sources, its pathology, and its cruelty. A fuller perception of this mingling of allegiances may enable us to appreciate the final equilibrium *Wuthering Heights* manages to establish between a total rejection of society and a reconciliation with the necessities of community.

In seeking an interpretative model to aid in reexamining the problem of the balance between passion and society in *Wuthering Heights,* I have been struck by

From *Philological Quarterly* 61, No. 4 (Fall 1982): 395–413.

the relevance of the theories of Erik H. Erikson. Historians of the family almost invariably cite Erikson as a guide in their efforts to acknowledge the importance of individual development, while describing the general social context of family structures.[2] In attempting to acknowledge the social significance of Emily Brontë's novel, as well as its powerful depiction of the unique and idiosyncratic in individual behavior, the literary critic may learn from Erikson as well. A sketch of his central notion about the interactions among generations in families may be in order here.

In *Identity: Youth and Crisis,* a sourcebook for his ideas about adolescence, Erikson defines the chief task of middle youth as assimilating the demands of adult society within the peculiar conditions of personal traits so as to arrive at the conviction of having a definable and continuous inner self—an identity. Many are the impediments to this achievement—the lack of coherent and worthwhile social ideals, the failure of confirmation from the preceding generation, the denial of prospects for sexual intimacy or productive work. In outlining these difficulties, Erikson also sketches the pathologies of adolescents who have been blocked in their efforts to attain maturity. He notes the strange blend of furious activity with passivity in young people who cannot find a core of being within themselves. He remarks on their tendency to ally themselves with rigid ideologies, excluding all but a favored few from a narrowed range of true believers. As the sexual and procreative imperatives develop, the disturbed adolescent may indulge in promiscuity that is devoid of affection or mutuality. Significantly, for our purposes, Erikson indicates that one of the most striking "symptoms" of identity confusion can occur in the adolescent's over-identification with a brother or sister. Young people who have no other basis for a sense of self may make the attachment to a sibling the psychological equivalent of identical twinship, only to panic upon the inevitable realization that the loved brother or sister cannot provide enough identity to go around.[3]

Such aspects of "identity crisis" are clearly at issue in *Wuthering Heights.* The question of who Cathy and Heathcliff are and what they are to become lies at the root of their attachment to one another. At moments of great emotional stress, each refers to the other as the sole source of personal being: "I *am* Heathcliff" (p. 102), Cathy tells Nelly Dean as she contemplates a decision to marry Edgar Linton. And Heathcliff, mourning Cathy's death later in the novel, exclaims, "Oh God! it is unutterable! I *cannot* live without my life! I *cannot* live without my soul!" (p. 204). If we are to realize the full significance of such statements, we must assess their source in the strange interplay of identities forced upon these two characters by the conditions of their adolescence.

That Brontë saw this source to lie in the generational interaction among the Earnshaw and Linton families may not be doubted: after all, she made her story a chronicle of three generations (I included Mr. Earnshaw in this family history as well as the grandchildren—Catherine, Hareton, and Linton). Structuring her narrative in this fashion, she takes care to establish the psychological etiology of her protagonists' behavior. And in making Nelly Dean her main narrator, she gives the family history a social context, accenting the norms applied to it by a traditional view of familial loyalties and limitations. Emily Brontë does not, then, present her characters' radical concern for identity simply as a symbolic confrontation of the sexes, a "pre-moral" disposition of nature, or a mystical search for grace. Rather, she celebrates the passionate energy of the ego as self-affirming, while showing that such energy, beating against the restrictions of a closed patriarchal system, can wear itself out by seeking to imprint its own deprivations upon the future.[4]

I

The first parent in *Wuthering Heights* is old Mr. Earnshaw, and the central mystery of his behavior is why he has brought Heathcliff home to usurp the places of his children. The novel offers scant analysis of the father's motives, suggesting thereby that sheer willfulness might be reason enough: "Not a soul knew to whom it belonged, he said, and his money and time being both limited, he thought it better, to take it home with him at once, than run into vain expenses there: because he was determined he would not leave it as he found it" (p. 45).[5] In arguing the demonic nature of Heathcliff's presence in the novel, Dorothy Van Ghent has observed that he is initially referred to with the impersonal pronoun, "it": he is not imagined as a human creature but as a supernatural force.[6] Nevertheless, the uses of Heathcliff's adoption indicate that Earnshaw senior has a "human" purpose in mind for him. Salvaging him through whim rather than a deeply contemplated act of adoption, Mr. Earnshaw promptly turns Heathcliff to use in chastizing his own offspring. It is significant that Heathcliff's accidental intervention has caused the father to forget the toys promised to his children. Hindley's and Cathy's resentment is natural, but Earnshaw seizes upon it to pit Heathcliff against them from the very start: ". . . and Cathy, when she learnt the master had lost her whip in attending on the stranger, showed her humour by grinning and spitting at the stupid little thing, earning for her pains, a sound blow from her father to teach her cleaner manners" (pp. 45–46). In making a weapon of one child against the others, Earnshaw establishes a mode of fatherhood that will be repeated in the generation to follow. It is a mode of violent self-assertion in the face of the child's assumption of prerogatives.

Fatherhood seems a matter of bewilderment to the elder Earnshaw. Indeed, in her depiction of his confusion, Emily Brontë participates in a thematic concern of such nineteenth-century critics of paternal authority as Austen, Dickens, and Butler.[7] She shows in Mr. Earnshaw the declining patriarch's lonely obsession with power, his resentment of the inheriting children and his effort to dominate the future by putting their patrimony in doubt. As Nelly Dean seeks to explain the current status of the Earnshaw family, she recounts how old Earnshaw sought to exacerbate the dependency of his blood heirs by preferring the child of adoption: "He took to Heathcliff strangely, believing all he said . . . and petting him up far above Cathy, who was too mischievous and wayward for a favorite" (p. 46–47). This preference for the silent and tractable child grows as Earnshaw becomes more jealous of his waning power: "A nothing vexed him, and suspected slights of his authority nearly threw him into fits" (p. 50). The loss of the moderating maternal affection of Mrs. Earnshaw removes all restraints to this paranoid response,[8] and Nelly emphasizes its effects on the legitimate son, Hindley: "So, from the very beginning, [Heathcliff] bred bad feeling in the house; and at Mrs. Earnshaw's death, which happened in less than two years after, the young master had learnt to regard his father as an oppressor rather than a friend, and Heathcliff as a usurper of his parent's affections and his privileges, and he grew bitter with brooding over these injuries" (p. 47).

Fiction has rarely portrayed the politics of familial competition more perceptively than the opening section of *Wuthering Heights*. Each child in the Earnshaw household is locked into a confused battle plan in which victory can be claimed only by proving himself or herself upon the other. Some critics have noticed an incestuous cast to the relations of brothers and sisters here, but it should be stressed that sensual experimentation is subordinate to maneuvering for power. A. O. J. Cockshut has remarked that the Romantics' fascination with love between brothers and sisters symbolizes, among other things, a "search for origins," and it is clear that Cathy and Heathcliff's bond involves an effort to transcend present confusion through an alliance with a purer, more original version of the self—one that has not been scarred by parental disapproval.[9]

And yet in seeking an identity in each other, the Earnshaw children also seek to please the parent. While Cathy chooses Heathcliff as an ally in order to gain the attention of her father, Hindley's enmity constitutes an acceptance of the nothingness proposed for him by old Earnshaw: in hating his stepbrother, the older son gains the distinction of having "lived up" to a minimal parental ideal. Heathcliff's passive participation in the father's program of revenge on his natural children, meanwhile, is charged with the stoicism of an outcast whose only validation is the parent's favoritism. Heathcliff asserts himself by instigating quarrels, like the one about his lame horse, which will bring Earnshaw's patronage into play. Thus the children bind themselves to each other in reaction to the father's effort to preside decisively over their developing selves. Each strives mightily to meet Old Earnshaw's expectations by acting out his worst fears about them: as Erikson has noted, children who can please their parents in no other way may take refuge in the terms of the parent's rejection—a negative identity, sanctioned by the parent's attention and emphasis, is better than none at all.[10]

Cathy is preeminently situated to illustrate this paradox. Her emotional authority over Heathcliff becomes her only source of contact with her father: "His peevish reproofs wakened in her a naughty delight to provoke him; she was never so happy as when we were all scolding her at once, and she defying us with her bold, saucy look, and her ready words . . . doing just what her father hated most, showing how her pretended insolence, which he thought real, had more power over Heathcliff than his kindness: how the boy would do *her* bidding in anything, and *his* only when it suited her own inclination" (p. 52). In displaying this form of inherited wilfulness, Cathy forfeits the mutual trust with adults upon which the child's sense of herself must depend. Disastrous results follow upon her occasional efforts at reconciliation, for each instance inspires a further rejection. At one point when she tries to make up, Earnshaw responds, "Nay, Cathy . . . I cannot love thee;

thou'rt worse than thy brother. Go, say thy prayers, child, and ask God's pardon. I doubt thy mother and I must rue that we ever reared thee!" (p. 52). Finally, on the day of his death, Earnshaw provokes the ultimate break with his daughter. Cathy sidles up to him affectionately, and he asks, "Why canst thou not always be a good lass, Cathy?" She responds with a question that can only vex him the more, attacking his faults while assenting to his declaration of her perversity: "Why cannot you always be a good man, father?" (p. 53). Shortly after this alienating exchange, Cathy discovers that her father has died in his chair. Heathcliff alone can console her now. Refused confirmation from her parent, where better to seek it than in the rival who has also been accomplice in her demands for recognition?

It is important to notice the emphasis that the elder Earnshaw has set upon rearing in his denouncement of his children. His curse to Cathy is specific: "I doubt that thy mother and I must rue that we ever *reared* thee!" (my italics). Though Hindley is sent away to school by his father, it is clear that formal education has little to do with the gift of some structured basis for selfhood: "Hindley was naught," his father remarks in assenting to his departure for college, "and would never thrive as where he wandered" (p. 50). The essential rearing that gives a child a sense of identity is more than formal schooling: it involves, as Erickson suggests, an interaction of the generations living within a family in such a way that a "meaningful hierarchy of roles" is provided for the young.[11] Many nineteenth-century novels record the deflection of such rearing through the banishment of the child to school; Hindley is the precursor of Ernest Pontifex, though he finds no benign maiden aunt to take charge of his rearing and thereby humanize him.

When Hindley returns from school to assume his own role as patriarch, he may have gained a surface culture, but within the family he bears the marks of the unreared child. He is sullen, bewildered, and incapable of consciously planned behavior. While Cathy clings to her playmate for self-identification, he clings to the childish bride he has brought with him.[12] When she dies in childbirth, Hindley's personality collapses, and he reenacts his father's most potent form of rejection. He stops all education for Heathcliff, hoping to revoke old Earnshaw's patronage. Cathy shares in this neglect, although the commercial expectation that she can "make" something of herself through a good marriage gives her a greater immediate freedom than Heathcliff has.

We have noted that Cathy is the most active rebel at Wuthering Heights. As the family heiress, she has some license to manipulate emotions and indulge in fits of imperiousness; such behaviors will form her arsenal as a mature woman in search of a suitable husband.[13] But the tragedy of her development derives not only from the artificiality of the role of flirt but from Cathy's need to continue playing it well into maturity. Nelly Dean's furtive enmity against her is in part the plain woman's rejection of lady-like airs and graces; what Nelly's common sense cannot fathom, however, is that Cathy's divisive flirtations both with Heathcliff and with Edgar Linton are strategies of sheer survival, disguised by the accepted stereotypes of feminine behavior.

Thus although she is partly motivated by a romance of the female self as a princess who can resolve familial discord through a magical marriage, Cathy's choice of Edgar Linton as her husband must also be read as an act of lacerating self-preservation against Heathcliff's need to become the sole justification for her existence. For after old Earnshaw's death, Heathcliff has had to develop in a void. Neither brother nor servant under Hindley's regime, he is deprived of most human contact. Indeed, his adolescence is marked by scenes in which he is barred both from the community of the family and the community of the kitchen—finding refuge in the anonymous landscape of darkness and storm from which Mr. Earnshaw had rescued him. Thus Heathcliff experiences nature as his only home; he receives some human solace when he has Cathy as company, but he sees no reflection of Nature's elemental vitality in the human society open to him. He therefore revels in the violent aspects of the moors; he embraces random wildness as his only model for behavior. Having allied himself with Cathy when her father was alive, he seeks to impose his anarchic energies upon her after Earnshaw's death. And with all the rigidity of adolescent need for ideological purity, he demands total loyalty. The conflict that this alliance makes for her may be seen in the staging of Cathy's first meeting with Edgar Linton.

Cathy has been on one of her jaunts with Heathcliff when they come upon the image of Edgar and Isabella Linton lit up in the window of their civilized home at Thrushcross Grange. The scene is by no means an amiable one; the Linton children are scrapping as usual. Their relationship illustrates the limitations of a family structure in which the children are shielded by parents from the testing arena of the natural world; they are quarreling over a miniature lap dog, and they are terrified of the intruders. Nevertheless, their family has continuity and comfort, and Cathy seems to respond to its security as much as she envies its social elevation. Her stay with the Lintons transforms her from an anonymous gypsy into a costumed young lady. When she returns home, Hindley greets her with a remark on her new self: "I should scarcely have known you—you look like a lady now . . . " (p. 65). She has preserved enough of her old self, however, to hope that she can force admittance for Heathcliff into a charmed circle of civilized life, but Cathy makes the error upon which the whole narrative revolves in imagining that she can extend the benefits of the Linton family to Heathcliff. Fixed at a stage of childhood development when life is a game in which arguments can be settled by asking each side to shake hands, Cathy has a limited understanding of the kind of fidelity that forms the basis for mature love. She is blind to the erotic realities that block her scheming to make her marriage with Edgar a means for shared intimacy with Heathcliff; indeed, her relations with both Edgar and Heathcliff are remarkably sexless.[14] And so the failure of familial affection, a misunderstanding of sexual loyalty, and the artificiality of female role playing have trapped Cathy in permanent childishness.

All of the difficulties of Cathy's marriage—her attraction to a weak man and her peculiar effort at once to reject and retain a bond with her foster brother—are understandable when we contemplate the liabilities of "twinship" with Heathcliff. She articulates those to Nelly Dean in the fateful conversation in which she analyzes her decision to marry Edgar Linton unaware—and unwarned by her confidante—

that Heathcliff may overhear. In the dream which, she tells Nelly, embodies her dilemma, she must either accept the false "heaven" of other people or the glorious "hell" of being cast out of the community of saints onto Heathcliff's moors. In telling Nelly that the barrier to marrying the socially engaged Edgar is her identity with Heathcliff, Cathy reveals the full nullity of her existence: "What were the use of my creation if I were entirely contained here?" she asks. The answer is that Heathcliff alone justifies her: "If all else perished, and *he* remained, I should still continue to be; and if all else remained, and he were annihilated, the Universe would turn to a mighty stranger. I should not seem part of it." This existential tie with Heathcliff is not only a rejection of ordinary human community but a rejection of the mutability of time and natural process as well. It is an effort to be free from the generative cycle that has failed to give either Cathy or Heathcliff any sense of their personal significance in its workings. In choosing Edgar, to be sure, Cathy will ally herself with the social world and with organic fruition, but she prefers a timeless security from change: "My love for Linton is like the foliage in the woods. Time will change it, I'm well aware, as winter changes the trees—my love for Heathcliff resembles the eternal rocks beneath—a source of little visible delight, but necessary" (p. 101–02).

This confrontation between the individual and the community, the eternal and the time-bound, being and becoming, are personified in the differences between Cathy and Nelly Dean, who are foster sisters, after all. Cathy represents the unbound ego, ever in a state of rebellious childhood, proclaiming its capacity to manipulate reality in its own image. Nelly is the generative figure in the novel, the nourisher of children, who rises above the ravages of time through her capacity to oversee the progress of one generation after another.[15] As such, she should be a source of reconciliation and maturity, but in this crucial episode, she plays the wicked stepsister rather than the wise nurse. With all her common virtues, Nelly Dean herself has been locked into a limited identity. The defensive, self-imposed isolation of her Yorkshire culture offers no outlet for the crucial dialectic between youth's drive to experiment with new freedoms and its respect for old ideals of order. In a vital society, the culture is secure enough in its own values to submit to the critiques of the young. Thus "generativity," as Erikson insists, is a mutual process where by the adolescent's search for identity constitutes an invigorating criticism of the culture in which it must finally be achieved.[16] At the very point at which Cathy pleads for understanding of her need to reconcile the desire for existential integrity with an almost pathetic drive for social stability, culture's representative not only turns a deaf ear but conspires with circumstances to insure that Cathy will fail.

II

Heathcliff leaves Wuthering Heights the day he discovers Cathy's decision to marry Edgar Linton. But before he disappears, he establishes a link with the Earnshaw generations that will be extremely important later. He saves Hareton, Hindley's son, from being destroyed. Following the death of his wife, Hindley has treated Hareton with the same willful abuse he suffered from old Earnshaw. Indeed, Hindley's behavior mirrors the extremes of doting fondness and brutal manhandling that characterize clinical accounts of child batterers.[17] Hindley has come home drunk and maudlin. Seeing Hareton in Nelly's arms, he reaches out to fondle the infant, becoming angry when Hareton shies away in terror; "Hush, child, hush! Well, then, it is my darling! whist, dry thy eyes—there's a joy; kiss me; what! it won't? Kiss me, Hareton! Damn thee, kiss me! By God, as if I would rear such a monster! as sure as I'm living, I'll break the brat's neck" (p. 92). As Hindley veers from stupid affection to violent rejection—and the word "rear" is significant here—he almost breaks Hareton's neck for sure. He has been holding the child out over the banister; in terror the child wrenches free and falls. Coincidentally Heathcliff is passing below and catches the boy. Much as Heathcliff might like to revoke this gesture to protect his foster brother's child, by the reflex of his act he has entered into some bond with Hareton. In the future, Hareton will be more a son to Heathcliff than his own blood offspring. Seeking to cast out Hareton as he has been cast out, Heathcliff will nevertheless have a tenderness for the boy who bears the greatest moral resemblance to himself as a child—and the greatest physical resemblance to Cathy.

Later on the day of this momentous act of "adoption," Heathcliff leaves the Heights to seek his fortune. Where he goes and what he does during his three-year absence is never quite clear, but his motive, and its connection with his attempt to establish a new identity, has been articulated for him long before in the words of Nelly Dean. Seeking to console him for his degradation Nelly has painted for Heathcliff a daydream as romantically wish-fulfilling as Cathy's dream of resolving everything through a fairy-princess marriage. "You're fit for a prince in disguise," she tells him. "Who knows, but your father was Emperor of China, and your mother an Indian queen, each of them able to buy up, with one week's income, Wuthering Heights and Thrushcross Grange together? And you were kidnapped by wicked sailors, and brought to England. Were I in your place, I would frame high notions of my birth; and the thoughts of what I was should give me courage and dignity to support the oppressions of a little farmer!" (p. 72).

With the return of a "new" Heathcliff intent upon enacting this program, the second half of *Wuthering Heights* takes on a new tone. The emphasis shifts from Cathy's confusions to Heathcliff's obsession with her betrayal, and with this shift, the novel's investigation of the nature of their mutually dependent identity is couched in the language of Heathcliff's rising hysteria. Though he speaks with compelling power in the great set-piece confrontations between the lovers that take place before Cathy's death, Heathcliff's speeches afterwards lose the dramatic validation of her responsiveness—becoming the rantings of a neurotic who seeks some obscure satisfaction in a revenge that his victims can scarcely understand.

Critics who are inclined to locate the total value of *Wuthering Heights* in its status as the instinctive product of the rapt Romantic imagination can be irritated and embarrassed by the closing half of the novel. For many, the story of Heathcliff's demise and the third generation's eventual happy marriage signals a lapse of imaginative energy—an awkward effort to mediate the disruptive power of myth through the means of a conventional happy ending.[18] Thus, for example, Terry Eagleton—who has decisively established the detailed responses to social and economic conditions as essential elements in the Brontës' fictions—ends his essay on *Wuthering Heights* by paying tribute to an ambiguity in the conclusion that defies all sociological or psychological analysis: " . . . there remains at the deepest level an ineradicable contradiction [between passion and society] which refuses to be un-locked, which obtrudes itself as the very stuff and secret of experience."[19] What-ever occurs at the deepest level, however, it is clear that at some level nearer the surface, Emily Brontë designed the ending of *Wuthering Heights* to answer the prob-lems posed by the beginning. And it is my contention that the children of the third generation enact a release from the agonies of negation suffered by Heathcliff and Cathy which is as dramatically necessary as it is psychologically sound. It is in clarifying the grounds of this contention that Erikson's emphasis on the natural "plot" of the stages of development in the human life cycle is most helpful.

Certainly Emily Brontë's structuring her novel upon a pattern of dialectical struggle from one generation to another suggests a richer mix of social and psy-chological realism in the conclusion of *Wuthering Heights* than has generally been acknowledged. The main interest in the resolution of *Wuthering Heights* lies in the countering of Heathcliff's hysteria by time's slow progress and the insistent psychic health of the second Cathy and Hareton. As Heathcliff embarks upon his plan to prove his own power of identity by acting the tyrant towards the remaining children, he continually neglects to reckon with the implacability of the future generation's capacity to discover its own identity through rebellion. Thus though he does manage to arrest his own development by refusing to accept the adult responsibility of nurture and care, he seeks the impossible when he attempts to halt the development of the children—working them like puppet players in the reen-actment of his own past.

As the image of Heathcliff's wounded youth, Hareton's dumb participation in the "courtship" between the second Cathy and Linton both disturbs and consoles Heathcliff. Heathcliff articulates his identification with Hareton to Nelly Dean as they observe the three children together. He admits his ambivalence; " . . . do you know that, twenty times a day, I covet Hareton, with all his degradation? I'd have loved the lad had he been some one else . . . " (p. 265). But then he enlarges upon the perverse sources of his attraction, accenting the adolescent confusion he shares with the boy: "He has satisfied my expectations—If he were a born fool I should not enjoy it half so much—But he's no fool; and I can sympathize with his feelings. Having felt them myself—I know what he suffers now, for instance, exactly—it is merely a beginning of what he shall suffer, though" (p. 267). It is important to note in his plans for Hareton how clearly Heathcliff connects the deprivation of rearing with the deprivation of identity. He exults that Hareton does not know himself well enough to be able to define his own suffering. And the encounter which Heathcliff and Nelly are watching illustrates the impact of the boy's enforced ignorance. Linton and Cathy are contemplating the writing over the entrance to the estate, and Cathy asks Hareton to read it out. His response reveals not only that Hareton is illiterate, but that illiteracy denies him access to a full knowledge of his heritage, his legal self, his right to future expectations. The writing over the entrance is, of course, his own name—"Hareton Earnshaw."

The conjunction of reading with the motif of proper names in *Wuthering Heights* demands a distinction between "book learning" and "rearing."[20] The first is personified in Linton, and it constitutes an escape from identity rather than an engagement with it. For Linton, reading has been a refuge from the conditions of his orphaned existence. For Cathy, books have also been a refuge in a protected childhood, but under the sensitive care of her father—a weak but nurturing man—reading has inspired in Cathy a lively imagination, generous emotions, and an eagerness for communication. Secure in her own sense of herself, Cathy must discover that mere bookishness has given Linton none of these qualities. Mistaking literacy for rearing can cause actual harm, and thus in her shock that Hareton cannot read, she joins with Linton in ridiculing Hareton's ignorance. She wonders if Hareton might be mentally deficient, not completely human—"Is he all as he should be?" she asks in the embarrassed bewilderment of inexperience.

When the question of Hareton's literacy rises again, a little later in the novel, Cathy is still the naive, home-bred girl. Though he painfully demonstrates that he has learned to read out the syllables of his name, she continues to mock Hareton's ignorance. The result is a furious battle between Hareton and Linton in which the true heir to Wuthering Heights thrusts the imposter out of the house, kicking the book he has been reading with Cathy after him. Not only does the issue of reading finally waken Hareton to some sense of his prerogatives, it also cause Cathy to perceive a difference between the well-read cousin and the unread one. Linton comes off second best, as Cathy relates to Nelly Dean, "He was not pretty then, Ellen—Oh, no! He looked frightful! for his thin face and large eyes were wrought into an expression of frantic, powerless fury" (p. 306).

Despite the initial carelessness and triviality, however, the second Cathy is the activating force for the liberation of the Earnshaw heir from the oppressions of the fathers. Heathcliff reserves for her his most pernicious hatred because she represents an impulse towards generational continuity that impelled even the weak Edgar Linton to at least some form of maturity in fatherhood. Renouncing all the generative capacities of adulthood. Heathcliff is unimaginably cruel to his blood son, Linton. But Linton is only an instrument of revenge; he is too weak and stupid to be a proper target for Heathcliff's attack on the promise of the life cycle itself. The second Cathy is the target, and in his dealings with her Heathcliff's actions must be read as clinical symptoms rather than poetic accounts of the triumph of demonic energy over the superego's longing for domestic peace. Emily Brontë does not flinch from the gory detail: " . . . he seized her with the liberated hand, and, pulling her on his knee, administrated with the other a shower of terrific slaps on both sides of the head, each sufficient to have fulfilled his threat [to knock her down] had she been able to fall" (p. 329). Heathcliff's gradual murder of his natural son and his displaced rape of Cathy's daughter are so vicious as to render stock Freudian interpretations somewhat frivolous.[21]

This violence is not essentially between male and female, but between parent and child, and its resolution must break the pattern of family politics which has pitted one child against another in order to give a sense of absolute power to a father who can achieve his sense of identity only in the exercise of physical coercion. The unexpected opposition to this kind of tyranny is the courage of the second Cathy. From her reclusive father and her doting nurse, she seems to have gained the emotional security which must serve as a foundation for self-assertion. Thus even when she is beaten down by superior physical strength, she maintains a sense of what she is and of what other human beings should be: "I've given over crying," she tells Heathcliff after her beating, "but I'm going to kneel here, at your knee; and I'll not get up, and I'll not take my eyes from your face, till you look back at me! No, don't turn away! *do* look! You'll see nothing to provoke you" (p. 334). Cathy has much to learn about Heathcliff's disdain for childish pleadings, but her sense of self is never worn away by it. She is imbued with the conviction—not always an attractive one—that once she is *seen* steadily by another, she will be acknowledged and her rights granted. Cathy's irrepressible sense of her right to exist impells her always to the aid of her cousins. And though she cannot salvage Linton—indeed, she succumbs to her mother's strange delusion that is is possible to give part of one's own identity to another in befriending him—her sufferings during the few weeks of their marriage ratifies her stature as the final source of redemption in the novel. And so, after experimenting with a withdrawn sullenness akin to that of the other inhabitants of Wuthering Heights, she is able to throw off the sulking child role, becoming with Hareton, in their mutual imprisonment, a kind of playmate.

Their play is not trivial, however, for it involves the important task of teaching Hareton how to read. This faltering education loosens Hareton's tongue and shows him what belongs to him by virtue of his birth. And the confederation leads to other kinds of important "play." Cathy makes Hareton an accomplice, significantly, in cultivating a garden. In this exploit, the two have infringed upon the domain of old Joseph, whose patriarchal Calvinism has made the identity of the saved (imaged in Lockwood's initial dream) a matter of mysterious law rather than human cultivation and effort. When Joseph complains to Heathcliff about the garden, Cathy confronts him with the facts of his usurpation of her and Hareton's birthrights. "You shouldn't grudge a few yards of earth, for me to ornament, when you have taken all my land!" she says, adding in increasing fearlessness, "And my money . . . And Hareton's land, and his money" (p. 588–89). Up to this point, Heathcliff's hold on the third generation has depended upon their vagueness about their status as heirs, but now Cathy can risk an open assertion of their legal rights. Heathcliff automatically threatens ultimate violence in return, but as he grabs Cathy by the hair, Hareton intervenes. At this crucial juncture, the legitimate son finally stands between the father and his revenge upon all the children.

Unable to repeat his earlier cruelty upon the inheriting children, Heathcliff turns to Nelly Dean to meditate aloud upon the impossibility of resolving the injustices of the past by reenacting it with childish players: "It is a poor conclusion, is it not," he observes, "An absurd termination to my violent exertions? . . . My old enemies have not beaten me—now would be the precise time to revenge myself on their representatives—I could do it; and none could hinder me—But what is the use?" Heathcliff has been forced to see the young as they are, naturally impervious to his will, but more real to him by that very fact: "Those two, who have left the room, are the only objects which retain a distinct material appearance to me," he tells Nelly, "and that appearance causes me pain, amounting to agony." The confident rebellion of the children has dispersed the illusions sustained by Heathcliff's obsession, forcing him to acknowledge the impossibility of molding the future to his will. As the children ally themselves against him, they also personify the unrooted and still restless elements of his own identity: "Well, Hareton's aspect was the ghost of my immortal love, of my wild endeavors to hold my right, my degradation, my pride, my happiness and my anguish—" (pp. 393–94). Assenting to the boy's alliance with Cathy, Heathcliff does not achieve any integration of self, but he does attain some measure of peace.

III

As Heathcliff hurries towards his death after the confrontation with Hareton and the younger Cathy, the household at Wuthering Heights is restored to a semblance of serenity. But the question of how to interpret Heathcliff's story remains to trouble and confuse its narrator. Nelly Dean poses the two contending interpretations of the history—the mythic and the realistic—in recounting Heathcliff's disintegration. At first, she contemplates the possibility of the demonic in Heathcliff's make-up: " 'Is he a ghoul, or a vampire?' I mused, I had read of such hideous, incarnate demons." But such ideas are finally rejected by the sensible Nelly, who has participated in the domestic events in Heathcliff's growing up and therefore must see him as an ordinary human being: "And then I set myself to reflect how I had tended him in infancy; and watched him grow to youth; and followed him almost through his whole course; and what absurd nonsense it was to yield to that sense of horror" (p. 403). Thus Nelly balances the critical issues involved in assessing the final meaning of *Wuthering Heights*: on the one hand, there is the mystery of evil; on the other, the human explanations that lie in knowing the "whole course" the thwarted development. Though Nelly is often seen as the single-minded speaker for the common-sense view, however, the eloquence of her narration of Heathcliff's death and burial exhibit the poise of a compromise. Thus she speaks Heathcliff's moving epitaph with a sad knowledge of the relationship between his lack of "some fit parentage" and his failure ever to achieve a name of his own.

But where did he come from, that little dark thing, harboured by a good man to his bane? . . . And I began, half dreaming, to weary myself with imagining some fit parentage for him; and repeating my waking meditations, I tracked his existence over again, with grim variations; at last, picturing his death and funeral; of which all I can remember is being exceedingly vexed at having the task of dictating an inscription for his monument, and consulting the sexton about it; and, as he had no surname, and we could not tell his age, we were obliged to content ourselves with the single word, "Heathcliff."   (p. 403)

The tragedy of a nameless stranger buried next to his lover/sister in a last gesture towards some kind of familial identity lingers in Nelly's hesitating acknowledgment to Lockwood of the growing legend that their ghosts haunt the moor. Her mordant common-sense attitude is mollified by a dim appreciation of the mythic dimensions of Heathcliff's story. Myth barely penetrates the imagination of Lockwood, however. He reacts against it; observing the young Cathy and Hareton together, he sees their happiness as casting out such images: "*They* are afraid of nothing . . . Together they would brave Satan and all his legions." Visiting the graves of the parents as his final act in the novel, Lockwood would like to have the case solved and the question of their demonic energy laid to rest as well. But his attempt at a last word must remain the unanswered question that ends *Wuthering Heights*—how "any one could ever imagine unquiet slumbers for the sleepers in that quiet earth" (p. 414).

Thus Emily Brontë's ending for *Wuthering Heights* teases the bystanders with questions of the ultimate significance of individual salvation and individual suffering alike. Of course, the novel is not a moral conundrum, any more than it is a psychological case history. And any effort to "solve" it through psychological theories is apt to seem as reductive as Lockwood's faint wish to lay all ghosts to rest with a passing sentiment about the healing power of Nature. What a modern theory as suggestive as Erikson's can help to do, however, is to reveal the total range of Emily Brontë's achievement by directing attention to two of the most singular aspects of her masterpiece—her clinically accurate depiction of adolescent identity confusion and her account of the dynamics of generational interaction as the central force in the formation of a sense of individual selfhood.

The concept of adolescence is relatively a recent one; it did not exist in Emily Brontë's time. Indeed, psychologists began to define and study adolescence as a crucial stage in human development only in the last two decades of the nineteenth century.[22] And although the interest in adolescence was intense at the beginning of the twentieth century, it lapsed in the twenties, only to revive in the last fifteen years or so. One reason for this lapse may have been the Freudian influence, for although Freud's psychology inspired an enormous interest in the effect of childhood, its emphasis on infantile experience tended to deflect concentration from the later stages of childhood. The interpretation of childhood in the Victorian novel has followed this tendency to neglect adolescence in favor of a focus on the images of earlier, more vulnerable childhood in such novels as *Jane Eyre, David Copperfield,* and *The Way of All Flesh;* thus *Wuthering Heights* has been oddly neglected as a significant study of childhood.[23] Jerome Buckley, for example, fails to include it as a *Bildungsroman* in his study of that genre. His lapse, however, drives from a formalist rather than a psychological predisposition. He defines the nineteenth century *Bildungsroman* as representing, by and large, the young hero's attempt to reach a suitable social accommodation.[24] Although Emily Brontë sponsored such an accommodation for the third generation of youth in *Wuthering Heights,* however, she departs from the general pattern by sponsoring, as well, the insubordination of adolescence in the face of intense family repression and abrupt social change. Thus her novel does not fit the nineteenth-century conception of the trials of adolescence. *Wuthering Heights* had no major sequels in the nineteenth century; its modern successors are novels like *The Story of an African Farm* or *The House with the Green Shutters*—late nineteenth-century stories of adolescents living in limited and repressive societies which conspire against any spontaneity of self-definition among the young.

Thus we must see Emily Brontë in a tradition wider than that of the romantic novel; she added immensely to the possibilities of depicting the crises of adolescence in English literature. She may have built her novel in part upon the rich, Byronic fantasies of her own youth, but she did not use these to imagine a regressive flight from reality: contemporary psychology shows how mature was her understanding of the social and psychological significance of childhood struggles in the "family histories" that she heard from her Yorkshire neighbors. Which is not to say that Brontë ever assented to the proposition that "mere" understanding could annul the tragedy involved in the thwarting of the human drive to declare a self. Indeed, the power of the last pages of *Wuthering Heights* results from the conjunction of the realist's insight into the "way things are" with the poet's refusal to be consoled.

NOTES

[1] "Editor's Preface to the New Edition of *Wuthering Heights,*" in Emily Brontë, *Wuthering Heights,* ed. Hilda Marsden and Ian Jack (Oxford: Clarendon Press, 1976), p. 442. Questions from *Wuthering Heights* in my text are from this edition.

[2] See, for example, John Demos, *A Little Commonwealth: Family Life in Plymouth Colony* (New York: Oxford U. Press, 1970), p. 129. For criticism of the Eriksonian model, see Lawrence Stone, *The Family, Sex and Marriage in England 1500–1800* (London: Weidenfeld and Nicolson, 1977), pp. 15–16. And David Hunt, *Parents and Children in History: The Psychology of Family Life in Early Modern France,* (New York: Basic Books, 1970), p. 25.

[3] *Identity: Youth and Crisis* (New York: Norton, 1968), p. 178.

[4] For classic "symbolic" readings see: Richard Chase, "The Brontës: A Centennial Observance (Reconsiderations VIII)," *Kenyon Review,* 9 (1947), 487–506; Barbara Hardy, "The Lyricism of Emily Brontë," in *The Art of Emily Brontë,* ed. Anne Smith (London: Vision Press, 1976), pp. 94–118; Lord David Cecil, "Emily Brontë and *Wuthering Heights,*" in *Early Victorian Novelists: Essays in Revaluation* (1935; rpt. U. of Chicago Press, 1958), pp. 136–82; and J. Hillis Miller, "Emily Brontë," in *The Disappearance of God: Five Nineteenth-Century Writers* (Harvard U. Press, 1963) pp. 157–211. Although Patricia Meyer Spacks's reading in *The Female Imagination* (New York: Knopf, 1975), pp. 171–89, analyzes the novel's insights into adolescent feminine psychology, her tendency to make the novel Catherine Earnshaw's (Heathcliff is in some way an "invention" of Catherine's adolescent narcissism) finally reaffirms the novel as romance and thus undercuts the "realistic" status that I want to emphasize here.

[5] The theory that Heathcliff might be Earnshaw's illegitimate son has been well argued by a scientist, Herbert Dingle, in his odd but refreshing *The Mind of Emily Brontë* (London: Martin Brian and O'Keeffe, 1974), pp. 69–74.

[6] *The English Novel: Form and Function* (1953; rpt. New York: Harper and Row, 1961), p. 54.

[7] I have discussed Jane Austen's treatment of patriarchy in "Mr. Bennet and the Failures of Fatherhood in Jane Austen's Novels," *Journal of English and Germanic Philology,* 74 (1975), 536–52.

[8] For a discussion of Mrs. Earnshaw's role in the novel, see Wade Thompson, "Infanticide and Sadism in *Wuthering Heights,*" *PMLA* 78 (1963), 69–74.

[9] Ellen Moers has made an intricate and interesting argument about the implications of childhood sexuality in the novel in *Literary Women* (Garden City, N.Y.: Anchor Books, 1977), p. 160. See also A. O. J. Cockshut, *Man and Woman: A Study of Love and the Novel 1740–1940* (London: Collins, 1977), p. 109.

[10] See *Identity,* pp. 172–76.

[11] *Identity,* p. 159.

[12] For a different reading of Frances's role in Hindley's scheme of patriarchy, see Sandra M. Gilbert and Susan Gubar, *The Madwoman in the Attic: The Woman Writer and the Nineteenth-Century Literary Imagination* (Yale U. Press, 1979), pp. 267–69.

[13] In *Myths of Power: A Marxist Study of the Brontës* (London: Macmillan, 1975), p. 105, Terry Eagleton has brilliantly analyzed Cathy's economic situation in terms of the commercial attention to geneology in the nineteenth century.

[14] In his "Introduction" to the Riverside Edition of *Wuthering Heights* (Boston: Houghton Mifflin, 1956), p. xiii, V. S. Pritchett has commented upon the sexlessness of the two characters as one impediment to the depth of their love story.

[15] Nelly's nurturing role is discussed by Anne Smith in her "Introduction" to *The Art of Emily Brontë,* p. 22.

[16] Erikson insists upon the crucial necessity for adolescent rebellion in cultural regeneration and change. *Identity,* pp. 188–91.

[17] For a summary account of the attitudes of parent child-batterers towards their children, see Letitia J. Allan, "Child Abuse: A Critical Review of the Research and Its Theory," in *Violence and the Family,* ed. J. P. Martin (Chichester: John Wiley and Sons, 1978), p. 52.

[18] The most extreme expression of this view is found in Thomas Moser's "What Is the Matter with Emily Jane? Conflicting Impulses in *Wuthering Heights,*" *Nineteenth-Century Fiction,* 17 (1962), 1–19.

[19] Eagleton, p. 100.

[20] The image of the book and its implications have been variously discussed. See Gilbert and Gubar (p. 281), who view the book as negative in its embodiment of patriarchal culture. Gilbert and Gubar also make the important observation that Catherine, like all girls, cannot know her own name (p. 276). In "The Image of the Book in *Wuthering Heights,*" *Nineteenth-Century Fiction,* 15 (1960), 159–69, Robert C. McKibben's analysis more nearly matches my own.

[21] Moser has a peculiar tolerance for the violence of this "memorable scene," arguing that it is a "poem to Eros" (p. 12).

[22] See John Demos and Virginia Demos, "Adolescence in Historical Perspective," *Journal of Marriage and the Family,* 31 (1968), 632–38.

[23] For example, neither Peter Coveney in *The Image of Childhood: The Individual and Society: A Study of the Theme in English Literature* (Baltimore: Penguin, 1967) nor David Grylls in *Guardians and Angels: Parents and Children in Nineteenth-Century Literature* (London: Faber and Faber, 1978) discusses *Wuthering Heights* as a central novel of childhood.

[24] *Season of Youth: The Bildungsroman from Dickens to Golding* (Harvard U. Press, 1974), pp. 17–18.

John T. Matthews

FRAMING IN
WUTHERING HEIGHTS

The Sinking Frame

Wuthering Heights is a novel preoccupied with the idea of boundary. In vast variations of single-mindedness, it haunts the sites of division—between self and other, individual and family, nature and culture, mortality and immortality.[1] It is not surprising, then, that Emily Brontë should be drawn to a formal expression of her concern with boundaries by enclosing her "central" story in an outlying narrative episode. What is the relation of the story *itself*—the chronicle of Earnshaw-Linton transactions crowned by Catherine and Heathcliff's love—to the story's *other* in its frame—Nelly Dean's entertaining account to her convalescent master Lockwood? Brontë means us to cross this question repeatedly in her deployment of the frame, in part because *Wuthering Heights* broods both at its center and in its margins on the problem of articulation. As in its structure, the novel's imagery and diction are saturated to the same purpose by the rhetoric of framing. Dorothy Van Ghent and others have written insightfully on the prominence of doors and windows as representations of the mind's and spirit's grasp of interior and exterior.[2] We will come to see, in addition, that the narrative frame is required by the incapacity of the central lovers to utter their relation. Perpetually frustrated, they cannot articulate the relation that would bind them, and so they leave a gap to be framed and filled by the loquacity of the narrators. Accordingly, Brontë brings into play a subtle and widespread terminology of framing that sounds almost all of its senses: to frame is to set off, to encompass, to edge, but also to invent, to lie, even—in the idiomatic "frame-off"—to cease, to leave off, to escape. Likewise, a frame may be a border, but also one's state of mind, skeletal build, or bodily condition. Brontë invites us to entertain the agreements between these kinds of framing as she considers how establishing a ground for the story's figure is indistinguishable from inventing the story "itself." Disclosure is enclosure. The discreteness of the frame wavers under the labor of setting off the story.

From *Texas Studies in Literature and Language* 27, No. 1 (Spring 1985): 25–61 (abridged).

The way painters use the term "frame" might confirm our understanding of the literary frame, since the frame refers both to the hidden understructure upon which the canvas is stretched and to the highly visible but unnoticed outer ornament. The frame is a double structure that opens the space of representation as it is covered over and closes the space of articulation as it mediates a boundary with the outer world. When Nelly describes old Earnshaw's declining health as "his sinking frame,"[3] she locates as well an image for the disposition of larger fictive entities in the novel, for the framing activities of *Wuthering Heights* are continually being noticed as forms of disappearance, as the creation of virtual presences that absent their own premises. Like Catherine and Heathcliff, Nelly and Lockwood remain palpable by virtue of their borderline fadings and absences.

The frame portion of *Wuthering Heights* sinks into the background of the monumental passion which it discloses. Unsurprisingly, interpretations of the novel readily ignore the circumstances of storytelling that appear in the opening and concluding pages and intermittently throughout. When Ellen Dean and Lockwood are discussed at all, their effects are confined largely to their status as characters *in* their story, not as its confabulators. Lockwood's "normalcy" or priggishness and Nelly's meddlesomeness or salt-of-the-earthness do bear on a few points of the central story—the moments of Lockwood's admiration for Heathcliff and attraction to Catherine the younger, or Nelly's protection of the innocent and censure of the indulged.[4] In those few instances in which their roles as narrators are taken up, however, what is emphasized is their passivity. The usual paradigm for Lockwood's part is as the dreamer of the story.[5] Nelly, perhaps because of her subservient marginality to the culture she describes and to the cultured gentleman for whom she describes it, typically comes across as a transparent narrator. But the transparency of narratorial disinterest we scarcely grant anymore, even to professionally objective narrators like historians.[6] There is little reason to expect that the equivocations of Lockwood's tremulous misanthropy or the gnarls of Nelly's ambivalence toward her supportive oppressors should not condition the story one transcribes as the other tells. My contention goes beyond the view that the narrators' personalities simply color the story they relate; rather, in this novel so absorbed by the instabilities of identity,[7] story becomes the only mode of being, a temporary shelter which permits the transient sense of stilled, collected selfhood for its telling tenants. Having encountered themselves in the passages of *Wuthering Heights*—the house of the narrative—the narrators sink back into the greater oblivion of all that is unframed.

The two principal narrators of *Wuthering Heights* are actively interested in their story, and thus they are intimated by it. Although their position as frame narrators implies that they simply transmit events that have already taken place, Brontë never wholly gives those narrators over to the dictates of the story. They reemerge regularly to remind us of their agency and the requirements of the telling scenes. In accepting the substance of the past, each narrator measures, revises, and preserves what he or she sees fit. Lockwood refers to his willingness to record the essence of Nelly's account: "I'll continue it in her own words, only a little condensed" (p. 132); but condensation is a form of composition. Elsewhere he accents the actual vigilance of the listener's apparent passivity; he is so intent on following the details of Nelly's narration that he will abide no leaping over spaces in the story. Nelly is impressed by the laziness of such a mood, but Lockwood protests that it is "a tiresomely active one. It is mine, at present, and, therefore, continue minutely" (p. 52). Lockwood's engagement with the story draws him into a version of a strenuously contemplative life, one he thinks Nelly enjoys in her isolated condition ("You have been compelled to cultivate your reflective faculties," p. 52). And she agrees that both experience and her reading have made her wise ("I have read more than you would fancy," p. 53). Both Lockwood and Nelly are careful to describe their states of mind during the reveries stimulated by the story as grounded in waking reality: Lockwood's dreams early in the novel and Nelly's fantasies on Heathcliff's behalf are varieties of "imaging" (p. 280),[8] a practice of suggesting active creation, or framing. As Nelly, encouraging the rude foundling Heathcliff, once puts it: "Were I in your place, I would frame high notions of my birth; and the thoughts of what I was should give me courage and dignity to support the oppressions of a little farmer!" (p.48). How Nelly specifically manages to frame herself is a question I shall take up shortly, but at this point we note that "imaging" requires exertion. Whatever impulses toward self-fulfillment and self-restraint Lockwood and Nelly exhibit, they emerge most forcefully in the aims and strategies of their narrating. An interpretation of the frame in *Wuthering Heights* must account not only for how the narrators take their story but what they make of it. The energies of desire, imaginative compensation, revenge, subversiveness, and ambivalence toward moral and social rectitude—the very stuff of the core story—have already been set off, are already under way, in the novel's frame. Brontë associates imagination with marginality (as the insinuation of Catherine's diary into the margins of Branderham's sermons confirms); what is imagined is the outside of what is possessed—the frame is for framing. If, as so many readers are willing to have it, Catherine and Heathcliff's passion involves a yearning for self-possession by means of the passage through the other,[9] then central to that passion is the sense of lack, of an interiority yearning for completion by (or through) its exterior. The structure of the core story is a synecdoche for the novel's structure, then, since the existence of the frame narrative signals that the central story lacks self-sufficiency, just as each of the lovers defines love as lack. The central story's compromised self-sufficiency actually constitutes its unity by calling forth the encircling frame. A silence, a reticence, some stunted power of speech in the lovers' relation requires the supplement of Nelly's telling and Lockwood's writing. The frame's preliminary nature requires completion by the central story it serves, but the self-insufficiency of the enframed story returns us to the required frame. This conceptual cycle is doubled by our actual reading experience of the novel, since we sink past the circumstances of the narrating scene only to rise back into the frame at the conclusion.

An Existence of Yours beyond You

Perhaps the millions of interpretive words which have come to encase this love story measure the incapacity of Catherine and Heathcliff to speak for themselves. Most readers register the ferocious privacy and thick silence which closes off Catherine and Heathcliff from the rest of their world. Such remoteness surely deepens our impression of their mysterious, suprapersonal passion, and it rallies our discontent with the oppressive institutions of civilization that conspire to frustrate their happiness. Yet it is the lovers' own powers of expression that fail to find a form or even to name the nature of their relation, and not merely the commonsensical incomprehension of Nelly and Lockwood or Brontë's respectful reticence. Catherine recognizes that somehow her need of Heathcliff involves his representation of all that she is not, including her language: "I cannot express it; but surely you and everybody have a notion that there is, or should be an existence of yours beyond you. What were the use of creation if I were entirely contained here?" (p. 70). Catherine wants to get at the notion that selfhood is distributed between one's contained identity and all it is not.[10] The "I" is also elsewhere, not "entirely here." In part, such a conception of selfhood stuns the potency of language because it blocks the clear passage of the word into the outer realm of the signified; that is, the zone of mind or experience that would complete Catherine, the "existence of yours beyond you," is not separate from her present state and so cannot simply be named as something else. Her words for it cannot break into that imagined space and represent it, since that space has no place of its own; instead, the conjoined self haunts the threshold of self and other, inside and outside, as if it were a site, though it is nothing more than the placeless line of differentiation. The lovers ceaselessly survey and traverse the line between themselves. Catherine resorts to the vocabulary virtually of figure and ground to elaborate this unutterable notion: "my love for Heathcliff resembles the eternal rocks beneath—a source of little visible delight, but necessary. Nelly, I am Heathcliff—he's always, always in my mind—not as·a pleasure, any more than I am always a pleasure to myself—but as my own being—so, don't talk of our separation again—it is impracticable" (p. 70). Ostensibly the separation but also the talk are "impracticable" in this situation, for there is no term, no form, for the relationship that would fulfill Catherine's and Heathcliff's wants. Like both sorts of framing, Heathcliff serves Catherine as the ground for her figure—the necessary foundation against which she distinguishes herself—and also as the imaged otherwise of herself—"the use of creation." In both regards he is the container that gives shape to the contained.

For all of the differences in Heathcliff's management of passion, he shares Catherine's grasp of an unspeakable edge of interlocking unity. When Catherine's death finally makes their incessant separations incurable, Heathcliff offers his own version of love's meaning: "You said I killed you—haunt me then! . . . Be with me always—take any form—drive me mad! only do not leave me in this abyss, where I cannot find you! Oh, God! it is unutterable! I cannot live without my life! I cannot live without my soul!" (p. 143). Heathcliff's words, like Catherine's, disappear into the abyss of the inexpressible, which is the lovers' boundary. Each is the other's ground and life, being and soul; each is the other's essence experienced as external, one's core the other's frame, and that frame the first's sought center. Nelly finds the suitable image for their state when they reunite on the eve of Catherine's passing:

"An instant they held asunder; and then how they met I hardly saw, but Catherine made a spring, and he caught her, and they were locked in an embrace from which I thought my mistress would never be released alive" (p. 137). The parts of the lock are indistinguishable to Nelly's modest eyes, but the configuration of interlocked-ness is what signifies their love to her.

It is this configural nature of Catherine and Heathcliff's attachment that stays them on the threshold of fulfillment throughout the novel, whether we employ the vocabulary of metaphysics, theology, psychology, sociology, or grammatology to characterize that nature. As the figure-ground relation might suggest, and the lock image might embody, the current that draws together Catherine and Heathcliff runs from the arbitrary opposition of their polarity rather than from any literal circumstances dividing them. What keeps them apart as it attracts them is less the simple facts of class discrepancy, or the conflict of natural appetite and social repression, or the incest prohibition, or the irretrievability of childhood's inno-cence—less these than the plain unavailability of a form for their bond. If we subscribe, for example, to the simple view that Catherine betrays her heart by marrying Edgar instead of Heathcliff, we ignore the lovers' own unquestioned devotion to *maintaining* the very barriers that keep them apart.[11] The kinds of prohibitions that seem to forestall their merging acquire force from being re-spected as actual obstacles when they are only virtual ones. It must strike every reader, for instance, that Catherine's prediction that marrying Heathcliff would degrade them seems a rationalization of some other reluctance to articulate their attachment in a common form: out of Heathcliff's hearing she elaborates that her love for him is fundamental to her "because he's more myself than I am" (p. 68), as if mere marriage were somehow simply beside the point of their relationship. Catherine thinks that she can concentrate on the strictly practical advantages of marriage because to her the potency of their love escapes confinement to any recognized container. Conversely, Catherine's match with Edgar is the soul of conventional romantic love; she furnishes a nice litany of the ordinary attributes of the beloved when she explains to Nelly her decision to marry him and concludes that she loves him "as anybody loves" (p. 66).

In other ways Catherine and Heathcliff are balked by their powerlessness to represent the union they crave. If the prospect of marriage is no answer, neither is the recovery of childhood. It has become one of the truisms of the novel's critical edifice that Catherine and Heathcliff suffer exile from a world of preconscious, natural intimacy which they struggle ever after to recover or recall.[12] But *Wuthering Heights* steadfastly resists picturing either such original moments themselves or even sharp memories of them. In childhood the times of companionship that Catherine and Heathcliff enjoy are always the *products* and *not* the *predecessors* of discord, violence, and the often brutal reestablishment of social order. Catherine and Heathcliff are never closer than when one has been momentarily hurt or banished by the family, against which they can maintain their separation. Lock-wood's acquaintance with the character of their love comes in the diary entry he happens upon in Catherine's former bed, and its first passage shows that the two children are thrown together by their rebellion against Hindley's "tyranny" and their mourning for old Earnshaw's patronage. The two are inclined to defy and mime the patriarchal order of the family, and yet they depend upon it to solidify their intimacy and purpose. Heathcliff's irruption into the Earnshaw household, of course, occasions his celebrated ostracism and objectification (he is "it"), and Nelly remarks that "from the very beginning, he bred bad feeling in the house" (p. 31). Heathcliff's very place in the family is the product of its rending, and his maintenance of his authority—from Earnshaw's favoritism through Hindley's oppressiveness to the foundling's eventual mastery—depends on his manipulation of the legalized violence of domestic arrangements. Likewise, his intimacies with Catherine, scrupulously concealed by the novel as they are, are indicated only by the constraints they habitually defy. The so-called fullness of childhood innocence rarely if ever appears in *Wuthering Heights;* it is a virtual condition made palpable by the incessant flights and breakings out of the two children as they seek "to have a ramble at liberty" (p. 39), liberty meaningful only in the context of tyranny. Even the paradisiacal state of unity, then, is already a curative ghost called forth by what was an intolerable present. The remembered wholeness of childhood is the memory of a dream that was to have redeemed what was already lost. Nelly's account of the earliest phases of Heathcliff's and Catherine's positions in the family (the fourth and following chapters) invariably demonstrates that separation is the condition of their attraction, displacement the location of their alliance, exile the origin of their union.

Neither marriage in the future nor memory of their past will serve to denominate the state sought by Catherine and Heathcliff. Instead, the object of desire owes its mass to the velocity with which it recedes before the pursuit of the lovers. The collapse of the distinction between natural and cultural forms contributes to this same air of desire without nameable content. One of the murkiest restraints on Heathcliff's and Catherine's relationship is the simulated incest prohibition that periodically grows legible. Q. D. Leavis has been the most emphatic champion of the taboo's evocation in the novel,[13] and though the evidence is striking, Brontë meticulously prevents it from being conclusive. Throughout *Wuthering Heights* it is always *as if* Catherine and Heathcliff were brother and sister: though he is named for the deceased, perhaps oldest, Earnshaw son, Heathcliff is not that son (and his missing surname forever declares the family's willingness to bring him in, but not all the way into, its lineage). Even the hint of Heathcliff's bastardy only draws half a line between brother and sister. Edgar identifies the nature of their relationship as all but siblings when he pouts to Catherine about "the sight of your welcoming a runaway servant as a brother" (p. 81). For reasons that may escape them, Catherine and Heathcliff often behave as if the barriers they take to separate themselves are the terms for their intimacy.

Our impression that their love constantly drives them to the moors from the drawing room may make us forget that the lovers strictly observe the structuring codes of society. As they accept the burden of class dictates and the restrictions of consanguinity, so their instincts have been made highly conventional. Since Heathcliff is so regularly misrepresented as the thrust of stormy nature at the foundations of culture, it might be worth pointing out that Heathcliff, having survived the Earn-shaws' instinctive equation of his swarthiness with bestiality, constantly surprises Nelly by being more refined, better mannered, and more amply furnished than the loutish gentry at which he takes aim. In the later, vaster stages of his revenge, Heathcliff leaves no doubt about the lawfulness of his design—from confining himself to the regulations of gaming in order to acquire Hindley's fortune to mastering the ins and outs of inheritance law.[14] Throughout his avenging career, Heathcliff follows the letter of the law, as he gives notice in warning Edgar through Nelly not to interfere with his marriage to Isabella: " 'But tell him also, to set his fraternal and magisterial heart at ease, that I keep strictly within the limits of the law' " (p. 129). Heathcliff's patient study of the ways of the world and Isabella's careless forfeiture of privilege for passion seem to create a reversal; in Nelly's view, "He was the only thing there that seemed decent, and I thought he never looked better. So much had circumstances altered their positions, that he would certainly have struck a stranger as a born and bred gentleman, and his wife as a thorough little slattern!" (p. 125). Nelly has an unconscious reason for repeatedly forgetting Heathcliff's advanced culture too (and I will take it up shortly), but even if she had simply remembered their shared childhood, she might have had a fuller appreci-ation of Heathcliff's polish.

The most striking facet of Heathcliff's early intimacies with Catherine is their refinement—however its youthful liveliness makes it jar on the ill and sobersided old Earnshaw. Indeed, when he dies Nelly is impressed by the wayward children's conversation: "no parson in the world ever pictured Heaven so beautifully as they did, in their innocent talk" (p. 36). Heathcliff's discoloration by the grime of the earth and his mental benightedness are the products of a "reform" (p. 43) in the order at the Heights, not his natural condition. Whatever further enameling Cath-erine picks up under the hands of the Lintons, it is certain that she is no savage to be transformed by them into a lady. It is Heathcliff and Catherine, staring through the Grange's windows, who already have an eye for luxury ("We should have thought ourselves in heaven!" [p. 40], Heathcliff reports to Nelly). When Heathcliff chooses to regress to a comparative state of nature upon Catherine's return, he acts with a sense of the gestural quality of his action; the dirt he bears signals his analysis of Catherine's too perfect absorption by the codes which are there to set off people, not pulverize them. Heathcliff's entire career from this point is a series of advances to be made against the pressures of exclusion and degradation; what he hopes to gain he is in fact simply regaining.

Even when Heathcliff behaves at his most despicable, he invariably turns out to be reflecting the violence inherent to the structure of social order. In the aftermath of Heathcliff's nearest disregard of the law, the kidnapping of Catherine the younger and her forced marriage to Linton, Brontë is careful to show that power, often exerted violently, is the condition of lawful order. Though Heathcliff detains Catherine against her will, she negotiates her own release by deciding that marrying Linton, a prospect she earlier pursues (with her father's belated approval, moreover), is an acceptable price to pay for rejoining Edgar before he dies. If

Heathcliff is fiendish in holding her to her earlier promises, his monstrosity in part just magnifies the flimsiness of one's word in common society and the coercive selfishness of affectional relations. When Nelly evaluates the state of Catherine's dispossession, furthermore, she is forced to conclude that Heathcliff's occupation of the Heights cannot be opposed "I suppose legally[;] at any rate Catherine, destitute of cash and friends, cannot disturb his possession" (p. 250). Nelly exposes how fully the protection of the law depends upon the exercise of simple power—cash and friends.

Heathcliff's advent into the family flushes this intrinsic violence to the surface: Catherine spits at the poor creature, "earning for her pains, a sound blow from her father to teach her cleaner manners" (p. 31). And Hindley, "who had learnt to regard his father as an oppressor rather than a friend" (p. 31), may owe less to Heathcliff's literal usurpation than to his own Oedipal, unconscious realization that every father is first his son's oppressor. Heathcliff masters the economy of civil brutality by accepting Hindley's blows as a kind of capital: when he wants to exchange his now lame pony for Hindley's, Heathcliff threatens to tell Earnshaw of Hindley's earlier beatings, "and, if I speak of these blows, you'll get them again with interest" (p. 32). It is no wonder that when Nelly looks for vestiges of Heathcliff's youth in the man, she finds at worst a "half-civilized ferocity" (p. 81) yet lurking, and when Catherine looks out onto the moors of her childhood, she can imagine having been at best "half savage and hardy, and free" (p. 107).

Brontë's strategy is folded, then, in a way too readily ignored by readers who want to identify the contents of the opposing wings of *Wuthering Heights.* The realms of nature and culture, person and family, and male and female, for example, bear features which seem to divide them on the basis of intrinsic content; but the force of Brontë's writing simultaneously evacuates the contents by showing that each realm is at once the outer zone defining the other and also the required, essential, central, interior supplement to the other's lack. The namelessness of Catherine and Heathcliff's relationship accents this situation and helps explain the odd pointlessness of the characters' schemes for satisfaction. Many critics imply that Catherine and Heathcliff simply miss or renounce possibilities for contentment available to them out there—as if with Heathcliff grinning at her side, Catherine might have had the roof removed from the Heights and set up an authentically natural household, with Nelly serving them supper on the moors.[15] I have sought to show instead how their longing cannot abide the congealment of representation.

However, Brontë does allow the narrative to propose two modes of being for the lovers' sought union that accord more exactly with their inexpressible nature: the image of the border and the gesture of effacement. Given the fusion that desire seeks, it is not surprising that the imagery of the margin, the shared boundary, the dividing line, rules the lovers' vision of their merging. Heathcliff's most spectacular description of uniting with Catherine depicts the confusion of their remains in the graveyard. Heathcliff demands of Nelly that his burial arrangements be respected; he threatens to haunt her if she does not see to it that the sexton performs the service he has agreed to:

"I got the sexton, who was digging Linton's grave, to remove the earth off her coffin lid, and I opened it. I thought, once, I would have stayed there, when I saw her face again—it is hers yet—he had hard work to stir me; but he said it would change, if the air blew on it, and so I struck one side of the coffin loose—and covered it up—not Linton's side, damn him! I wish he'd been soldered in lead—and I bribed the sexton to pull it away, when I'm laid there, and slide mine out too, I'll have it made so, and then, by the time Linton gets to us, he'll not know which is which!"   (p. 244)

Heathcliff makes central the space of the barrier between them, the interval that both interferes with and makes possible a site for their reunion. The thickness of the missing coffin boards corresponds to the emptied forms of desire throughout the novel; the disfigured coffin frames open a virtual space that is the trace of the missing borderline.

That the space between desire and its object has been made a fetish in *Wuthering Heights* helps explain other prominent images to which the lovers resort. Catherine, for example, interpreting her dream about exile from childhood, concentrates less on her innocent pleasures or marital sufferings than on the gap opened by the sundering "stroke": "the whole last seven years of my life grew a blank" (p. 107). The imagery of her dream elaborates the derangement of being lost in that gaping blankness, the placeless line that cuts adulthood out of childhood: "But, supposing at twelve years old, I had been wrenched from the Heights, and every early association, and my all in all, as Heathcliff was at that time, and been converted, at a stroke into Mrs. Linton, the lady of Thrushcross Grange, and the wife of a stranger; an exile, and outcast, thenceforth, from what had been my world—You may fancy a glimpse of the abyss where I grovelled!" (p. 107). The abyss is the space that measures and makes the margin of desire, the barrier literally imaged in the window frame through which Catherine looks as she says this sentence and contemplates her return to her "all in all." She looks from the Grange's bedroom into "the outer darkness" (p. 109), where her home in the kirkyard lies; yet she also sees her candlelit room at the Heights, another home that awaits her. As throughout the novel, it is the "journey," "a way," the passage, that preoccupies the lovers, and not any destination privileged in its own right.

In that each lover thinks of the other as, paradoxically, an essential supplement to himself or herself, each encounters that other as a kind of pressing blankness gives contour to the self. In *Wuthering Heights* the blankness of desire also attaches to the desired, and Catherine and Heathcliff each become, as lovers, the haunting specter of the other. Catherine promises that she will never rest "till you are with me" (p. 108), and Heathcliff welcomes just such a possession: "haunt me then! . . . Be with me always" (p. 143). The odd, satisfying change that seems to overtake Heathcliff at the end of the novel arises from closer approach to Catherine's blankness; having arranged for the communication of their remains underground, Heathcliff begins to "see" Catherine. At breakfast soon after, "he cleared a vacant space in front" of him and "gazed at something within two yards distance" (p. 281).

According to my argument, such an emanation is as full a representation of the beloved as may be drawn; Catherine's haunting Heathcliff simply perpetuates the spacing and separation which constitute desire. We might not be as surprised as Nelly to find that "the fancied object was not fixed, either" (p. 281).

Edgar Linton's presence in Heathcliff's vision of perfectly possessing Catherine adds one final significance to blankness in the core story. Throughout their struggles to represent their relationship, Catherine and Heathcliff draw on context, ground, and margin to distinguish their love by what it is not. Linton's character is the structural embodiment of this principle, since he is invoked constantly to foil the lovers' sameness by his difference. Heathcliff pictures Edgar's belated arrival in the grave's decomposing processes to set off his own merging with Catherine. Catherine needs Linton's feeble courtship and marriage proposal to articulate the substance of Heathcliff's uniqueness. Nelly intuitively recognizes Linton's function when she notices that Heathcliff has discarded a lock of the husband's hair in Catherine's locket and substituted his own; Nelly reports that she retrieves Linton's: "I twisted the two, and enclosed them together" (p. 144). A curious gesture, and one that marks the inescapably triangular nature of this represented love. In his contempt for his plight, Heathcliff names Linton's function by referring to him as "the cipher at the Grange" (p. 177). Edgar as cipher sounds monotonically, marking a place that has no intrinsic value in order to let the other figures signify.

As the configuration of their coffins will suggest, the frame and framing of each lover is the boundary, the pressing edge of the other, that might give way to allow passages of communication. As their physical frames decompose, they will merge in the empty space opened by the removal of the casket sides. In Heathcliff's view, their union is less the accumulation of a new entity than the motion of eternal transit; it is as if the bodies will cross and recross the space that demarcates separation and reparation. This idea has consequences for two other crucial registers of *Wuthering Heights,* the language and gestures of transport. We have seen that the terminology of love in the novel falls toward inexpressibility; likewise, the vocabulary reserved for the satisfaction of desire effaces the object and emphasizes movement. In the following passage, for example, Catherine envisions her fast possession of Heathcliff in heaven; yet her prepositional desperation betrays the absence of place for such a state: " 'he's in my soul. . . . I'm tired, tired of being enclosed here. I'm wearying to escape into that glorious world, and to be always there; not seeing it dimly through tears, and yearning for it through the walls of an aching heart; but really with it, and in it. . . . I shall be incomparably beyond and above you all. I *wonder* he won't be near me!' " (pp. 136–37). Although Catherine's utterance appears to describe the state of union, in fact her language fails to consolidate the divergent ideas that Heathcliff is both already within (her soul) and also to be joined out there (beyond and above). One can hardly be "with" and "in" at the same time: to be with Heathcliff is for Catherine to be beside him; to be in Heathcliff is to obliterate the very boundary that makes the concept of "with" possible. The effect of seeking what is in, through, with, beyond, and above is to void the notion of "there." Beside the namelessness of their relationship, then, we might place this second class of verbal behavior, in which what is desired as central can be called only the outside.

The equivalent for this state of language in the novel is the largely unremarked oscillation of the characters' actions. If perfecting their passion were a question of getting hold of something or someone, any gesture might set off a genuine precipitation of action in the plot. As I have argued, however, there is nothing for the lovers to say or do, and so they clench, separate, and fade into the parting of potential reunion. Heathcliff follows a course deprived of destination throughout *Wuthering Heights*. Perhaps the most eerie example is the first occasion of his visit to Catherine's grave. He describes the scene to Nelly:

> "Being alone, and conscious two yards of loose earth was the sole barrier between us, I said to myself—
>
> " 'I'll have her in my arms again!...'
>
> "I got a spade from the toolhouse, and began to delve with all my might—it scraped the coffin; I fell to work with my hands; the wood commenced cracking about the screws, I was on the point of attaining my object, when it seemed that I heard a sigh from some one above, close at the edge of the grave, and bending down.... but as certainly as you perceive the approach to some substantial body in the dark, though it cannot be discerned, so certainly I felt that Cathy was there, not under me, but on the earth."
>
> (p. 245)

Heathcliff's mad effort to thrust below and within produces the sensation that Catherine is above and without: he is "unspeakably consoled. Her presence was with me" (p. 245). This incessant reversal of interior and exterior, origin and destination, governs virtually all of the lovers' movements. Heathcliff is constantly coming in from the outside (from Liverpool, the stables, the moors, the Grange, the American war for independence, the conditions of dispossession and subservience, the position of Catherine's brother or servant), only to be driven, or to drive himself, back outside. Likewise, Catherine stands at windows looking out upon freedom, but once out (in nature, in childhood, in heaven), she longs to return inside. Late in the novel, on the eve of his death, Heathcliff signals the positioning of his desire when Nelly enters his room: "He was leaning against the ledge of an open lattice, but not looking out; his face was turned to the interior gloom" (p. 279). Heathcliff occupies the threshold of the casement frame, and his posture reflects the attitude of the novel toward the centrality of the open barrier. Heathcliff's pose predicts his death scene, in which "the lattice, flapping to and fro, had grazed one hand that rested on the sill" (p. 284), and recalls his lover's hand, which thrusts through the locked window, wanting to enter, only to be cut by the threshold's half-broken pane. The lovers incessantly flee from enclosure to expanse and back, reversing themselves at the moment of their "arrivals," encountering each other as remains left in the space between.

Finally, we might see Heathcliff's devotion to a revenge he cannot come to execute as the most telling example of love's dependence on the gestures and language of inefficacy. What has struck all readers is how demeaning and uncharacteristic Heathcliff's revenge plot is. The rise of the second generation of lovers and Heathcliff's descent into grumpy sniping threaten to break the coherence of *Wuthering Heights* structurally, as indeed its coherence endures strain at other points as well. Yet Heathcliff's determination to usurp Hindley's fortune and lands lawfully and his assumption of authority over Catherine the younger and the Heights constitute more than simply an effort to correct the ills he has suffered in childhood. While Heathcliff surely succeeds in rewriting the past in part, forcing Hareton into a parody of his own degradation and exclusion, the motives of an avenger, oddly, also empower his attraction to Catherine the elder from the beginning. The origin of Heathcliff's affection for his new stepsister is not clear, but a measure of it seems to be an initial appetite for revenge and restitution. Heathcliff's study of the Earnshaw family teaches him that people must *take* that to which they are entitled.[16] This puzzle—that law is force and acquisition robbery—licenses Heathcliff to seize the place of the firstborn and to reach for both the rights of the oldest brother (the father's favor, lands, and wealth) and the rights of a brother-in-law (Hindley's sister). By responding to Catherine's love, then, Heathcliff entrenches his tenuous position within and without the family. We need not attribute a conscious motivation to Heathcliff to read his determined rise and return to Catherine's favor as inextricably bound up with a self-made gentleman's advance. More profoundly, Heathcliff not only loves because he seeks revenge, he avenges because he loves.

The formless love required by Catherine and Heathcliff frequently drives them to gestures of cancellation to indicate their desire. When Heathcliff returns from his financial exploits, surely he cannot intend to marry Catherine. What he wants somehow is to *un*marry her from Edgar, whether by loosening the grounds of her affection or by alienating her husband's devotion. Heathcliff seeks to recover the state of the threshold, the blank abyss, that demarcates their relation. As the nature of revenge demands, Heathcliff is left with eradicating an action by repeating it, with curing exclusion by destroying the inside. It is not surprising that Heathcliff sees that such gestures finally express the futility of expression. Just as there is not destination for his or Catherine's career as lovers, so there is no point to the machine of his revenge:

> "It is a poor conclusion, is it not," he observed, having brooded a while on the scene he had just witnessed. "An absurd termination to my violent exertions? I get levers and mattocks to demolish the two houses, and train myself to be capable of working like Hercules, and when everything is ready, and in my power, I find the will to lift a slate off either roof has vanished! My old enemies have not beaten me—now would be the precise time to revenge myself on their representatives—I could do it; and none could hinder me—But where is the use?"   (p. 274)

The answer that the novel frames in all but words is "nowhere."

NOTES

[1] Two central examples are J. Hillis Miller's study of the opposition in *Wuthering Heights* of virtue and joy in his chapter on Emily Brontë in *The Disappearance of God* (New York: Schocken, 1965) and Dorothy Van Ghent's consideration of the unconscious and the conscious, or nature and culture, in *The English Novel: Form and Function* (New York: Rinehart, 1953).

[2] Van Ghent's essay on *Wuthering Heights* is in many respects still the most perceptive and capacious we have. She isolates the importance of the imagery of thresholds to argue that the novel concerns the "tension between two kinds of reality: the raw, inhuman reality of anonymous natural energies, and the restrictive reality of civilized habits, manners, and codes" (p. 157). I take issue with Van Ghent by maintaining that the opposition of natural innocence and civilized corruption is a false dichotomy in Catherine and Heathcliff's desire and that Lockwood manages—through his narrative procedures—to evade the glimpse of nature within him (a recognition Van Ghent points to in passing). Moreover, Van Ghent specifies the content of the other as dark, savage instincts while I think that the novel shows the radical arbitrariness of all that is other.

[3] Emily Brontë, *Wuthering Heights*, ed. V. S. Pritchett (Boston: Houghton Mifflin, Riverside Edition, 1956), p. 34. I shall quote from this edition throughout.

[4] See, for example, John K. Mathison, "Nelly Dean and the Power of *Wuthering Heights*," *Nineteenth-Century Fiction*, 11 (September 1956), 106–29, and James Haffey, "The Villain of *Wuthering Heights*," *Ninetenth-Century Fiction*, 13 (December 1958), 199–215.

[5] An example is Edgar F. Shannon, Jr., "Lockwood's Dreams and the Exegesis of *Wuthering Heights*," *Nineteenth-Century Fiction*, 14 (September 1959), 95–110. Even in a recent and shrewd application of Derridean deconstruction to *Wuthering Heights*, Carol Jacobs emphasizes the narrators' passivity before the requirements of interpretation and the intractable nature of language ("*Wuthering Heights*: At the Threshold of Interpretation," *Boundary 2*, 7 [Spring 1979], 49–71). This article represents an early stage in deconstructive reading as it follows the dislocating effects of *écriture*: the conditions of imperfect repetition, usurpation, homelessness, and wandering that yoke the central characters and their inter-preters. But Jacobs ignores the creative work of reading and the spectral products of writing in her deconstruction. Brontë's text confronts the kind of haunting presences produced by textual exertions, and not the absolutes of absence.

[6] Consider Hayden White's study of the narrative tropes that organize the writing of history in *Tropics of Discourse* (Baltimore: John Hopkins University Press, 1978).

[7] See Leo Bersani, *A Future for Astyanax: Character and Desire in Literature* (New York: Little, Brown, 1969), pp. 197–229, for a study of the self as the other and the subversion of identity in *Wuthering Heights*.

[8] Emended by Charlotte Brontë in the 1850 edition to "imagining" (*Wuthering Heights*, ed. Hilda Marsden and Ian Jack [London: Oxford University Press, Clarendon, 1976], p. 476).

[9] In addition to Bersani, see Miller's *Disappearance of God*.

[10] My focus on the alterity of selfhood differs from both Miller's and Bersani's treatments by concen-trating on the prominence of the border or the space between the lovers' desire. Miller, somewhat like Van Ghent, probes the paradox that "a person is most himself when he participates most completely in the life of something outside himself. This self outside the self is the substance of a man's being.... It is the intimate stuff of the self, and it is also that which 'stands beneath' the self as its foundation and support" (p. 172). Miller goes on to situate this alienation in a theological context: the individual's estrangement from God. In a second essay on the novel, Miller finds a similar dismantling of unitary identity in the register of textual meaning (*Fiction and Repetition* [Cambridge: Harvard University Press, 1982]). *Wuthering Heights* demonstrates, according to Miller, that interpretation produces multiple valid readings, not a single master reading. Though he contributes to our understanding of how the struggles of interpretation are one of Brontë's themes, Miller does neglect the scenes of narration in which Lockwood and Nelly focus these issues.

Besides several studies of the textuality of *Wuthering Heights* that I shall cite in the course of my argument, a recent exchange in *Critical Inquiry* explored the problematics of interpretation by centering on the novel. See James R. Kincaid, "Coherent Readers, Incoherent Texts," *Critical Inquiry*, 3 (Summer 1977), 781–802; Robert Denham, "The No-Man's Land of Competing Patterns," *Critical Inquiry*, 4 (Autumn 1977), 194–202; and James R. Kincaid, "Pluralistic Monism," *Critical Inquiry*, 4 (Summer 1978), 839–45.

Bersani extends the line on the alterity of identity by arguing that an individual's sense of an essential other destabilizes the possibility of unitary identity. Eve Kosofsky Sedgwick proposes the importance of the barrier and the equivalence of the states it divides in her examination of *Wuthering Heights* in *The Coherence of Gothic Conventions* (New York: Arno, 1980), pp. 104–27, and in her more general study of veil imagery in Gothic fiction, "The Character in the Veil: Imagery of the Surface in the Gothic Novel," *PMLA*, 96 (March 1981), 255–67.

[11] See Sandra M. Gilbert and Susan Gubar, *The Madwoman in the Attic* (New Haven: Yale University Press, 1979), for an account of Catherine's suffering under patriarchal domination. Although their feminist analysis of Catherine's predicament is occasionally insightful, Gilbert and Gubar seem to me to subvert the power of their critique of repressive social institutions by implying that Catherine should have married Heathcliff (pp. 278ff.). It is not the person of Edgar which disappoints Catherine; it is the very contamination with repression of all social forms—along with their ameliorative future forms—that blocks Catherine's hope to fulfill her true desire. As I go on to argue, the very ideology of desire's fulfillment depends on the mechanism of repression and testifies to the deepseatedness of discontentment as the condition of civilization.

[12] Miller typifies the view: "The violence of Emily Brontë's characters is a reaction to the loss of an earlier state of happiness" (*Disappearance of God*, p. 170).

[13] Q. D. Leavis, "A Fresh Approach to *Wuthering Heights*," *Lectures in America* (with F. R. Leavis) (New York: Pantheon, 1969), pp. 85–138, as reprinted in *Wuthering Heights*, ed. William M. Sale, Jr. (New York: Norton Critical Edition, 1972), pp. 306–21. William R. Goetz ("Genealogy and Incest in *Wuthering Heights*," *Studies in the Novel*, 14 [Winter 1982], 359–76) perceptively studies the novel from the standpoint of kinship systems. He argues that the story of Catherine and Heathcliff is shaped by the force of the incest taboo to determine so-called free choice; the first part of the novel is based, then, on Catherine's rejection of Heathcliff as "the renunciation of incest" (p. 363). Goetz also analyzes the distinction between nature and culture that is represented by the authority of the incest taboo, finding (after Lévi-Strauss) that the apparent succession of nature by culture in *Wuthering Heights* is illusory and that society for Brontë is constantly threatened by the collapse into incest and nature.

[14] C. P. Sanger, *The Structure of Wuthering Heights* (London: Hogarth, 1926).

[15] This is the point of Gilbert and Gubar's analysis. Their championing of Heathcliff as the man who might have filled Catherine's dreams reentrenches the dependence on masculine energy and on patriarchal models of self-realization that they want to challenge. They make a belated attempt to correct this drift by claiming that Heathcliff is feminine in his attractiveness; aside from having little textual support, this strategy further consolidates the stereotypes of gender.

[16] See Terry Eagleton's Marxist analysis of Heathcliff's threat to class structure and property in *Myths of Power* (New York: Barnes & Noble, 1975), pp. 97–121.

Robert M. Polhemus

THE PASSIONATE CALLING: *WUTHERING HEIGHTS*

There are staggering similarities and even corresponding or inter-changeable characteristics in the two systems, erotic and mystical.

—Georges Bataille[1]

With a human love replacing the divine, Emily pursued in the novel the theme of spiritual union that can be made to triumph over the divisions of physical existence. —Winifred Gérin[2]

If the mystic says: "I am because I am God," or if Descartes says he is because he thinks, Cathy must say: "I am Heathcliff, therefore I exist." Her hyperbole is the climax and endpoint of the long tradition making love a private religion in which the loved one is God and there is a single worshipper and devotee. —J. Hillis Miller[3]

I

In 1842, the year that Emily and Charlotte Brontë went to school for a time on the Continent, *Giselle* was first performed in Paris. Like *Wuthering Heights,* that enduring ballet is one of the nineteenth-century testaments of erotic faith. Though the story lines of ballets and operas often read like the sport of drunk comedians, details of *Giselle*'s plot bear looking at. A morally flawed hero capable of evil loves a girl of the country. These two, though very much in love, separate for reasons of class, and pathetic Giselle dies in a mad passion at the midpoint of the piece. The man visits her grave and her spirit haunts him; without her love, he is a damned and doomed man. A supernatural spell hangs in the atmosphere. The two lovers call and reach poignantly to one another from the opposite sides of death. He is willing

From *Erotic Faith: Being in Love from Jane Austen to D. H. Lawrence* (Chicago: University of Chicago Press, 1990), pp. 79–107.

to join her, but, as it happens, their mutual love gives each a form of life. For a time they dwell together in a night world of cruelty, erotic longing, loneliness, and extraordinary beauty. It's a hard, enchanted world where love's fatality literally gives you the Wilis. At the end, Giselle, a sacrificial figure, is absorbed into nature—into earth, grass, and flowers—where, the dancers mime, her beloved will join her in immortal love.

The fragile intensity of their love can be profoundly moving. Betrayal, bad faith, resentment, erotic victimization, sadism, and revenge fill the ballet; but, if the dancers' skill is good, all that fades in the audience's mind. The two lovers have a special calling. The motions, figures, and patterns of their love can make their experience appear worthwhile, lovely—even transcendent.

I push the comparison between Emily Brontë's novel and the ballet to point up how erotic faith permeates the art of the century. This ballet is a composite, synthetic work, so it reflects what's in the air.[4] In both works love is the most important thing, and it is all-consuming for the man as well as for the woman. Its frustration causes anguish and guilt, which then motivate behavior and haunt life. In both we sense a powerful erotic paganism clashing with a tepid or unsympathetic Christianity. Love is the true vocation. Other pursuits and concerns—like normal marriages, occupations, and worldly calculations—though inescapable, seem trivial, or the mere gathering of so many sour grapes. And both *Giselle* and the novel imply that lovers in death can find immortality.

There is one great difference, however, between the protagonists of these two works. Giselle's lover is a count; Heathcliff is as common as a Liverpool slum. Before Brontë, the great lovers—the devotees, in their various courtly and romantic fashions, of erotic faith, such as Tristan, Troilus, Romeo, Don Juan, Lovelace, Valmont, Werther, Emile, Fabrizio, Darcy, Ravenswood, and even the real-life Marquis de Sade and Lord Byron—had almost always been upper class, or, in the rare cases when they were not, at least they were of noble mind. Brontë mongrelizes Heathcliff, gives him a plebeian origin, makes him a dirty, degraded boy, shows him scrambling for money. Her passionate lover is a base-born marauder of bourgeois manners and morals, a true underdog. In creating him, she thus imagines love and erotic faith as potential motivating force and solace for the despised. To understand the power of *Wuthering Heights,* we need to grasp this idea: As divinity could appear in a stable or strike a persecuting tax collector in the road, so transfiguring passion might come to a manic, miserly sinner amid squalid conditions. As no figure had quite done before, Heathcliff—bad, impossible person—holds out the hope of erotic redemption.

Georges Bataille writes, "The lesson of *Wuthering Heights,* of Greek tragedy and, ultimately, of all religions, is that there is an instinctive tendency towards divine intoxication which the rational world of calculation cannot bear."[5] Heathcliff, showing how, in the modern age, romantic intensity and the capacity to love and attract love, like religious fervor historically, were becoming means for asserting self-worth and superiority, puts the case of erotic individualism this way: "If he [Edgar, Cathy's genteel husband] loved with all the powers of his puny being, he couldn't love as much in eighty years as I could in a day. And Catherine has a heart as deep as I have. . . . It is not in him to be loved like me."[6] Heathcliff seems to be describing an alternative capitalism of the heart, where subjective feeling and defiant devotion are wealth. Through him, Brontë gets at a revealing tension in nineteenth-century culture, for Heathcliff, in fact, has a genius for amassing property. His acquisitiveness, she shows, sublimates frustrated love, but she also shows that the amazing force of his erotic desire coexists with his passion and talent for appropriation. Thus erotic faith could both defy the quantifying money society and teach the necessary paradigms of desire that would make the system work. Heathcliff, in whom Emily Brontë makes the religion of love more catholic and democratic than it had ever been, stands between the religion of Christianity and the religion of capitalism, a rebel against the values of both, but with obvious ties to each. A grubbing messiah of unlimited spiritual desire, a miser who would rescue love from death, he looms as a figure of world-historical significance.

II

What happens to you after you die? Many people find that religious faith helps them face that question without falling into despair. Desire for transcendence, not just of the self but of the self's mortality, has motivated the will to faith since the first syllable of recorded time; and, if love is a faith, we ought to find that some of its devotees see it as a hope in confronting—or avoiding—the problem of personal death and annihilated consciousness. Death haunts Emily Brontë's *Wuthering Heights,* as it so terribly haunted the Brontë family, and in its pages she imagines a mystical, passionate calling as a way of facing the immanent and imminent mortal agony. The book, as earthy a piece of Victorian fiction as there is, grounds grand romantic passion in the gross texture of everyday life. Nevertheless, it is a crucial text of mystical erotic vocation, raising and forcing most of the critical issues that swirl about romantic love in the post-Renaissance era.

Emily Brontë's characters talk repeatedly about afterlife. No novelist's imagination has ever bound love and death more closely together, and no nineteenth-century writer more clearly shows the relation between the menace of unredeemed, meaningless death and the rise of popular faith in romantic love. Hating and fearing death, people have often professed to welcome it as a release into eternal joy. If you are good, you may go to heaven when you die; you may find "peace." Some form of that idea has been a traditional solace of religion. In one of her famous speeches, Catherine Earnshaw, to the chagrin of conventional Nelly Dean, rejects such orthodoxy. "If I were in heaven, Nelly, I should be extremely miserable. . . . I dreamt, once, that I was there. . . . heaven did not seem to be my home; and I broke my heart with weeping to come back to earth; and the angels were so angry that they flung me out, into the middle of the heath on the top of Wuthering Heights; . . . That will do to explain my secret" (IX, 72). It will do also to explain the novel's title: "Wuthering Heights" means the rejection of heaven. Reject

heaven and you reject angels—even angels-in-the-house. We have here the complaint of romantic individualism that Christian heaven—theocratic authority called
bliss and made perpetual—does not seem to be an inviting place or a satisfactory
consolation for death.

But it is one thing for advanced poets like Blake, Byron, and Shelley to side
with Satan's rebellion against heaven, and another for a Yorkshire parson's daughter
to find the dogma of afterlife wanting. We are confronting a growing crisis for
orthodox faith. *Wuthering Heights* is filled with a religious urgency—unprecedented
in British novels—to imagine a faith that might replace the old. Cathy's "secret" is
blasphemous, and Emily Brontë's secret, in the novel, is the raging heresy that has
become common in modern life: redemption, if it is possible, lies in personal desire,
imaginative power, and love. Nobody else's heaven is good enough. Echoing Cathy,
Heathcliff says late in the book, "I have nearly attained *my* heaven; and that of
others is altogether unvalued and uncoveted by me!" (XXXIV, 259). Even Cathy II
and young Linton imagine their own ideas of the perfect heaven (XXIV, 198–99).
The hope for salvation becomes a matter of eroticized private enterprise.

Faith tries to reconcile what, to reason, is irreconcilable. Consciousness of
death and of the self defines us as human, and yet human beings try to deny the
death of the self. Catherine and Heathcliff have faith in their vocation of being in
love with one another. Says she, "If all else perished, and *he* remained, I should still
continue to be; and, if all else remained, and he were annihilated, the Universe
would turn to a mighty stranger. I should not seem a part of it" (IX, 74). He cries
that "nothing"—not "death," not "God or Satan" (XV, 135)—has the strength to
part them. They both believe that they have their being in the other, as Christians,
Jews, and Moslems believe that they have their being in God. Look at the mystical
passion of these two: devotion to shared experience and intimacy with the other;
willingness to suffer anything, up to, and including, death, for the sake of this
connection; ecstatic expression; mutilation of both social custom and the flesh; and
mania for self-transcendence through the other. That passion is a way of overcoming the threat of death and the separateness of existence. Their calling is to *be*
the other; and that calling, mad and destructive as it sometimes seems, is religious.

Wuthering Heights features the desire to transgress normal limitations, and
that desire accounts for its violence and for the eccentric, fascinating flow of libido
in it. If we think of the three major acts and areas of erotic transgression for the
nineteenth-century imagination—sadism, incest, and adultery—and then consider
how the Cathy-Heathcliff love story touches on them, we can see why the novel
has had such a mind-jangling effect. It's a very kinky book, replete with polymorphous perversity, sadomasochism, necrophilia, hints of pedophilia, and even a bent
towards polyandry, as well as incest and adultery. All this, however, figures in the
urge to free the spirit from social conventions, the world, and the galling limitation
of the body. That dispersed eroticism, shocking as it is, connects with an underlying
drive for the breaking of boundaries—transgression as a means to transcendence.

Consider the question of Brontë's pervasive sadism: she seems to revel in
rendering pain. One of the first things we find out about Cathy, even before
Heathcliff comes, is that when her father asks her what present she would like, she

opts for a whip. That choice characterizes her life. Like Heathcliff, she behaves with a prodigal disregard of physical well-being, almost as though will and love could turn pain to pleasure—which is the point of libidinal sadism. The lovers' sadism ought in part to be seen in the same light as disdainful war on the flesh by early Christian ascetics. Their erotic faith claims a passion superior to physical circumstances. The pain that figures so deeply in the novel's view of erotic psychology impinges upon Christianity's emphasis on the Christian Holy Passion. Few writers get so directly at the petulant fury of love—that anger at a limited state of being that frustrates free and timeless erotic connection. The author, like Cathy and Heathcliff who starve their bodies, seems furious at fleshly matter because it confines souls and keeps beings apart from one another and from nature. Bearing pain—or even inflicting it—tests lovers and the strength of love; it helps induce heightened states of ecstasy and insight, proves one's spiritual devotion, and defies the way of the world. Mortifying the flesh for being mortal, Emily Brontë rebels against materialism for confining love.

Spiritual quest shapes the life of the book. Says Catherine to Nelly, "I cannot express it; but surely you and everybody have a notion that there is, or should be, an existence of yours beyond you. What were the use of my creation if I were entirely contained here?" (IX, 73–74). Those are the words of religious seeking. She is talking about the difficulty and the necessity of making manifest the ineffable but common inner mysteries of spiritual desire, talking about the wish for an immortal soul. The Christian characters—Joseph, the brimstone-ranting fundamentalist; Nelly, charitable voice of conventional, pragmatic Anglicanism; and even Lockwood, tepid defender of orthodoxy—could all subscribe to those two sentences of Cathy's.

That is not true of the famous enunciation of her creed that follows: "My love for Linton is like the foliage in the woods. Time will change it, I'm well aware, as winter changes the trees. My love for Heathcliff resembles the eternal rocks beneath—a source of little visible delight, but necessary. Nelly, I *am* Heathcliff" (IX, 74). Here Brontë is setting out a heretical erotic creed. Being so much in love, Cathy imagines abrogating the physical boundaries of bodies and souls, as if she *were* a heavenly creature. Freud would later psychologize Cathy's miraculous feeling: "At the height of being in love the boundary between ego and object threatens to melt away. Against all the evidence of his senses, a man who is in love declares 'I' and 'you' are one, and is prepared to behave as if it were a fact."[7]

"I *am* Heathcliff" proclaims the erotic vocation—to dissolve the limits of the self by achieving absolute intimacy with the beloved. Notice the language: for Cathy, Heathcliff is like a "rock of ages," a "rock" upon which she founds her identity and faith. And the passionate assertions of Cathy and Heathcliff in their moments of transport dismiss conventional religion. In death, they seek union with one another, not with God.

III

The Christian text becomes an erotic text. Brontë, in an early passage, uses imagery that symbolizes a major theme of my study: Scripture turns into the novel, and the novel is haunted by being in love. Letters preserve the spirit of the dead, and what starts as a marginal form of literature, a gloss on holy writ, becomes, in itself, a means to immortality: Our first knowledge of Catherine Earnshaw comes when the narrator Lockwood, spending the night at Wuthering Heights, finds her name written all over the ledge by his bed. When he closes his eyes, "a glare of white letters started from the dark, as vivid as spectres—the air swarmed with Catherines" (III, 25). (The mind jump between writing and ghostly figures, as we shall see, is anything but random: both preserve the past.[8]) He then peruses her margin-annotated "library," including her defaced "Testament," in which she, as a girl—notice that one of the most renowned loves in fiction begins as a marginal figure—recounts the disgust she and Heathcliff feel for Sunday services and Joseph's long-winded, sanctimonious bullying. They rebel against religion, and, ripping up Christian books, they run away for a romp on the moors. Lockwood falls asleep reading some bitter sectarian tract, which gives him a nightmare about a chapel congregation falling into a violent free-for-all. From the start, Christian practice appears harsh and life-denying, a form that has degenerated from sacred mystery.

What then follows is, literally, erotic vocation: the callings of Cathy and Heathcliff set in a mediated, dreamlike atmosphere of pain and absurd chaos that epitomize the world of *Wuthering Heights*. Lockwood, the gentleman, mixing dream and wakefulness, reaches out the window and feels the grip of the long-dead Cathy's ice-cold hand:

> "Let me in—let me in! ... I'm come home. ...'
>
> As it spoke, I discerned, obscurely, a child's face looking through the window. Terror made me cruel; and, finding it useless to attempt shaking the creature off, I pulled its wrist on to the broken pane, and rubbed it to and fro till blood ran down and soaked the bed-clothes: still it wailed, "Let me in! ... I've been a waif for twenty years!"   [III, 30]

Lockwood, in his dream, piles up books to keep the ghost out; but, when the specter threatens to enter through the massed words, he cries out, rousing Heathcliff. Half awake, they argue, and Lockwood, babbling the language of desiccated faith, exclaims, "Catherine Linton, or Earnshaw, or however she was called—she must have been a changeling—wicked little soul! She told me she had been walking the earth these twenty years: a just punishment for her mortal transgressions, I've no doubt!" (III 31–32). Such a remark in the context of his sadistic nightmare indicates how big a part sadism can play in religious feeling and doctrine. Later, when Heathcliff thinks himself alone, Lockwood observes him: "He got on to the bed and wrenched open the lattice, bursting, as he pulled at it, into an uncontrollable passion of tears. 'Come in! come in!' he sobbed. 'Cathy, do come. Oh, do—*once* more! Oh! my heart's darling, hear me *this* time—Catherine, at last!' " (III, 33).

Out of banality, cruel hallucination, and stumblings in the night come the mysterious calling and desire that spell love for Emily Brontë. "Let me in!" and "Come in!" are signifiers of the lovers' vocation. They express the longing for infinite vulnerability to the other. *Their calling is to call to the other, to desire impossibly, trying, through passion and imagination, to overcome physical and temporal reality.* Through love, they seek identity even in, and beyond, death; they strive to nullify natural law and merge in oneness, but a oneness that is personal, distinct, and unique—not abstract.

Heathcliff's outburst, a genuine prayer if there ever was one, is an important piece of narrative strategy. It wins sympathy for him, sympathy he cannot entirely lose, despite his many sins, because he appears early on so naked and helplessly sincere in his love. Such feeling is impressive. Readers who remember nothing else about the book remember Heathcliff, Cathy, and their love because—no matter what Nelly Dean, Lockwood, or conventional moralists say—passion is the star of the show.

Later in the book we find out that Heathcliff has prayed to Cathy once before, just after her death. That prayer and his passion help us to understand this narrative introduction to Cathy's presence/absence and to Heathcliff's love: to Nelly Dean's trite sentiment, "Her life closed in a gentle dream—may she wake as kindly in the other world!" he answers, "May she wake in torment! . . . Where is she? Not . . . in heaven—not perished—where? . . . I pray one prayer—I repeat it till my tongue stiffens—Catherine Earnshaw, may you not rest, as long as I am living! You said I killed you—haunt me, then! . . . Be with me always—take any form—drive me mad! only *do* not leave me in this abyss, where I cannot find you! Oh, God! it is unutterable! I *cannot* live without my life! I *cannot* live without my soul!" (XVI, 139). Heathcliff's prayer to the beloved, deceased *other,* his "God," again spells out the opposition between orthodox and erotic faith. It also gives one plausible answer to the question of what happens when you die, which is that you might haunt the living. Immortality, at least figuratively, might be a diffusive and lasting, if various, haunting—through memory, image, spiritual infusion, word of mouth, legend, and writing. And haunting might depend upon alienated love and the desire to overcome erotic separation.

IV

Two things seem especially puzzling about this episode: Why does Cathy appear in the reserved Lockwood's dream, and what is that awful piece of torture, the bloody wrist-rubbing incident, doing there? The answer would seem to involve "the return of the repressed" and the rhetorical status of Lockwood, the unimaginative principal narrator with whom the story begins and ends. (Though Nelly Dean narrates much of the time, she tells her tale to and through him.) He mediates the novel for us, assumes common social conventions, gains our general credence; thus we are implicated in his dream and its cruelty.

I want to suggest a trope: As the dream-waif Cathy is to the dreamer Lockwood, so *Wuthering Heights* is to its readers. His dream enacts the agonizing internal war of the self on the past and past love—love that might threaten present life. It renders the spooky hunger for love of the enduring, importuning child within—battered and rubbed a thousand wrong ways—who is the past self's denial of love to others and also the self denied love in the past. Cathy is not only the passionate lover; she is also the erotic history of childhood—the needs and urges formed back then and inefficiently suppressed later—that so terribly and inexorably haunts consciousness, all consciousness. This child is mother to the man and the woman too. Erotic desire is the mother of imagination and the shaper of fate. How else account for the hold of this odd book, not just on the romantic temperaments of the passionate and young, but on some much closer to Lockwood and Nelly than to Cathy and Heathcliff? One more trope: This chapter and dream can stand for the continuing creative process of life and literature. Language plays upon memory and emotion to make new forms and images which create new combinations of language for the imagination.

Dreams matter intensely to the mystical Emily Brontë. Cathy, later, makes two notable comments on the subject: "I've dreamt in my life dreams that have stayed with me ever after, and changed my ideas; they've gone through and through me, like wine through water, and altered the colour of my mind" (IX, 72); and "my dreams appall me" (XII, 106). Both apply to Lockwood's dream. The first statement asserts that dreams are in some sense true and have consequences. Recall Cathy's dream of rejecting heaven or think how Lockwood's blood-red dream colors the novel and you see how strongly Brontë supports that idea. Dreams shape and are shaped by how we perceive things, and, as psychology now stresses, the reporter of dreams reconstructs them in the waking context of present urgencies. They display, as phenomena, in extreme form, the force of individualism: the self, like a god, orders—or disorders—a world. And they give glimpses of a realm of wonder, of supernatural possibilities where normal limitations do not hold. Dreams, like fiction, tell us that, however we try to repress the knowledge, life is partly out of control and fantastic. It *is* mysterious; we are all touched truly, if unconsciously, by the visionary power of imagination.

Foppish Lockwood, in the first chapter, reports that he had recently fallen "over head and ears" in love but was too shy to communicate his feelings to the woman and, driving her away, thereby "gained the reputation of deliberate heartlessness" (I, 15). His dream, then, makes good psychological sense. His repressed guilt at spurning love and his repressed need for love haunt him. The "characters" of Catherine's name and writing swarm into his brain with his memory of lost love to give dream life to a girl-child imploring him to let her come in from the cold world of the dead.

But the unconscious imagination of a dreamer may receive impressions that the rational daytime mind cannot precisely catalogue or comprehend. Any number of separate reasons can be given why Lockwood dreams the dream he does, or why the whole novel is as it is: indeterminacy is Brontë's queen and the critic's chance. Dorothy Van Ghent has plausibly suggested, for instance, that the oak-panel closet is like a coffin and thus its occupier would be open to a death-haunted dream (Heathcliff, in fact, will die here at the end).[9] One possibility is that the amorous drive to overcome the separation of death inevitably touches and infects to some degree the lives of almost all people, even if they be as passive and mediocre as Lockwood. The strength of love might be so intense and at the same time so diffuse that it can in effect produce an intersubjectivity of imagination, even though we cannot trace exactly how. Emily Brontë, for example, might imagine that the force of the Heathcliff-Cathy erotic desire might—through the words of Cathy and Heathcliff's bearing—sink into Lockwood's dreaming mind.

The dream, however, *is* appalling. It previews the pain and violence to come. It quickly establishes that the panorama of cruelty that defines life in the novel is not something alien to a "civilized" person, nor some weirdness beyond the pale in the wilds, but an inescapable part of "normal" reality. "Terror made me cruel," says Lockwood, this conventional filter of our knowledge, and then in his mind he commits what may well seem the most sadistic act in this compendium of sadism. A desperate quality of hurt the hurt (i.e., if you can't stop the pain, revel in it!) comes through in his dream act, and that spirit permeates the narrative. It is as though Brontë were trying, by rendering the bleeding dead flesh, the hanging dogs, the slaughtered rabbits, and all the other acts great and small of bestial cruelty in the book, to retaliate against existence for giving us the excruciating knowledge of death and loneliness: as though, in suppressed rage, she were saying, "If you think cutting a girl's wrist on a windowpane or destroying puppies is terrible, what about an earth and a life in which you and every person you ever love will die, and you can never really repress the fact of your own unquenchable loneliness?" In *Wuthering Heights,* the impulses and effects that arise from the love-frustrating, death-plagued conditions of existence flicker in the consciousness of all souls, be they mild-mannered, colorless, well-meaning, or savage and vengeful. That is the kind of world Emily Brontë lived in and imagined.

Of the interpretation of dreams there is no end, but let me make four more suppositions about the dream scene.

1. A paradox in Lockwood's dream is that the dead can bleed. That might suggest that there is an unending flow of consciousness in which people have a kind of immortality. It can also suggest that imagining pain is one way of overcoming the blankness of nonbeing that threatens us. If losing the power to feel is one of the terrors of modern life, then contemplating and feeling pain at least proves some sort of emotional vitality. That notion might help us to understand the strange link between sadism and eroticism, a connection that often appears in this novel. Sadomasochism would seem to be a desperate strategy to break through the wall of numb otherness, a fanatical attempt at intimacy and abnormally intense communication through the sharing of pain—the inflicting and the bearing of it. In Brontë, spiritual strength comes from a resolve to disdain the flesh by mortifying it and, beyond that, a will to mortify death itself. John Donne, the Christian, says, "Death thou shalt die."[10] Brontë, the erotic mystic, imagines that if we can't make death die, at least we can make it bleed.

2. The intrusion of death upon the living, a permanent feature of psychic and social life, terrifies people and provokes violent reactions. We hate and instinctively

want to punish the knowledge of death, and we want no part of it. But, of course, we want exactly the opposite too: information and witnesses from beyond that tell us that death is an illusion. Hence we get the ambiguity and tension in the dream and the novel about the barrier between life and death which the recurrent liminal imagery symbolizes—here, the reach from outside to inside, the grip of the dead hand, the attempt to "cut" oneself off from fleshly connection with death, and the penetrating voice of the girl insisting on a return to mortality. The blood is sacrificial—homage to the power of imagination and love, both of which are bound up with the knowledge of suffering. It proclaims that human life as we know it rests upon the reality of cruelty and death. Culture and civilized comfort require their toll of blood, as does vital fecundity.

3. We will later learn that Lockwood's closet was the place where Heathcliff and Cathy slept together until, to her chagrin, Hindley separated them when they reached thirteen and twelve, respectively—approximately the age of puberty. This blood that "ran down and soaked the bed-clothes," therefore, could be imaginatively fused with the menstrual blood that causes painful alienation and loss of innocence. One meaning of the image might be: *blood shuts out childhood.*

4. Another is: *the privileged and the civilized are willing to shed the blood of others to protect themselves.* Rich tortures poor; male tortures female; insider tortures outsider. Brontë's imagination does associate blood with transitional states of being. The dream also shares the color and violence of an event that separated Cathy and Heathcliff. Going for their run on the fatal Sunday that Lockwood reads about before his dream, Heathcliff and Cathy look in at the refined elegance of Thrushcross Grange: "We . . . saw—ah! it was beautiful—a splendid place carpeted with crimson, and crimson-covered chairs and tables, and a pure white ceiling" (VI, 47). When the Lintons, the "civilized" insiders, hear them, they loose a bulldog, and Cathy, this time a living child outside the window, suffers bloodshed that connects with Lockwood's image: "The dog was throttled off, his huge, purple tongue hanging half a foot out of his mouth, and his pendant lips streaming with bloody slaver" (VI, 48). The result is that she is drawn away from Heathcliff into the Linton world, class distinction, and womanhood. There is such hurting and mindless torture loose in this world—and it is so ingrained in the texture of things—that pride in refinement and virtue looks like the wildest delusion, if not hypocrisy.

Putting an act of violence in Lockwood's mind prepares us for Emily Brontë's overall vision. All are brothers and sisters in the collective agony of human fate. Her world cries out for some sort of redemption and expiation. Hence the vocation of love. In the words and actions of Heathcliff and Cathy, Brontë creates a love so strong and a passion so interesting that she imagines they could break through into the Lockwoods of the world by the sheer force of energy they generate.

V

The calling of Heathcliff and Cathy is to seek oneness. That sounds like a single-minded, if mystical, quest, but it is not, since living in time gives them disor-

derly, destructive character traits and contradictory desires that hold them apart.
When they grow up they both betray their calling. Their passion for each other gets
mixed up with secondary obsessions about class, culture, wealth, and vengeance.
They never, however, lose their vocation.

In nineteenth-century fiction, the condition of motherlessness, or a deep and
special alienation from the mother, seems repeatedly to motivate passionate love.
Brontë locates the germ of erotic faith and grand passion in childhood. In their
respective states of literal and figurative orphanhood, Cathy and Heathcliff immerse
themselves in each other and in nature, where they find instinctive intimacy and
an antidote to motherlessness. *Wuthering Heights* gives us an eroticized and unsentimental version of a Wordsworthian vision. These two are not trailing pre-
natal clouds of glory. Deprivation and fierceness—especially in the victimized
Heathcliff—mark their lives from the beginning, but their early years together call
to them in retrospect as paradise lost.

Their vocation points in two directions. Sometimes it seeks to recover lost
time by regression to childhood intimacy; sometimes it moves towards a longed-for
unity in death. Emily Brontë deserves more credit than she usually gets as an
explorer of juvenile experience and its decisive psychological importance. There is,
as critics have noted—sometimes disparagingly—an infantile quality about the love
between Heathcliff and Cathy;[11] but the novel is onto something. These two seem
to experience a sadistic joy in love for each other. Everyone senses the lack of
inhibition in these characters. In *Wuthering Heights* we seem often to be in a realm
that is not so much *beyond* good and evil as *before* them. The lovers have in them
a spirit of infantile sexuality that antedates moral system, a trace of erotic aggression
that we might fathom if we could recall the libidinous pleasure of *biting*. When
Heathcliff exclaims famously, "I have no pity! I have no pity! The more the worms
writhe, the more I yearn to crush out their entrails! It is a moral teething, and I grind
with greater energy, in proportion to the increase of pain" (XIV, 128), the words
may sound insane. But if we consider the impulses behind the words, if we try to
imagine where we have encountered anything like them, we may remember
tremendous emotions and transgressive acts of narcissistic rage against otherness
and alienated existence that spring from childhood. Infantile erotic desires for
absolute freedom to use everything—any and all flesh, blood, and animated spirit—
for pleasure may not be noble, but they are formative emotions and demand
outlet.

Part of the fascination of Cathy and Heathcliff lies in their high style of verbal
and physical cruelty. They touch on basic erotic desires of omnipotence, but Emily
Brontë knows that such desires have a history that reaches back to the time when
the processes of socialization are just beginning and children resent them. Like
Wordsworth, she knows growing up can bring deplorable loss; but unlike him, she
offers no moralized innocence of first years. She does, however, show how a
moment of quiet in Cathy's young life becomes a spot of time that the lovers—
soon separated from one another—long ever after to recapture: "[S]he leant
against her father's knee, and Heathcliff was lying on the floor with his head in her

lap" (V, 43). Heathcliff's whole existence, right up to his attempt to merge with Cathy's spirit, can be seen as a frustrated longing to recapture that lost time.

Cathy, fevered and terminally ill, gives one speech that sounds just like a prolegomenon to the great twentieth-century fictional study of eroticism and early life, Proust's *A la recherche du temps perdu.*

> "Nelly. . . . I thought . . . that I was enclosed in the oak-panelled bed at home; and my heart ached with some great grief which, just waking, I could not recollect. . . . I was a child; my father was just buried, and my misery arose from the separation that Hindley had ordered between me and Heathcliff. I was laid alone, for the first time, and, rousing from a dismal doze after a night of weeping. . . . memory burst in—my late anguish was swallowed in a par-oxysm of despair."   [XII, 107]

For Proust's narrator the critical trauma is the nighttime separation from the mother; for Cathy it is the ban on sleeping with Heathcliff that biology, social custom, and kinship structure dictate. For both, primary, semi-incestuous urges for closeness fix vocation and make it strong.

In her delirium, Cathy imagines a supernatural state of eternal childhood in roaming the moors: "It's a rough journey, and a sad heart to travel it. . . . We've braved its ghosts often together. . . . But Heathcliff, if I dare you now, will you venture? If you do, I'll keep you. I'll not lie there by myself; they may bury me twelve feet deep, and throw the church down over me, but I won't rest till you are with me. I never will!" (XII, 108). Her vocation, asserting the power of erotic faith even—and expressly—over Christian faith, carries her backwards in memory and forwards to death, which paradoxically liberates her into past time.

In the lovers' calling, death appears both as the dreaded severer and as the unifier of loving souls. Cathy and Heathcliff at times wish for death because earthly life keeps them apart. In a sense they, with their fasting, both commit a kind of suicide. Yet they fear and rant against death, too, and have no consistent view of what it is or what sort of existence they want in death. The different, contradictory views of death that emerge are projections into the future of their passions. (Cathy says, "Heathcliff! I only wish us never to be parted," but in her very next speech, "I'm wearying to escape into that glorious world" [XV, 133–34]). They imagine that the dead lover can haunt the living, that they can find some sort of unified tran-quility, that the moment of death can bring the desired release, that the grave will and will not part their souls, that they will both keep and lose one another.

Let us take one phase of Heathcliff's vocation: after Cathy's death, he lives possessed—first by impulses of necrophilia, then by his long perception of her tormenting presence just beyond the reach of his senses, and then, near the end, by his jealous concern about the fate of his own and her material remains. He tells Nelly, "I could *almost* see her, and yet I *could not!*" (XXIX, 230). He has the man who digs Edgar Linton's grave open Cathy's coffin. After seeing "her passionless features" (XXIX, 229), Heathcliff bribes the sexton to arrange it so that he will be buried next to Cathy with the sides of their coffins removed. Though Edgar's coffin on Cathy's other side will disintegrate, says Heathcliff, "by the time Linton gets to us, he'll not know which is which!" (XXIX, 228–29).

The morbidity of this burial scheme actually shows the fantastic power of the erotic imagination. Heathcliff's love is so strong that he simply must project through eternity an intimate physical connection and identity with his beloved. Think of the animating force of a creature who can *imagine* and rejoice in a scene in which two corpses thoroughly moulder into one another so that their simple material essence is indistinguishable, while a third moldering corpse, completely disintegrated but somehow retaining consciousness, finds that the remains of his wife and his rival have become one. An eternal triangle indeed! It would be wildly comic, if it were not so pathetic and oddly moving. In Heathcliff's vision, Emily Brontë really does try to confront the physical inanimacy of a dead beloved and a dead self, but she shows that the force of human attachment is so great that it overcomes the idea of death as an impersonal nothingness and imbues even mortal dust with fiery, amorous spirit.

Generalizing from Heathcliff, we can say that the passionate vocation of love depends upon desire that separation creates; and death, the great divider, makes this vocation all the stronger. Love and death so often flow together in the human mind, not because romantic passion is world-hating or life-denying and thus seeks death,[12] but because death, changing and removing the material presence of the beloved, is the ultimate obstacle and test for lovers. Love is what makes the diffusion of death personal and creates an afterlife, though that afterlife exists in the minds of particular people. Heathcliff does not wish to have no life; he wants a permanent life identified with Cathy. Her death, by which she loses corporeal reality and becomes identical with his love—that is, his own spiritual desire, memory, and projection of her—transforms her into his own enduring perception of her desirability and his agonizing, frustrated longing to be at one with her. His state is like that of a religious mystic conscious of, and constantly seeking, oneness with God: "In every cloud, in every tree—filling the air at night, and caught by glimpses in every object by day, I am surrounded with her image!" (XXXIII, 255).

Why doesn't Brontë have Heathcliff kill himself soon after Cathy's death, feeling as he does? A logical answer would be that his love, that is, his passionate need for her, lives within him, even though it torments him; he knows her very existence depends upon his own agony and separation. She has been translated into his passion. For two decades, he does not want to risk destroying his love, even though her physical absence parches his spirit and makes him terrible to himself and others. She exists after death in his suffering.

VI

In Heathcliff's confrontation with death, the pattern his vocation of love follows is this: personal grief and crazed desire to possess unchanged the body of the deceased; frustrated and tormenting quest for sense communication with an existent but intangible spirit; acceptance of material transformation to impersonal matter, and physical, objective—*not* subjective—integrity with the beloved; seeming consciousness of perfect identity at the moment of his own death (he dies in triumph, according to Nelly, a "frightful, life-like gaze of exultation" in his eyes [XXXIV, 264]); fusion into the imagination and legends of others; and finally, a peaceful unity with nature and all being which, however, mysteriously depends upon erotic faith and diffusive subjective perception.

Heathcliff and his fate show how being in love, rendered in art, has a modern, specialized vocational impact as a calling that serves other people's lives and needs. On Nelly, on Lockwood, on the neighborhood folk, on readers, the professed passion leaves its mark. The country people feel the presence of the lovers as ghosts who together rove the area. In the minds of some, the two have overcome death and joined together in eternal youth, specters—as Cathy foretold—of the continuity of past and present and of the power of love. The text suggests that for Lockwood, both as a typical nineteenth-century bourgeois man and as a surrogate for a romance-hungry audience, Heathcliff performs the function of an erotic surrogate through whom the splendid agonies of love can be experienced vicariously and the sins of love taken away; *as for passionate loving and suffering, the characters in our novels will do that for us.*

Nelly finds and describes him dead in the panel closet where he slept with Cathy as a child: "Mr. Heathcliff was there. . . . His eyes met mine so keen and fierce, I started; and then he seemed to smile. . . . he was perfectly still. The lattice, flapping to and fro, had grazed one hand that rested on the sill; no blood trickled from the broken skin, and when I put my fingers on it, I could doubt no more—he was dead and stark! . . . I tried to close his eyes—to extinguish, if possible, that frightful, life-like gaze of exultation" (XXXIV, 264). Flowing blood signifies corporeal life and suffering. Lockwood's dream of Cathy, who bleeds, and Nelly's final view of Heathcliff, who does not, fit together in a perfect symmetry of image, narrative, and the wish fulfillment of dreams. Private erotic desire and obsession fuse with public erotic imagination, and we seem to have at last both Heathcliff's individual perception of identity with Cathy—and thus his triumph and self-transcendence in death—and the immortality of the lovers in the perception of others.

The much-noted ambiguous ending of the novel shows how reverberant the lovers' vocation and afterlife can be. Lockwood, with stories of ghostly rovers in his head, visits the graves of Heathcliff, Cathy, and Edgar: "I lingered round them, under that benign sky; watched the moths fluttering among the heath and hare-bells; listened to the soft wind breathing through the grass; and wondered how any one could ever imagine unquiet slumbers for the sleepers in that quiet earth" (XXXIV, 266). To a sensibility like his, they have become memory and consoling moral *exempla* who reconcile us to personal death. The violent lifelong passion finally ends, and contemplating it all, in the lovely wholeness of nature, we can feel that the mortal fate of dreamless sleep, where there is no pain, nothing to fear, no hellish desire, constitutes a practical happy ending.

But, as many have pointed out, this last complex paragraph is deeply ironic.[13]

Language gives us social areas where meanings coincide while at the same time calling up uncontrollable personal associations. For example, the moth that flutters about the heath might remind a reader of the lover who flutters about the flame of Heathcliff, and such an association might mean that the passage would connote something different for that reader than for Lockwood. I prefer to take the question and expressed wonder as literal rather than rhetorical. As the local folk—not to mention their author—prove, the easiest thing in the world is to imagine "unquiet slumbers" for Heathcliff and Cathy. The rhetoric of their speech and actions have such power that it is hard to imagine them peacefully contained. The novel, in the formal structure of its telling from the point of view of unreliable narrators and in the way it features the force of private emotions, stresses subjectivity and personal vision. We know that for some those lovers can rise right out of the grave.

The evocative beauty of the final sentence, however, cannot be missed. Heathcliff and Cathy are once more, as in childhood, immersed in nature, death now replacing love as the unifier. The end suggests Wallace Stevens's line, "Death is the mother of beauty";[14] but my corollary would be, after Emily Brontë, that "the expression of love is the mother of death and beauty." Love creates death as many men and women come to know it because it makes them conscious of its primary meaning for them: the agony of loss.

Behind the traditional sentiment of Lockwood—in effect, "rest in peace"—Brontë is working out in her prose a faith in transubstantiation that points to continuous life. She chooses to write *heath* and *hare-bells,* words that denote flowering life, but also conjure up, in a mode of verbal magic, associations with Heathcliff, Hareton, the heather that Cathy loves, and the erotic history that she has just imagined. The imagery and the diction bring out the connection and continuity of all natural life in a world whose matter, though it metamorphoses endlessly, is finite. For Emily Brontë, the power of metaphor and metonymy do actually mean that we live in a world of transubstantiation. Fusion and mutual interflow between characters, their passions, inanimate matter, growing and living things, language, and imaginative perception *take place* in this final passage. Within the novel, when death comes, love has the power of transubstantiating the dead into continuing life—spirits, flowers, or circulating words, for example. Erotic faith, does, therefore, meet the test that we said all religions face: it offers a dissolution of death.

I want to suggest something more: in Brontë's imagination, the moving force creating metaphor is the drive for love. Set next to the novel's ending those most famous words of Cathy: "My love for Linton is like the foliage in the woods. . . . My love for Heathcliff resembles the eternal rocks beneath. . . . I *am* Heathcliff." The basic condition of our being is to live in the metaphorical, metonymical medium of language; to understand and become part of the world, we say one thing is like another; we want to attach this or that quality or constellation of being to ourselves. Language, then, is the means of seduction and expropriation, and by mutual expression we merge with the other and join a process that extends beyond our death. The desire for attachment beyond alienated being manifests itself as love. The maddening imperative of the erotic calling in *Wuthering Heights,* to transcend the self and join in the identity of another, is really the involuntary vocation of being human. Being in love and trying to say it epitomize the human condition.

VII

Emily Brontë enunciates the vocation of love mainly in the speeches of Cathy and Heathcliff to Nelly Dean or to each other. These erotic professions have such frenzied force that, though they can make some people feel ill at ease, they go through the minds of readers, staining them, if not changing them. They always grow out of the pain of threatened or real separation. Cathy's cry, "I am Heathcliff," for example, comes when he has already gone, and nearly all of Heathcliff's eloquence comes when Cathy is dying or dead. Nelly, as a professional servant who depends upon stable social arrangements that violent erotic feeling can upset, deplores these verbal displays of passion, and often appears as a sensible skeptic of socially unsanctioned love. But Nelly's prosaic mentality cannot address the most profound needs and problems of individual existence that the lovers try to express. In their context, these manic, engulfing speech acts proclaim the drive to mate spiritual with physical being. The lover's cliché "soul-mate" points out one of the strongest of all human longings and the obsession of *Wuthering Heights:* the desire to be at the same time a bodiless spirit and a material creature too.

Wuthering Heights renders directly the problem that love and its representation in the arts of "the Western world" pose: is the emotional exaltation of romantic eroticism worth the human waste and sorrow that it seems to cause? Many theorists of love, including Freud, Denis de Rougemont, Ortega y Gasset, and even Irving Singer, often appear to bemoan overwhelming amorous passion.[15] They see that it violates common sense, bends nature, mistakes another person for projected internal desires, kills tranquility, and often ends in tragic misery. Few philosophers would agree with the Judgment of Paris; most, it seems, would like to award the apple to a goddess of piety, wisdom, or power. That myth, however, conveys the magnetism of erotic love. Emily Brontë, especially in the frenzied last meeting of Heathcliff and Cathy (XV), dramatizes the case for transfiguring passion. The wild, sadomasochistic love that spews out in the dialogue and action of this chapter—a love that harms the perdurance of life—can work rhetorically to persuade readers that erotic experience brings existence to its highest pitch, that it is the most sacred thing life has to offer.

Brontë composes for the dying Cathy a shrewd speech to Heathcliff in which she mocks practical attitudes towards love:

> "I care nothing for your sufferings. Why shouldn't you suffer? I do! Will you forget me—will you be happy when I am in the earth? Will you say twenty years hence, 'That's the grave of Catherine Earnshaw. I loved her long ago, and was wretched to lose her; but it is past. I've loved many others since—my children are dearer to me than she was, and, at death, I shall not rejoice that

I am going to her, I shall be sorry that I must leave them!' Will you say so, Heathcliff?"   [XV, 133]

She actually frames the essential argument of almost all who distrust erotic love and insist that the tedious "long run" matters more than ecstasy, whose subjective and unquantifiable value time always dilutes. But the whole scene—and it is largely the inscribed passion of this chapter, a touchstone in the literature of love if there ever was one, that has propelled Heathcliff and Cathy into popular consciousness— renders the counterargument.

Brontë imagines for Heathcliff and Cathy what I shall call *the individualism of two*. In their climactic interview, they express themselves completely in all their rage, pain, self-contradiction, and vitality, and then they close together in a momentary, doomed embrace. The extremity of their situation allows a wonderful candor. They can say anything to each other—do anything—without disguise, and thus they can, even if just for a short time, *be* themselves completely. One of the great appeals of eroticism is that it offers a chance for openness, no holding back of the self. It allows a liberation from the repression that social life demands, and we mistake its force if we think only of sexual repression. We long to be known wholly by another being in all the savage need, inconsistency, and passion of our being—known and *still* loved—in fact loved all the more for this knowledge.

Cathy says to Heathcliff things like, "I shall not pity you, not I. You have killed me—and thriven on it. . . . How many years do you mean to live after I am gone?" (XV, 132). He berates her for "infernal selfishness" (XV, 133) in this time of her dying—never pretending to her that she *isn't* going to die: "I have not one word of comfort. You deserve this. You have killed yourself. . . . You loved me—then what *right* had you to leave me?" (XV, 134–35). They can talk this way because they identify so closely with one another that nothing the other says, nothing the other reveals, not even those flashes of hatred and pure aggression that boil in lovers, can threaten their love. In their shameless state, Emily Brontë then imagines the kind of atoning, ecstatic communication that such a relationship can induce.

> "Let me alone. Let me alone," sobbed Catherine. "If I've done wrong, I'm dying for it. It is enough! You left me too; but I won't upbraid you! I forgive you. Forgive me!"
>
> "It is hard to forgive, and to look at those eyes, and feel those wasted hands," he answered. "Kiss me again; and don't let me see your eyes! I forgive what you have done to me. I love *my* murderer—but *yours!* How can I?"   [XV, 135]

If we think of the impassioned speeches of this chapter as the most vitally charged expression of desire, faith, personality, and being for these particular depicted characters, Catherine Earnshaw Linton and Heathcliff; if we see Emily Brontë pushing, like Wagner in *Tristan und Isolde,* to find artistic utterance that conveys the complexity of desire and the resourceful power of the self to engage with another, to merge oceanic emotion into an oral epiphany of the most intense

consciousness human beings can feel—we can begin to comprehend the conse-
crating function of the lover's vocation.

Violent love in this operatic scene shows forth in action as well as in speech.
The two grab one another, kiss madly, go into breathing paroxysms, tear hair, cause
bruises, squeeze the life out of each other, and altogether behave ferociously. Nelly
witnesses their final, shocking union: "An instant they held asunder; and then how
they met I hardly saw, but Catherine made a spring, and he caught her, and they
were locked in an embrace from which I thought my mistress would never be
released alive" (XV, 134). This is a very pregnant woman who would rather die
holding the man she loves than live comfortably with the nice husband who has
impregnated her. Fighting and shrieking to hang on to her lover while her husband
approaches the room, Catherine cries, "I shall die!" (XV, 136) and passes out in
Heathcliff's arms; she gives birth to her daughter and dies without regaining consciousness.

Without reproducing the whole chapter, it is almost as hard to convey the
force of this scene and its passion as it is to convey the erotic force of Wagner's
Tristan without playing the music. Nelly reacts to it all with bewilderment, like a
Christian watching heathen rites, "in great perplexity" and "very uncomfortable"
(XV, 134, 135). The erotic energy and the mad eloquence overwhelm the decent
social convention which helps to sustain everyday life—and drain it of its mystery.
The expression of requited, cruel, anguished love is so fully imagined and suggestive
that the scene embodies and challenges readers with the primary claim of romantic
faith: that the value of life lies in the quality and intensity of feeling.

Something Edward Albee writes in *The Zoo Story* illuminates this chapter and
the whole novel: "I've learned that neither kindness nor cruelty by themselves
independent of each other creates any effect beyond themselves. And I've learned
that the two combined are the teaching emotion. And what is gained is loss."[16] This
"teaching emotion" Emily Brontë knew. "Cruelty" and "kindness" provoke the
dialectic that inheres in being; *Wuthering Heights* renders it. "The teaching emotion"
inheres in eroticism and points to the idea of *sacrifice*—sacrifice, the act upon
which religion is founded. And a feeling of sacrifice, the painful beauty of violent
passion, is what makes love religious in the novel.

I go back to my hackneyed phrase for what astonishingly happens in the
episode: Heathcliff truly and in a double sense *squeezes the life out of* Cathy. I
suggested before that the phrase, "love is the mother of death and beauty," characterizes Emily Brontë's vision. Fierce love provokes Catherine's death and the
premature birth of Cathy II, who, in the plot of her happy, melioristic love with
Hareton, will redeem normal, worldly life in the novel. (The text suggests that had
not Cathy been stunned into labor, she would have died without giving birth to a
living child.) I sense here also a trope—intended or not—for the violent, cruel,
erotic process of regeneration. Human reproduction, regarded historically, is a
system of propagation so dangerous, painful, and melodramatically charged that it
almost defies belief. Another subliminal message here might be, "if you think this
chapter is emotionally overwrought, consider the circumstances and conditions in

which women have given birth; or think of the act of crazy fury, gentleness, selfishness, pleasure, intimacy, and physical wildness that leads to birth!"

VIII

Cathy and Heathcliff alike reject "the real world" if it denies them the love they want. She, for example, turns the "double standard" on its head and professes to be in love with two men at once, who both love her. Brontë, through Cathy's polyandrous feeling, is getting at the limitlessness of desire and a feminine will to power through erotic drive. Wanting to be infinitely lovable—"I thought, though everybody hated and despised each other, they could not avoid loving me" (XII, 104)—she dreams of herself as a mediating redemptress. She embodies the need, in love, for both identity and complementarity, claiming Heathcliff as her true self and Linton as the not-self which draws her. The contradictory logic of desire is both "like with like" and "opposites attract."

An ambiguity and ambivalence about sexuality in the book has puzzled critics.[17] Some have wanted to see the plot's first triangle in conventional Freudian terms; that is, the idlike Heathcliff is sex, and cultured Edgar Linton is civilization with its repression and discontents.[18] And yet Cathy early on finds Edgar physically attractive, wants his person as well as his status, and chooses without ado to become his sexual partner; loving Heathcliff soulfully, she seems much more interested in claiming Heathcliff's spirit than his flesh. Near her death, she tells Edgar, "What you touch at present, you may have; but my soul will be on that hilltop before you lay hands on me again. I don't want you, Edgar. I'm past wanting you" (XII, 109). Soul and body play out their usual bitter debate in the novel, but both refuse to speak their conventional lines. The soul seems earthy and sexy, the body ethereal; and each partakes of the other in the complexities of erotic vocation. The passionate current of libido in the novel does not especially seem to have a genital focus.

Though there are moments when the author seems at war with sex, in general the text neither condemns conventional sexual feeling nor exalts it. Sex is a worldly process leading to both reproduction and destruction of the flesh (Cathy's, for instance); in itself, sex is not transcendence. Brontë conveys intense desire and physicality—much more so than most Victorian novelists—with lots of violent, polymorphous touching and animal spirits; but much of the sexuality expresses pre-adult impulses. The grown-up Heathcliff has an obvious erotic magnetism, but his sexual maturity means for Cathy that she can no longer sleep with him. Sex also means here the curse of gender definition, with its fixed roles, functions, and desires channelled by custom, and thus more boundaries to curb the spirit.

There is a specter haunting *Wuthering Heights*, the specter of incest. The novel, with the original love bonding of Cathy and Heathcliff, eroticizes childhood and floats this ghost. It ties love to children's history and dramatizes, without the usual repression, the erratic libidinal spirit, combining the feeling of a hothouse and a Roman arena, that so often marks the emotional atmosphere of the close, nuclear family. As so often with Emily Brontë, she creates a powerful effect by heightening—not downplaying—the contradictions of profound desires. The historical development of family life and affections in a world of change could make memories of early sibling affinities a reassuring psychological refuge in the face of the uncertain, alien nature of adult existence. But as familial relationships became increasingly close, emotionally charged, and idealized, the culture would more urgently feel the threat of incest, the force of the incest ban, and the need to stress it. The subject would naturally take on the glamorous mystery of taboo and transgression. Brontë makes Heathcliff an outsider who looks like a gypsy child, but she also poses the question of Earnshaw's paternal relation to him and imagines him growing up like a brother to Cathy. She thereby holds in provocative tension the strong attraction and repulsion of the impulse to sibling incest that emerges in nineteenth-century literature, psychology, and family life.

Her conception is brilliant. It allows Heathcliff to be 1) an intrusive figure of exogamy at odds with the semi-incestuous Earnshaw-Linton harmony, class smugness, inbreeding, and potential spiritual degeneration; 2) a subversive tempter showing the dangerous appeal of incestuous transgression; 3) a mystic defier of time and social reality who desires a pregenital existence where there is no such thing as incest or the adult preoccupation with sexuality. One reason for the nineteenth-century cult of childhood is that it honors the erotic intimacy of the family, even as it denies the threat of incest by focusing on a period that predates it. If Cathy's wraith could come to Heathcliff in the flesh, they would be children again, and incest would be out of the question.

IX

There are many ways of being in love in *Wuthering Heights* besides the passion of Heathcliff and Catherine. They range from Lockwood's trivial crushes and Isabella's disastrous infatuation, through Hindley's brief and pathetic love match with Frances, Edgar's real but unsatisfactory love for Cathy, and the puppy love of Cathy II and Linton, to the civilizing, happy-ending love of Cathy II and Hareton. The high drama of Cathy I and Heathcliff, however, overwhelms all the rest of Brontë's anatomy of love—even that constructive, redeeming love at the end.

The Cathy II–Hareton love match promises a well-adjusted erotic union attuned to the reality principle and social continuity, the would-be goal of almost all "love" experts since the middle ages.[19] Though some find it pale and contrived, it seems credible enough. Even its admirers, however, tend to see it in the shadow of a greater love. J. Hillis Miller calls the primary process of the novel's action "the establishment of a valid community based on mediated love"; but even stressing the rational, benevolent love that develops in the second generation, he writes, "The love of Hareton and the second Cathy appears to be possible only because Heathcliff and the first Cathy have broken through life into death, and have liberated energies from the region of boundless sympathy into this world."[20] Getting at the mystical nature and intentions of the book, he concludes, "The breakthrough into God's world of Heathcliff and Cathy has not only made possible the peaceful love of Hareton and the second Cathy; it has also made institutionalized religion unnecessary. The love of Heathcliff and Cathy has served as a new mediator between heaven and earth, and has made any other mediator for the time being superfluous."[21] That sounds a bit too sanguine, and the phrase "God's world" seems questionable; but it reinforces the idea that when we talk of Heathcliff and Cathy we are talking about serious religious feeling, aspiration, and function, and that the effect of their vocation touches others.

Brontë chooses to stress that the Cathy II–Hareton love is mediated by reading and books. Again she imagines a symmetry with the novel's beginning: Cathy I's writing plunges Lockwood into the love story, and in his dream he shores up books to keep out her ghost; Cathy II teaches Hareton to read and gives him books as a sign and a means to love. Cathy I and Heathcliff throw their religious books away and become erotic demons; Hareton, taught by Cathy II, picks up books suffused in love, and, being in love, they read together. We have a true Brontë-sisters and Victorian wish fulfillment. The woman's power over the word leads the man to love. The importance of the nineteenth-century myth of cultural and moral redemption of men by women that recent critics and historians, for example, Nina Auerbach and Ann Douglas,[22] have been analyzing gets strong support from the Cathy II–Hareton relationship. The image of a loving, competent, pert woman training the savage beast to read and be a gentleman says a lot about the history of women and the faith in the reforming power of love.

The fusion, in a book, of love and developing literacy offers a paradigm not only for "the rise of the novel" but for the English novel itself, one motive for which might well be described as "the establishment of a community based on mediated love." The union also shows the socializing power of the word and the laying to rest, in a book, of the ghosts of erotic desperation. One strain in Brontë is a hope that the novel can teach proper love, as, say, *Pride and Prejudice* does. But *Wuthering Heights* is much better at starting erotic ghosts than at containing them. Conflict exists between the mediation of love through literacy and books—reading and writing—and the drive, erotic in itself, for unmediated love.

Hareton, happy graduate of Cathy II's course, is not the hero of love. Heathcliff is. Brontë gives him what Hareton lacks—the charismatic quality Blake names when he says, "energy is eternal delight." Charlotte Brontë, whose notorious 1850 preface sometimes reads as if Nelly wrote it, says of her sister's hero, "Whether it is right or advisable to create beings like Heathcliff, I do not know: I scarcely think it is. But this I know: the writer who possesses the creative gift owns something of which he is not always master—something that at times strangely wills and works for itself."[23] What Emily wills to express through Heathcliff is the insatiable need for permanent love and a furious resentment against a moral, social, and natural order that inevitably creates impossible desires and thwarts personal freedom. Through imagined love, she wants to identify with and expropriate domineering male power and also to show this power devoted, finally, to a woman who, in this fantasy of real but conflicting desires, is both separate from and identical with the man. Through Heathcliff and his relationship to Cathy, she renders the human imagination of love violently at war with "objective reality."

The trouble with the Cathy II–Hareton match is that it, like literature for this novelist, may contain, but cannot requite, the deepest desires in her text: *the longing for a pre-incestuous world, for self-assertive transgression of boundaries, and for the transcendence of personal death.* Unlike the other love relationships, even the paltry ones, the surviving couple is not threatened by time and extinction. The heart of Emily Brontë's vision is a passion to confront and overcome—through totalizing, immediate love—the separation of death that she sees inexorably testing human relationship. The basic contradiction in *Wuthering Heights* is that faith in such love can only be formed, expressed, and sustained by writing and narrative.

X

Love, like religion and politics, is power—often the power that destroys. In her own reading, Emily Brontë found that out mainly from Walter Scott and Byron. She owes much to the erotic subtexts of gothic fiction and the stark fatalism of the Scottish ballads, but much more to Scott, the novelist who manifested history and country as areas of desire. He feeds her text. As a child, she chose him as one of her heroes,[24] and as a novelist she formed the names Heathcliff and Earnshaw from his hero in *The Black Dwarf,* Earnscliff, a figure caught between love and family vengeance. As Lucy Ashton read and absorbed romance, so, no doubt, did Emily Brontë read of Ravenswood, Lucy, the sexual politics of the Ashton family, and the latent force of love passion. Absorbing Scott's eroticization of history, she went on to make the fatal significance of erotic desire in the world unmistakably clear. And she learned from him how to mix romance and earthiness. From his matter-of-fact portrayal of common life in novels like *The Bride of Lammermoor* comes the hurly-burly and physical detail of day-to-day life at Wuthering Heights—Balderstone and Ailsie Gourlay would be right at home there. The pattern and direction of the novel can even be seen to follow Scott's overall perception of history: glamorous, exciting, but deadly passion in the past that gives way to the more rational, if less emotionally compelling, compromises and civilizing process of the present.

But Scott, important as he is, was not the major outside literary influence on the Brontës. Behind Heathcliff, and behind the love and lovers in much Victorian literature, looms the figure of "Byron," that is, the amalgam in the popular imagination of Byron the man, the poet, and the Byronic hero. "Byron" conjures up the heroics of eros and an erotics of individualism. In him flow together the romanticized, positive conceptions of Milton's Satan, Prometheus, Don Juan, and other defiers of orthodox authority. For the young Brontës, and for thousands of other romantic young people in the nineteenth century, "Byron's name was synonymous with everything that was forbidden and daring."[25] He was the embodiment of the

Romantic movement, and his name, work, and example set libidos swirling. If Heathcliff is Emily's brother, Branwell, romanticized, he is equally "Byron" fantasized—"novelized" we might better say—in the gritty Yorkshire world.

Traces of the Byronic figure show up in nearly all British literary renderings of love down to our own time, so we must pay attention to him. Helen Moglen writes definitively,

> Byron's hero was modeled upon the role which the poet himself had chosen to play. Misanthropic and adventurous, he also defined himself as rebel. He not only rejected the ugliness of the new world he saw coming to birth, but also the old repressions of the world from which it had descended. Central to his rebellion was the assertion of a self freed from external limitations and control. Without religion, he proclaimed himself his own God. . . . Emerging from a mysterious past, he was without apparent familial ties. . . . Because his isolation is unbearable, he undertakes the romantic quest: to resolve aesthetically or erotically the subject-object conflict—obliterating the division between the "I" and the "not-I" by fusing the two in a redemptive state of feeling. To those who were part of Byron's cult, the drive for integration was focused in eroticism.[26]

The persona "Byron," in the popular mind, offered a cult of youth, a cult of art and the imagination, a cult of self-assertion, and skepticism about stultifying creeds and customs.[27] Notorious as a seducer who would transgress any erotic ban in the pursuit of love, he—"mad, bad, and dangerous to know"—was most sensationally of all the breaker, with his half-sister Augusta, of the incest taboo.[28] For the Brontë children—Charlotte, Emily, Branwell, and Anne—given the circumstances of their physical and psychological isolation and the intensity of their relationship, "Byron" expressed the drive for psychic, social, and erotic freedom. To read him and study his life and work in their formative years was a heady moral teething, and their writings—from the juvenilia of Angria and Gondal to *Jane Eyre* and *Wuthering Heights*—would be inconceivable without his example.

But Emily Brontë is, to borrow Harold Bloom's term, a "strong" writer who moves beyond the vision of Byron or anyone else to her own; and Heathcliff, as we have seen, is a revolutionary figure. He's no gentleman, and he gets dirty. Byron writes, "Man's love is of man's life a thing apart,/'Tis a Woman's whole existence."[29] Brontë insists—it is the point of her narrative—that it is Heathcliff's whole existence, too. The novel gets rid of Byronic posing, abstraction, and self-pity. It is the least self-righteous and pretentious, but the most mystical, of Victorian novels—descriptive terms that do not fit Byron at all well.

XI

At the end, Heathcliff speaks of his "one universal idea" to be ecstatically united with Cathy: "I have a single wish, and my whole being and faculties are yearning to attain it" (XXXIII, 256). Nearing his goal and death, yet not there, he says, "I'm too happy, and yet I'm not happy enough. My soul's bliss kills my body, but does not satisfy itself" (XXXIV, 262). That is like Saint Theresa's "I die that I can not die."[30] Think of his final "life-like gaze of exultation" and of Catherine's last moment of consciousness holding desperately onto her lover with "mad resolution on her face," crying "Heathcliff, I shall die! I shall die!" In *Wuthering Heights,* love as vocation is literal, not metaphorical. It seems fitting, then to use one of the most famous representations of mystical transport, Bernini's sculpture *The Ecstasy of Saint Theresa* (1645–52),[31] to help illustrate and understand the passionate calling in the novel.

The face of Theresa, rapt, by love possessed, matches the passion of Heathcliff and Cathy. It does not fit the emotion of Cathy II or Hareton, and that negative fact tells us why irrational, ecstatic love sometimes drowns the appeal of rational affection. Theresa's visage, the scene and image of blinding love, not only expresses faith, it somehow countenances it and calls it up in beholders. Her eyes are closed, her vision inward and subjective. The experience belongs to her, and the world cannot judge its value. We know the strength of emotion from the open mouth and the general demeanor of one transported. This woman's status and social relations in the world are beside the point. The suggestion of orgasm, the bare flesh, the sensuous folds of the drapery, the handsome angel who so closely resembles Cupid (he has been compared to Caravaggio's Eros in *Amor Vincit Omnia*[32]), and the phallic imagery all point to the high tide of libidinous energy in religious experience. The golden arrow that the angel wields, the smile on his face, and the expression of the woman encompassing joy, agony, and worldly oblivion stress the inseparability of suffering and pleasure, hope and cruelty in the time of true passion. Two particularly striking features of Bernini's art set up a reverberating tension: first, the integration of the group—Theresa, the angel, his wings, the clouds blending both heaven and nature and supporting the figures, all flow into one another to make a unity; and, second, the individual passion on the love-struck human face upon which wonder fixes. We see the whole process and the rendered balance—we see how things fit together—but the intensity of personal emotion itself is what seems miraculous. So it is with *Wuthering Heights.*

In a celebrated religious text, Theresa describes "the Transverberation": "In his hands I saw a long golden spear and at the end of the iron tip I seemed to see a point of fire. With this he seemed to pierce my heart several times so that it penetrated to my entrails. . . . The pain was so sharp that it made me utter several moans; and so excessive was the sweetness caused me by this intense pain that one can never wish to lose it, nor will one's soul be content with anything less than God."[33] Being in love is something like this for Cathy at the end of her life, and for Heathcliff: an amazing experience and an excruciating calling. If we avoid the temptation to read the passage and the art it provoked in the reductive terms of crude Freudianism (i.e., it's just a sublimated wish for genital sex), we can see how they and Brontë's novel bring into focus the complex, irresistible human drive for ecstasy that comprehends and makes use of both theology and sexual activity.

Yes, some might say, but the comparison is all wrong: Theresa is a saint; Cathy and Heathcliff are selfish, cruel characters; and juxtaposing the blindingly beautiful love of Christ with one sinner's erotic love for another is either trivializing speciousness or blasphemous special pleading. One work of art depicts experience leading to beatitude, the other describes destructive, juvenile, antisocial behavior. But surely both express the heartbreaking compulsion to get beyond the physical self through love and identification with another being, and that drive is religious as well as erotic. Being in love for the novel's characters is rendered as an experience of comparable magnitude to Theresa's rapturousness: *that* is the heresy of the age of individualism.

Heathcliff and Cathy enact a quest for salvation, a quest to make and keep something they (and perhaps *we* as well) struggle to name in the word *soul.* Cathy: "Whatever our souls are made of, his and mine are the same" (IX, 72). Heathcliff: "I *cannot* live without my life! I *cannot* live without my soul!" (XVI, 139). We can read this kind of emotion on the face of Bernini's Theresa, as we can find there the ecstasy of their last living embraces and the passion of Heathcliff's own countenance at the moment of his death. In light of *Wuthering Heights,* his expression conveys the passionate faith of both its lovers. The comparison can help us with the ontological questions, why does this figure of Saint Theresa exist, and why does the last meeting of Heathcliff and Cathy exist? The works, in conjunction, make it obvious that there is something erotic about religious faith and something metaphysical and sacred about libidinal love; and, when erotic and religious feeling come together, we can sense the full aesthetic power of each.

Bernini's *Ecstasy* bears on *Wuthering Heights* in another way. Let me take the face as a metaphor, not this time for Heathcliff, Cathy, or their experience, but for a humanity that has been prodded and pierced repeatedly by the shaft of insistent, obsessive, pain-dealing love. Heathcliff and Cathy come together to goad one another and their audiences to erotic consciousness. The vocation of love might appear sometimes to ravish the world. *Amor vincit omnia,* "love conquers all," and that could mean that many get killed, wounded, and sacrificed. But the hope in Brontë's text is that the faith somehow evolves by touching others.

Just as religious rhetoric might persuade many normal people that Christian faith is good and that it would have been a fine thing to be a fanatically devoted follower of Christ wandering in the desert or out from Avila, so the rhetoric of Emily Brontë's fiction might also persuade some with romantic tendencies that love is good and that it would be a marvelous thing to be a possessed lover like Heathcliff. To many the mysterious frenzy of the lovers' last interview might seem as bizarre as the flaming heart of Saint Theresa, but to others that ecstatic devotion might arouse as much sympathy as does the religious passion of god-struck saints. What counts for others about the seekers of transcendence is not their personalities—in social context, mystics are liable to be difficult, crazed, highly unpleasant people—but the power of their emotion, the form of their expression, and the example of their faith.

Heathcliff and Cathy would continue to haunt the modern imagination as they were reported to haunt the countryside. Laurence Olivier, arguably our century's most distinguished actor, stars as Heathcliff in the 1939 William Wyler film of *Wuthering Heights,* and Luis Buñuel, one of the greatest of all filmmakers, makes the novel into a movie, *Los abismos de pasion* (1954), focusing on the conflict between religious orthodoxy and erotic passion.[34] You can hear, in the transistor age, Kate Bush's keening lyrics "Wuthering, Wuthering, Wuthering Heights! . . . Heathcliff! It's me! Cathee! I've come home."[35] A high school student in the 1980s writes to his brother, "I love *Wuthering Heights!* It's so powerful for me. Just imagine the strength of that love. Wow! I love it because I feel that I could love someone that much myself and I know you have the passion, the sensitivity and the desire to love someone as Heathcliff and Cathy do. . . . P.S. Here is my favorite line: 'Be with me always—take any form—drive me mad! Only do not leave me in the abyss, where I cannot find you! Oh God!' "

The question to all this again is, why? What gives Heathcliff and Cathy such a continuing fascination? I suspect that the attraction of erotic passion, especially for the young, comes not so much out of lust as out of a longing to gain identity and feel important. One of the appeals of love is the implicit promise of most faiths: that the last shall be first and live at the heart of things. People long to believe that the miracle of significance, of ecstasy, of felt passion might strike anywhere—even where they stand (or thrash about). Emily Brontë has imagined intercessors for erotic faith. If Sartre can write "Saint Genet," we can certainly proclaim, after nearly a century and a half in the canon of love, "Saint Catherine, Saint Heathcliff"!

NOTES

[1] Georges Bataille, *Erotism: Death and Sensuality* (San Francisco, 1986), p. 226.

[2] Winifred Gérin, *Emily Brontë* (Oxford, 1971), p. 190.

[3] J. Hillis Miller, *The Disappearance of God* (Cambridge, Mass., 1963), p. 175.

[4] See Cyril W. Beaumont, *The Ballet Called Giselle* (New York, 1969).

[5] Georges Bataille, "Emily Brontë and Evil," trans. Alistair Hamilton, in *Emily Brontë: A Critical Anthology,* ed. Jean-Pierre Petit, pp. 151–63 (Harmondsworth, England, 1973), p. 156.

[6] Emily Brontë, *Wuthering Heights: An Authoritative Text with Essays in Criticism,* ed. William M. Sale, Jr. (New York, 1963), Norton Critical Edition, chap. 14, p. 126. All subsequent citations, by chapter and page, are to this edition.

[7] Sigmund Freud, *Civilization and Its Discontents,* in *The Standard Edition of the Complete Psychological Works,* ed. and trans. James Strachey (London, 1953–66), vol. 21, p. 66.

[8] Belief in ghosts, whose broad social function can in part be said to preserve and make memorable figures, voices, and influences from the past ("beyond the grave"), ebbed as literacy spread. Writing—letters, printed material, books—gradually took over the function in the last three centuries of memorializing the past and preserving, as it were, dead voices and the reality and influence of the deceased.

[9] See Dorothy Van Ghent, *The English Novel: Form and Function* (New York, 1953), pp. 160–61.

[10] *The Poems of John Donne,* ed. Herbert Grierson (London, 1937), Holy Sonnet 10, p. 297.

[11] See, for example, Bataille on "Emily Brontë and Evil," p. 153; Irving H. Buchen, "Emily Brontë and the Metaphysics of Childhood and Love," *Nineteenth-Century Fiction* 22 (June 1967): 63–70; Margaret Homans, *Bearing the Word: Language and Female Experience in Nineteenth-Century Women's Writing* (Chicago, 1976), pp. 73–77, who stresses the Lacanian hypothesis of child development in her reading of *Wuthering Heights.*

[12] See Denis de Rougemont, *Love in the Western World,* trans. Montgomery Belgion, revised and augmented (Princeton, 1983), pp. 42–46, 50–53, for the counterargument.

[13] See, for example, Thomas C. Moser, "What Is the Matter with Emily Jane?" *Nineteenth-Century Fiction* 17 (June 1962): 1–19.

[14] Wallace Stevens, "Sunday Morning," in *The Collected Poems* (New York, 1972), pp. 66–70.

[15] See, for example, de Rougemont, *Love in the Western World;* Freud, "Being in Love and Hypnosis," in *Works,* vol. 18, pp. 111–16; José Ortega y Gasset, *On Love: Aspects of a Single Theme,* trans. Tony Talbot (New York, 1958); Singer, *The Nature of Love,* vol. 2, *Courtly and Romantic* (Chicago, 1984), pp. 14–15, 298, 432–87 (Singer, however, is well aware, as all his work shows, of the power, the appeal, and the emotional payoff of passionate love).

[16] Edward Albee, *The Zoo Story,* in *The Plays* (New York, 1981), vol. 1, p. 44.

[17] See, for example, the discussion of Thomas Moser and, in *Bearing the Word,* Margaret Homans.

[18] See Moser, "What Is the Matter with Emily Jane?" and Terry Eagleton, *Myths of Power* (London, 1975).

[19] See the introductory chapters in both volumes 1 and 2 of Irving Singer's *The Nature of Love.*

[20] J. Hillis Miller, pp. 209–10.

[21] J. Hillis Miller, p. 211.

[22] See, for example, Nina Auerbach, *Woman and the Demon: The Life of a Victorian Myth* (Cambridge, Mass., and London, 1982), and Ann Douglas, *The Feminization of American Culture* (New York, 1977).

[23] "Editor's Preface to the New Edition of *Wuthering Heights* (1850)," in *Wuthering Heights,* by Emily Brontë, ed. William M. Sale, Jr., p. 12.

[24] See Winifred Gérin, *Charlotte Brontë: The Evolution of Genius* (Oxford, 1967), p. 31.

[25] Winifred Gérin, "Byron's Influence on the Brontës," *Keats-Shelley Memorial Bulletin* 17 (1966): 2.

[26] Helen Moglen, *Charlotte Brontë: The Self Conceived* (New York, 1976), p. 29.

[27] For an informative discussion of Byron, romantic love, romantic irony, and the potential influence of "Byron" in nineteenth-century erotic history, see Anne K. Mellor, *English Romantic Irony* (Cambridge, Mass., 1979), pp. 31–76.

[28] See Leslie Marchand, *Byron: A Biography* (New York, 1957), vol. 1, p. 328.

[29] Byron, *Don Juan,* Canto 1, stanza 194.

[30] See Bataille, *Erotism: Death and Sensuality,* p. 240.

[31] For discussion of Bernini's Saint Theresa, see Robert T. Petersson, *The Art of Ecstasy: Teresa, Bernini, and Crashaw* (New York, 1970); Rudolf Wittkower, *Gian Lorenzo Bernini* (London, 1966), especially pp. 216–17; Howard Hibbard, *Bernini* (Harmondsworth, England, 1965, reprinted 1976); Hans Kauffman, *Giovanni Lorenzo Bernini: Die figurlichen Kompositionen* (Berlin, 1970); Robert Wallace, *The World of Bernini: 1598–1688* (New York, 1970), especially pp. 143–48.

[32] See *The Age of Caravaggio* (New York, 1985), p. 277: "There is no figure more closely analogous to this triumphant Cupid than Bernini's smiling angel who directs his arrow towards Saint Teresa."

[33] See Bataille, *Erotism,* p. 244, which cites the language of the Transverberation. See also *The Life of Saint Theresa,* trans. J. M. Cohen (Harmondsworth, England, 1957), p. 210.

[34] Luis Buñuel, *Los abismos de pasion* (Produciones Tepeyac, 1954).

[35] Kate Bush, "Wuthering Heights," on the album *The Kick Inside,* EMI America (Capitol) CDP7-46012-2, 1978.

W. David Shaw

THE BURDEN OF SIGNS
IN *WUTHERING HEIGHTS*

Consciousness in *Wuthering Heights* is a product of the fall into language. In paradise there would be no language: only music or silence. The more disjunction there is between the sign and what it signifies, the more intense but falsifying is the self-consciousness that language generates. If Heathcliff's feeling for Cathy were indeed unutterable, could he utter anything about it, including his utterance that it is unutterable? If the sign were truly intrinsic, it would be the thing-in-itself, and there would be no need of language. That is what paradise or death would be like. And paradise and death are hard to distinguish in this novel. Total unconsciousness would dispense with signs, and it would be either to reenter Eden or to descend into hell. To be Mrs. Edgar Linton is to be consigned to limbo. But to be merged with Heathcliff, ostensibly a very different fate, appears to come in the end to the same thing. To generate an alternative fate as the faithful catalyst of heightened consciousness, Cathy must betray Heathcliff, and life must interpose delay after delay between Cathy's death at the middle of the novel and Heathcliff's at the end. If everything is a sign, then nothing is a sign. There is an empty god term at the center of *Wuthering Heights,* or at least no god term we can compass in words, and hence no paradisal state of primal identity and unconsciousness we can aspire to or be conscious of.

Originally despised and dismissed as a mere demonic supplement to the civilized norms, Heathcliff soon reverses these priorities. Not only does he move into the center of the picture, but he also erodes the boundaries between picture space and frame. Once divisions between light and dark, heaven and hell, love and hate are allowed to appear, they generate a process of atomic fission, of dismemberment or desynonymizing, as futile and regressive as Jabes Branderham's division of his sermon into 490 parts (chap. 3). Heathcliff forgets, however, that without such partitioning there can be no definition (from *finis,* a limit or end). Only by making boundaries and assigning limits can the nameless be named. The alternative

From *Victorians and Mystery: Crises of Representation* (Ithaca, NY: Cornell University Press, 1990), pp. 53–61.

is Heathcliff's Nietzschean desire to stand beyond good and evil, annihilating every division of words in a black hole or void.

The scribes and reporters in *Wuthering Heights* are usually low-energy transformers like Nelly and Lockwood who tame the voltage that threatens to strike down the real centers of energy. The great exception to that statement is the sequence of events culminating in Cathy's death, where Cathy and Heathcliff are finally allowed to speak for themselves. To help them say what is otherwise not strictly sayable, Brontë carefully contrasts Heathcliff's division from Cathy with Edgar's division from Isabella. Linton, who refuses to answer his sister's letter in chapter 14, will do nothing to mend the division caused by her marriage. Though Heathcliff finds the division Cathy has placed between them just as intolerable, he is passionate in its denunciation, whereas Edgar is icily aloof. Even Edgar's anger is geared down into a decorous, civilized "sorry." Like his deficient fraternal affection for Isabella, his love for Cathy seems sisterly and weak.

When Heathcliff and Nelly talk, they do not really use words in the same sense: they talk past each other (chap. 14). "Cathy's life is spared," she reports, then warns Heathcliff that he must "shun crossing her way again." In fact, Heathcliff will help falsify the first statement by ignoring the second. To cross Cathy's way is not just to appear on her path but also to vex her, to cross her will. In playing verbal tennis with Nelly, Heathcliff picks up her phrase "humanity and duty," then in two italicized passages throws the words back at her with a curve, repeating them in reverse order. As if to cross Nelly's will, Heathcliff uses the cross trope, chiasmus, to mock the dull shape of Edgar's weak "humanity," "duty," "duty," "humanity." What is left out of the chiastic vise is passion, the quantity Heathcliff resolves to establish as the primary term. Common humanity and duty must be made weakly specialized uses of passion rather than the other way round.

An incorrigible parasite, Heathcliff feeds remorselessly on what is prior, only to reverse the priorities and break down the divisions that the idea of priority assumes. To define what Catherine means to him, Heathcliff must first define what Isabella can never mean. His wife is a mere unruly child, whom he sends upstairs for punishment. Her simpering pretense of loving Heathcliff is a more degrading form of her brother's love for Catherine. True love is excluded from such shameless performances: it is their missing supplement, which Heathcliff and Cathy can alone supply. Heathcliff is a little like Browning's duke of Ferrara, with Nelly as Linton's envoy, sent over from the Grange. Before this captive auditor he must assimilate the word "pity" and its conventional opposite, "cruelty," into some larger unit of meaning where normal divisions cease to apply. Though what has to be uttered is never fully utterable, it can at least be gestured at through nonnaming tropes like oxymoron and catachresis, the tropes traditionally used to cancel divisions in an effort to restore inclusive categories. " 'I have no pity! I have no pity! The worms writhe, the more I yearn to crush out their entrails! It is a moral teething, and I grind with greater energy, in proportion to the increase of pain' " (chap. 14). Does Heathcliff mean that the more his victims writhe like worms, the more he yearns to crush them? Or does he mean that the more he yearns to destroy, the more the worms inside himself writhe? The odd transfer across the comma of the comparative adverb "more," which might more logically modify "writhe" than "yearn," erodes the boundary between Heathcliff's internal and external enemies. And few phrases could be more oxymoronic than "moral teething." Morality generally entails control and mastery. "Teething," by contrast, is a painful process we suffer passively. The control implicit in "moral" is half canceled by the passivity implicit in "teething." Moreover, to "grind" is generally to impede efficiency. But here the grinding increases energy, in apparent defiance of Newton's laws. Heathcliff's paradoxes invite us to construct a totally novel universe—one where laws of motion cease to apply, even metaphorically.

In chapter 15, the deathbed scene itself, Heathcliff takes all his cues from Cathy, as in the previous scene he had picked up Nelly's words and thrown them back at her. As Cathy's rhetoric breaks apart, the silent spaces between the dashes circumscribe the true center of meaning, which cannot be translated into words. " 'You have killed me—and thriven on it, I think . . . Will you forget me—will you be happy when I am in the earth?' " (chap. 15). Though the concessive "I think" mutes the force of the words that follow the dash, the first break mimes the wrenching of her soul, as one unspeakable aftermath of Cathy's death is forced into words. Will Heathcliff live to say, "I've loved many others since—my children are dearer to me than she was"? The silence of this third dash is a pause in which to gather up strength, as if to say the unsayable. As the anaphora "Will you," hurled at Heathcliff four times, is used as a club to beat him into submission, each dash is like a knife wound, enacting the sharp breaks and thrusts of her words. Now Cathy assumes the part played by Nelly in the preceding scene. Taunting Heathcliff with forgetting her, Cathy describes exactly what Heathcliff can never do. In setting the terms of Heathcliff's own response, she does the opposite of what she thinks: she writes the script that Heathcliff will act out to his dying day.

As Heathcliff overwhelms Cathy with a barrage of short questions, made more emphatic by anaphora, it is clear that Cathy not only has taught him how to be cruel and false, she has also taught him the use of words, the use of morally charged words like "murder" to describe her betrayal. Heathcliff is morally superior to Cathy, since he can love his own murderer but not *her* murderer. He loves the one Cathy, the victim, so much that he must hate the other Cathy, the murderess. His culminating paradox is that he hates her *because* he loves her. He would be less cruel were he not so loving. Only oxymorons that cancel each other out can begin to express the paradox that great love and great hate are inseparable. Heathcliff's play on words is really shredding them to bits in an agony of despair. Even in breaking down distinctions that normally apply between pity and cruelty, love and hate, Heathcliff uses oxymoron to express terrible distress of mind.

In Heathcliff's and Nelly's vocabularies the words "good" and "evil" have different meanings. Their incommensurability becomes explicit in Heathcliff's cruel play upon Nelly's use of the verb "lies." Her benedictory phrase, "she lies with a sweet smile on her face" (chap. 16), modulates by way of an elided pun into the bitter exclamation, "Why, she's a liar to the end!" The alarming multiplication of dashes in Heathcliff's speech fittingly culminates in his discovery that what he has to say is "unutterable." The knives and spears with which Nelly says Heathcliff is goading himself to death are also knives and spears of elision. His lament that he *"cannot* live without [his] life" comes perilously close to tautology, the most reserved and withholding of tropes. As his words begin to reach into silence, the worst torment he can conceive is the torment of existing in an abyss emptied of meaning. The unconscious is literally the "unutterable," the plentitude or void that exists on the far side of silence. To the degree that Cathy agitates and torments Heathcliff, she keeps eroding and destabilizing all the falsifying divisions that Heathcliff's language is tempted to place between them. But without divisions there can be no consciousness or speech.

The experience of reading *Wuthering Heights* is often the experience of discovering that what we had taken for an accepted norm or center is a mere margin. The frame or supplement to one picture turns out to be the center of the next one. What is excluded, for example, from the first picture of Heathcliff's throwing himself on Cathy's grave, like a crazed Hamlet, becomes the subject at the center of a second picture. In chapter 17 everything is seen from the peripheral perspectives of Isabella and Nelly. Isabella's narrative of Heathcliff's demented praying like a Methodist, full of directionless enthusiasm, incites more grim humor than tragic pity. Heathcliff's madness is that of a ruffian, physically violent, dashing his head repeatedly against the flagstones. This last detail recalls its omitted supplement: the desire to dash Hareton's infant skull against the steps when Heathcliff saves him from possible death in chapter 9. What Heathcliff has experienced at Cathy's grave is not yet told. Even in chapter 29, which provides the supplement to the potential crudities of chapter 17, the marginal experience is given first. The opening of Cathy's coffin and the discovery that her face is still recognizable are mildly horrific. Having experienced the shock, we are prepared for something more subtle and compelling, first in Heathcliff's dream of sleeping the last sleep beside Cathy, and then in a disclosure of Heathcliff's being strangely elated at the time of Cathy's burial.

His extraordinary experience at her grave is one of the novel's most striking reversals of insides and outsides, of picture spaces and margins. Instead of being inside the coffin, Cathy is outside, looking down at Heathcliff from the edge of the grave. If Heathcliff is physically outside the coffin, he is spiritually inside it. And if Cathy is physically entombed, she is also spiritually outside, wandering the earth as a disembodied ghost. There could be few more arresting metaphors for the failure of bodies to incarnate spirits or for the failure of words to incarnate their meanings. Heathcliff is willing in this scene to entertain any wild surmise to validate the fantasy of holding Cathy alive again in his arms. If she is cold, he will blame the north wind; if she is motionless, he will indulge the pathetic fallacy that she sleeps. But the truth turns out to be stranger than any of these desperate fictions. Instead of being under him and inside the coffin, she is standing on the earth outside the coffin, breathing in his ear. As Heathcliff turns "consoled at once, unspeakably consoled" (chap. 29), the weighted adverb, coming between the repeated past participle, reminds us, like his earlier use of the adjective "unutterable," that what is most worth saying cannot be said. To be told that laughter is a possible reaction at precisely the moment it becomes an inappropriate and impossible response is to be alerted to the distance we have unknowingly traveled. Though Heathcliff is talking to a spirit, no reader now considers him mad. His most irrational and absurd convictions belong to an order of things that matter more than ordinary reality and that therefore ought to exist.

Wuthering Heights threatens to become a tragedy without a catharsis, a tragedy in which Heathcliff's vision of something noble, speaking to him across his death in the grave scene, is smothered under stifling revenge codes. But toward the end of the novel Heathcliff speaks enigmatically of the approach of some "strange change" (chap. 33), which he himself only partly understands. Heathcliff's unmotivated elation, which translates itself inadequately as "a strange joyful glitter" (chap. 34), is a mark of the "unutterable." The rhetoric is a glorious failure, illustrative of Brontë's inability to incarnate a truth that is signless. One way to intimate such a truth is to use animal similes that are at once strange and familiar, like Heathcliff's inhuman, feline breathing, "fast as a cat['s]" (chap. 34), which recalls the earlier warm breathing Heathcliff felt when standing in Cathy's grave (chap. 29). Temporal dislocations place these two accounts of breathing closer together in Brontë's narration than they occurred in the actual chronology. The flashback in chapter 29 to an event first described in chapter 17 is a way of narrowing the space between Cathy and Heathcliff just before it disappears altogether.

This sense of contracting space is confirmed by Heathcliff's declaration that he is "within sight" of his "heaven." "I have my eyes on it—hardly three feet to sever me!" (chap. 34). Heathcliff may be referring either to the few feet of earth thrown over Cathy's coffin in chapter 29 or to the few feet of space separating him from Cathy's apparition, which a few moments later in chapter 34 he claims to see only two yards away. At first we think of the earth, but after Heathcliff gazes at the apparition, visible to no one but himself, we may surmise that he has actually communicated with the dead. It adds greatly to the sense of mystery that we cannot tell with certainty what Heathcliff means. The whole concluding sequence resonates mysteriously with subliminal recollections of earlier scenes. In particular, the sound of the murmuring valley stream, audible only at certain times of the year, recalls the sound that was heard at the time of Cathy's death. The space and time intervals between the events described in chapters 15 and 34 are already in a state of rapid collapse as Heathcliff prepares to cross the last divide himself.

To speak at all is to use the language of partition and division. But once the process begins, can it ever be stopped? Lockwood's odd use of the word "divide" alerts us to the dangers in the opening paragraph. "A perfect misanthropist's heaven," he observes, "and Mr. Heathcliff and I are such a suitable pair to divide the desolation between us" (chap. 1). How can one divide something so empty of content as desolation? To divide in this case is to multiply, to divide up the emptiness so it can proliferate without end. Moreover, no two people could be more divided: any division of solitude, far from drawing them together, is only going to increase the distance that separates them. Even Lockwood protests against the brainless divisions of Jabes Branderham's sermon on the forgiveness of trespasses, which are themselves a trespass on the listener's patience. In Matthew 12:25, as one commentator has observed, the unforgivable sin entails another instance of division: the division of a house against itself (Parker, 1983, 54). Because Branderham's replication of the Gospel's injunction to forgive until seventy times seven in a discourse divided into 490 parts is itself a dreamlike replication of the book-length sermon on the Gospel text that catches Lockwood's eye before he falls asleep, its partitioned discourse is also a further partitioning of experience into waking events and dream. When Lockwood in his nightmare rises to protest against the method, the irate preacher brands him as the ultimate transgressor, "The First of the Seventy-First," who would arrest the process of dividing up language by trying to collapse all words back into a primal word or synonym.

Such a synonym is Cathy's bold equation, "I *am* Heathcliff" (chap. 9), which, if valid, reverses the mindless partitioning of the sermon. Desynonymizing also yields to the recovery of one primal name as the three Cathys inscribed in the diary Lockwood has been reading—Catherine Earnshaw, Catherine Linton, and Catherine Heathcliff—are collapsed into a single identity. What is the common root, the matrix, from which Catherine and Heathcliff have sprung? They seem to belong to that small, queer margin at the very apex of the pyramid that cannot be housed inside the walls of language. Their names compose some primal word that has fallen into syntax. And only through dream vision and analogy can Cathy begin to clarify the mysteries that lie beyond the frontier of language. To be homesick in heaven, she tells Nelly, is to be estranged from her earthly home with Heathcliff (chap. 9). Linton is to Heathcliff what the moonbeam is to lightning and frost is to fire. But in heaven we expect to find the very elements that Cathy ascribes to earth and Heathcliff. What she calls heaven is really hell or the fallen world, and what she calls earth is heaven, whatever the angry angels may say. She has to use Nelly's biblical vocabulary to express reversals that profoundly alter Nelly's values. Her verbal confusion comes from the need to express revolutionary moral insights in a language inherited from the very culture and code that the insights are designed to subvert.

Ironically, the speech that most movingly attests to Cathy's at-onement with Heathcliff leads Heathcliff to think she means to divide herself from him. He stays to the point where he hears her say that to marry Heathcliff would degrade her. But it is not really Cathy who betrays Heathcliff. It is her language that betrays him—the burden of the endlessly dividing signs she must use to gesture beyond them in a retreat from the word toward ever deepening silence. Public divisions of any kind, including Cathy's removal from Heathcliff, which is really a division of herself from herself, are acts of desynonymizing, of making different, what should remain one indivisible identity. There are three Cathys who collapse into two people; and Catherine and Heathcliff are said to have a single nature. But who *is* Heathcliff? As we approach the one primal word, language falls back into untranslatable tautology. Because Heathcliff's origin like his end is a mystery, there is no fitting gravestone inscription for him. Part of his inscrutability is his lack of any surname. In its fragmentary state, his proper name is suitably improper. And yet no proper name can escape the pathos of the capital letter, which must divest even a word like "Heathcliff" of its indeterminate properties. By the time the novel's most important equation, "I *am* Heathcliff," has managed to restore a measure of intrinsic symbolism, language is already in a state of rapid retreat from the world. We are moving from definition to tautology, from rhetoric to equation. Indeed, in obliterating all sustaining difference, "I *am* Heathcliff" is no definition at all, but a return to silence and mystery.

Analysis is a kind of murder, because it breaks apart the primal language of equivalence. To divide such a language is to suffer the fate of Milo, who was devoured by beasts for splitting a tree (chap. 9). Jabes Branderham is a kind of theological Milo (chap. 3), and so is every author who carries the process of desynonymizing language to its logical conclusion. As a marital Milo, dividing his wife from her true husband, Linton, according to Cathy, can no more break her at-onement with Heathcliff than winter can change the trees or erode "the eternal rocks" beneath the earth (chap. 9). If no marriage to another can annihilate their at-onement, then no atonement in the biblical sense is necessary. Unfortunately, Heathcliff labors under the burden of a more extrinsic symbolism. Imprisoned by language and trapped by its antinomies, he can never allow Cathy to use the word "marriage" in both of these contrasting senses. He feels that Cathy's betrayal of their at-onement requires something like atonement in the biblical sense, even though he rejects biblical values elsewhere. Who is being inconsistent, Heathcliff or Cathy? Each is inconsistent, because each uses ideas like at-onement and marriage both in the limited extrinsic sense of their adversaries and in the more primary intrinsic sense that represents their own truest understanding of such concepts.

To be intelligible and "utterable" at all is to be partitioned. But to be endlessly partitioned by self-replicating signs, in the kind of infinite regress that Kant associates with the mathematical sublime, is to slide further and further down the slope of words. To be sublime is to remain at the apex of the pyramid. But it is also to be nameless or "unutterable." To understand *Wuthering Heights* one has to play Wagner. Music, according to Susanne Langer, is an unconsummated form of symbolism, because its sounds lack specific denotations. The unity that Brontë celebrates between Catherine and Heathcliff is necessarily unconsummated in words, "unconsummated" in Langer's sense of the word, just as their spiritual at-onement is never consummated physically.

CONTRIBUTORS

HAROLD BLOOM is Sterling Professor of the Humanities at Yale University and Henry W. and Albert A. Berg Professor of English at the New York University Graduate School. He is a 1985 MacArthur Foundation Award recipient, served as the Charles Eliot Norton Professor of Poetry at Harvard University (1987–88), and is the author of twenty books, the most recent being *The American Religion* (1992). Currently he is editing the Chelsea House series Modern Critical Views and The Critical Cosmos, and other Chelsea House series in literary criticism.

MIRIAM ALLOTT was Andrew Cecil Bradley Professor of Modern English at the University of Liverpool and later Professor of English at Birkbeck College, University of London. She is the author of *Elizabeth Gaskell* (1958) and a bibliography of the Brontës (1973) and the editor of many anthologies of criticism, including Wuthering Heights: *A Casebook* (1970, rev. 1992), *The Brontës: The Critical Heritage* (1973), and a casebook on *Charlotte Brontë:* Jane Eyre *and* Villette (1973). She has edited the poems of John Keats (1970) and Matthew Arnold (1979).

WALTER L. REED is Professor of English at Emory University in Atlanta. He has written *Meditations on the Hero* (1974) and *An Exemplary History of the Novel: The Quixotic versus the Picaresque* (1981).

RONALD B. HATCH, Associate Professor of English at the University of British Columbia in Vancouver, is the author of *Crabbe's Arabesque: Social Drama in the Poetry of George Crabbe* (1976).

JOHN BEVERSLUIS is Professor of Philosophy at Butler University in Indianapolis. He has written *C. S. Lewis and the Search for Rational Religion* (1985).

WALTER E. ANDERSON is Associate Professor of English at the University of California at Los Angeles. He has written on Jane Austen, George Eliot, Henry James, Joseph Conrad, Katherine Mansfield, and D. H. Lawrence.

MARY BURGAN is Professor of English at Indiana University. She has written articles on Jane Austen, Charlotte Brontë, James Joyce, D. H. Lawrence, Katherine Mansfield, and on women and music in nineteenth-century fiction.

JOHN T. MATTHEWS is the author of *The Play of Faulkner's Language* (1982) and The Sound and the Fury: *Faulkner and the Lost Cause* (1990). He is Professor of English at Boston University.

ROBERT M. POLHEMUS is Professor of English at Stanford University. His major publications include *The Changing World of Anthony Trollope* (1968), *Comic Faith: The Great Comic Tradition from Austen to Joyce* (1980) and *Erotic Faith: Being in Love from Jane Austen to D. H. Lawrence* (1990).

W. DAVID SHAW is Professor of English at Victoria College, University of Toronto. He is the author of *The Dialectical Temper: The Rhetorical Art of Robert Browning* (1968), *Tennyson's Style* (1976), *The Lucid Veil: Poetic Truth in the Victorian Era* (1987) and *Victorians and Mystery: Crises of Representation* (1990).

BIBLIOGRAPHY

Baldridge, Cates. "Voyeuristic Rebellion: Lockwood's Dream and the Reader of *Wuthering Heights*." *Studies in the Novel* 20 (1988): 274–87.

Barreca, Regina. "The Power of Excommunication: Sex and the Feminine Text in *Wuthering Heights*." In *Sex and Death in Victorian Literature*, edited by Regina Barreca. London: Macmillan, 1990, pp. 227–40.

Benvenuto, Richard. *Emily Brontë*. Boston: Twayne, 1982.

Berman, Jeffrey. "Attachment and Loss in *Wuthering Heights*." In *Narcissism and the Novel*. New York: New York University Press, 1990, pp. 78–112.

Bersani, Leo. "Desire and Metamorphosis." In *A Future for Astyanax: Character and Desire in Literature*. Boston: Little, Brown, 1976, pp. 189–229.

Black, Michael. "*Wuthering Heights:* Romantic Self-Commitment." In *The Literature of Fidelity*. New York: Barnes & Noble, 1975, pp. 125–51.

Bloom, Harold, ed. *Emily Brontë's* Wuthering Heights. New York: Chelsea House, 1987.

Bosco, Ronald A. "Heathcliff: Societal Victim or Demon?" *Gypsy Scholar* 2, No. 1 (Fall 1974): 21–39.

Buckler, William E. "Chapter VII of *Wuthering Heights:* A Key to Interpretation." *Nineteenth-Century Fiction* 7 (1952–53): 51–55.

Buckley, Vincent. "Passion and Control in *Wuthering Heights*." *Southern Review* (Adelaide) 1, No. 2 (1964): 5–23.

Burns, Marjorie. " 'This Shattered Prison': Versions of Eden in *Wuthering Heights*." In *The Nineteenth-Century British Novel*, edited by Jeremy Hawthorn. London: Edward Arnold, 1986, pp. 31–46.

Burns, Wayne. "On *Wuthering Heights*." *Recovering Literature* 1, No. 2 (Fall 1972): 5–25.

Caine, Jeffrey. *Heathcliff*. New York: Knopf, 1978.

Carson, Joan. "Visionary Experience in *Wuthering Heights*." *Psychoanalytic Review* 62 (1975–76): 131–51.

Champion, Larry S. "Heathcliff: A Study in Authorial Technique." *Ball State University Forum* 9, No. 2 (Spring 1968): 19–25.

Chitham, Edward. *The Brontës' Irish Background*. New York: St. Martin's Press, 1986.

———. *A Life of Emily Brontë*. Oxford: Basil Blackwell, 1987.

Clayton, Jay. "*Wuthering Heights*." In *Romantic Vision and the Novel*. Cambridge: Cambridge University Press, 1987, pp. 81–102.

Collins, Clifford. "Theme and Conventions in *Wuthering Heights*." *Critic* 1, No. 2 (Autumn 1947): 43–50.

Craik, W. A. *The Brontë Novels*. London: Methuen, 1968.

Daleski, H. M. "*Wuthering Heights:* The Whirl of Contraries." In *The Divided Heroine: A Recurrent Pattern in Six English Novels*. New York: Holmes & Meier, 1984, pp. 25–46.

Davies, Cecil W. "A Reading of *Wuthering Heights*." *Essays in Criticism* 19 (1969): 254–72.

Davies, Stevie. *Emily Brontë*. Bloomington: Indiana University Press, 1988.

———. *Emily Brontë: The Artist as a Free Woman*. Manchester: Carcanet Press, 1983.

Dawson, Terence. "The Struggle for Deliverance from the Father: The Structural Principle of *Wuthering Heights*." *Modern Language Review* 84 (1989): 289–304.

De Grazia, Emilio. "The Ethical Dimensions of *Wuthering Heights*." *Midwest Quarterly* 19 (1977–78): 176–95.

DeLamotte, Eugenia C. "Boundaries of the Self as Romantic Theme: Emily Brontë." In *Perils of the Night: A Feminist Study of Nineteenth-Century Female Gothic.* New York: Oxford University Press, 1990, pp. 118–43.

Dervin, Daniel. "The Subjective Phases of Creativity in Emily Brontë." In *Creativity and Culture: A Psychoanalytic Study of the Creative Process in the Arts, Sciences, and Culture.* Rutherford, NJ: Fairleigh Dickinson University Press, 1990, pp. 47–60.

Dingle, Herbert. *The Mind of Emily Brontë.* London: Martin Brian & O'Keeffe, 1974.

———. "The Origin of Heathcliff." *Brontë Society Transactions* 16 (1971–75): 131–38.

Dodds, M. Hope. "Heathcliff's Country." *Modern Language Review* 39 (1944): 116–29.

Duthie, Enid L. *The Brontës and Nature.* New York: St. Martin's Press, 1986.

Eagleton, Terry. *Myths of Power: A Marxist Study of the Brontës.* London: Macmillan Press, 1975.

Ellis, Kate Ferguson. "Emily Brontë and the Technology of the Self." In *The Contested Castle: Gothic Novels and the Subversion of Domestic Ideology.* Urbana: University of Illinois Press, 1989, pp. 207–22.

Evans, Margiad. "Byron and Emily Brontë." *Life and Letters* 57 (1948): 193–216.

Farrell, John P. "Reading the Text of Community in *Wuthering Heights.*" *ELH* 56 (1989): 173–208.

Fike, Francis. "Bitter Herbs and Wholesome Medicines: Love as Theological Affirmation in *Wuthering Heights.*" *Nineteenth-Century Fiction* 23 (1968–69): 127–49.

Ford, Boris. "*Wuthering Heights.*" *Scrutiny* 7 (1938–39): 375–89.

Frank, Katherine. *A Chainless Soul: A Life of Emily Brontë.* Boston: Houghton Mifflin, 1990.

Gates, Barbara. "Suicide and *Wuthering Heights.*" *Victorian Newsletter* No. 50 (Fall 1976): 15–19.

Gérin, Winifred. *Emily Brontë: A Biography.* Oxford: Clarendon Press, 1971.

Gerster, Carole. "The Reality of Fantasy: Emily Brontë's *Wuthering Heights.*" In *Spectrum of the Fantastic,* edited by Donald Palumbo. Westport, CT: Greenwood Press, 1988, pp. 71–80.

Gleckner, Robert F. "Time in *Wuthering Heights.*" *Criticism* 1 (1959): 328–38.

Goetz, William R. "Genealogy and Incest in *Wuthering Heights.*" *Studies in the Novel* 14 (1982): 359–76.

Goff, Barbara Munson. "Between Natural Theology and Natural Selection: Breeding the Human Animal in *Wuthering Heights.*" *Victorian Studies* 27 (1983–84): 477–508.

Gordon, Felicia. *A Preface to the Brontës.* London: Longman, 1989.

Gordon, Marci M. "Kristeva's Abject and Sublime in Brontë's *Wuthering Heights.*" *Literature and Psychology* 34, No. 3 (1988): 44–58.

Gose, Elliott B., Jr. "*Wuthering Heights:* The Heath and the Hearth." *Nineteenth-Century Fiction* 21 (1966–67): 1–19.

Grove, Robin. "*Wuthering Heights.*" *Critical Review* No. 8 (1965): 71–87.

Grudin, Peter D. "*Wuthering Heights:* The Question of Unquiet Slumbers." *Studies in the Novel* 6 (1974): 389–407.

Hafley, James. "The Villain in *Wuthering Heights.*" *Nineteenth-Century Fiction* 13 (1958–59): 199–215.

Hagan, John. "Control of Sympathy in *Wuthering Heights.*" *Nineteenth-Century Fiction* 21 (1966–67): 305–23.

Haggerty, George E. "The Gothic Form of *Wuthering Heights.*" *Victorian Newsletter* No. 74 (Fall 1988): 1–6.

Hannah, Barbara. "*Wuthering Heights.*" In *Striving towards Wholeness.* New York: Putnam's, 1971, pp. 208–57.

Harpham, Geoffrey Galt. "Walking on Silence: The Lamination of Narratives in *Wuthering Heights.*" In *On the Grotesque: Strategies of Contradiction in Art and Literature.* Princeton: Princeton University Press, 1982, pp. 79–105.

Harris, Anne Leslie. "Psychological Time in *Wuthering Heights.*" *International Fiction Review* 7 (1980): 112–17.

Hewish, John. *Emily Brontë: A Critical and Biographical Study.* London: Macmillan, 1969.

Hochman, Baruch. "*Wuthering Heights:* Unity and Scope, Surface and Depth." In *The Test of Character: From the Victorian Novel to the Modern.* Rutherford, NJ: Fairleigh Dickinson University Press, 1983, pp. 91–110.

Holderness, Graham. *Wuthering Heights.* Milton Keynes, UK: Open University Press, 1985.

Homans, Margaret. "The Name of the Mother in *Wuthering Heights.*" In *Bearing the Word: Language and Female Experience in Nineteenth-Century Women's Writing.* Chicago: University of Chicago Press, 1986, pp. 68–83.

———. "Repression and Sublimation of Nature in *Wuthering Heights.*" *PMLA* 93 (1978): 9–19.

Jacobs, Carol. "*Wuthering Heights:* At the Threshold of Interpretation." *Boundary 2* 7, No. 3 (Spring 1979): 49–71.

Jefferson, Douglas. "Irresistible Narrative: The Art of *Wuthering Heights.*" *Brontë Society Transactions* 17 (1980): 337–47.

Justus, James. "Beyond Gothicism: *Wuthering Heights* and an American Tradition." *Tennessee Studies in Literature* 5 (1960): 25–33.

Kavanagh, James H. *Emily Brontë.* Oxford: Basil Blackwell, 1985.

Kermode, Frank. "A Modern Way with a Classic." *New Literary History* 5 (1973–74): 415–34.

Klingopulos, G. D. "The Novel as Dramatic Poem (II): *Wuthering Heights.*" *Scrutiny* 14 (1946–47): 269–86.

Knapp, Bettina L. *The Brontës: Branwell, Anne, Emily, Charlotte.* New York: Continuum, 1991.

Knoepflmacher, U. C. "*Wuthering Heights:* A Tragicomic Romance." In *Laughter & Despair: Readings in Ten Novels of the Victorian Era.* Berkeley: University of California Press, 1971, pp. 84–108.

Landon, Bette. "*Wuthering Heights* and the Text between the Lines." *Papers on Language and Literature* 24 (1988): 34–52.

Langman, F. H. "*Wuthering Heights.*" *Essays in Criticism* 15 (1965): 294–312.

Lavers, Norman. "The Action of *Wuthering Heights.*" *South Atlantic Quarterly* 72 (1973): 43–52.

Lehman, B. H. "Of Material, Subject, and Form: *Wuthering Heights.*" In *The Image of the Work* by B. H. Lehman et al. Berkeley: University of California Press, 1955, pp. 3–17.

Liddell, Robert. *Twin Spirits: The Novels of Emily and Anne Brontë.* London: Peter Owen, 1990.

Loxterman, Alan S. "*Wuthering Heights* as Romantic Poem and Victorian Novel." In *A Festschrift for Professor Marguerite Roberts,* edited by Frieda Elaine Penninger. Richmond, VA: University of Richmond, 1976, pp. 87–100.

McGuire, Kathryn B. "The Incest Taboo in *Wuthering Heights:* A Modern Appraisal." *American Imago* 45 (1988): 217–24.

McKibben, Robert. "The Image of the Book in *Wuthering Heights.*" *Nineteenth-Century Fiction* 15 (1960–61): 159–69.

Macovski, Michael S. "*Wuthering Heights* and the Rhetoric of Interpretation." *ELH* 54 (1987): 363–84.

Madden, William A. "*Wuthering Heights:* The Binding of Passion." *Nineteenth-Century Fiction* 27 (1972–73): 127–54.

Mengham, Rod. *Emily Brontë:* Wuthering Heights. Harmondsworth: Penguin, 1989.

Miller, J. Hillis. "*Wuthering Heights:* Repetition and the 'Uncanny.'" In *Fiction and Repetition.* Cambridge, MA: Harvard University Press, 1982, pp. 42–72.

Mitchell, Giles. "Incest, Demonism, and Death in *Wuthering Heights.*" *Literature and Psychology* 23, No. 1 (1973): 27–36.

Moglen, Helene. "The Double Vision of *Wuthering Heights:* A Clarifying View of Female Development." *Centennial Review* 15 (1971): 391–405.

Moser, Thomas. "What Is the Matter with Emily Jane? Conflicting Impulses in *Wuthering Heights.*" *Nineteenth-Century Fiction* 17 (1962–63): 1–19.

Newman, Beth. "'The Situation of the Looker-On': Gender, Narration, and Gaze in *Wuthering Heights.*" *PMLA* 105 (1990): 1029–41.

Oates, Joyce Carol. "The Magnanimity of *Wuthering Heights.*" *Critical Inquiry* 9 (1982): 35–49.

Paglia, Camille. "Romantic Shadows: Emily Brontë." In *Sexual Personae: Art and Decadence from Nefertiti to Emily Dickinson.* New Haven: Yale University Press, 1990, pp. 439–59.

Paris, Bernard J. "'"Hush, hush! He's a human being"': A Psychological Approach to Heathcliff." *Women and Literature* NS 2 (1982): 101–17.

Parker, Patricia. "The (Self-)Identity of the Literary Text: Property, Propriety, Proper Place, and Proper Name in *Wuthering Heights.*" In *Identity of the Literary Text,* edited by Mario J. Valdés and Owen Miller. Toronto: University of Toronto Press, 1985, pp. 92–116.

Patterson, Charles I., Jr. "Empathy and the Daemonic in *Wuthering Heights.*" In *The English Novel in the Nineteenth Century,* edited by George Goodin. Urbana: University of Illinois Press, 1972, pp. 81–96.

Reed, Donna K. "The Discontents of Civilization in *Wuthering Heights* and *Buddenbrooks.*" *Comparative Literature* 41 (1989): 209–29.

Roberts, Mark. "The Dilemma of Emily Brontë." In *The Tradition of Romantic Morality.* London: Macmillan Press, 1973, pp. 156–97.

Sedgwick, Eve Kosovsky. "Immediacy, Doubleness, and the Unspeakable: *Wuthering Heights* and *Villette.*" In *The Coherence of Gothic Conventions.* New York: Arno Press, 1980, pp. 104–53.

Senf, Carol A. "Emily Brontë's Version of Feminist History: *Wuthering Heights.*" *Essays in Literature* 12 (1985): 201–14.

Shapiro, Arnold. "*Wuthering Heights* as a Victorian Novel." *Studies in the Novel* 1 (1969): 284–96.

Sherry, Norman. *Charlotte and Emily Brontë.* New York: Arco, 1970.

Smith, Anne, ed. *The Art of Emily Brontë.* London: Vision Press; Totowa, NJ: Barnes & Noble, 1976.

Sonstroem, David. "*Wuthering Heights* and the Limits of Vision." *PMLA* 86 (1971): 51–62.

Spark, Muriel, and Derek Stanford. *Emily Brontë: Her Life and Work.* London: Peter Owen, 1953.

Stevenson, W. H. "*Wuthering Heights:* The Facts." *Essays in Criticism* 35 (1985): 149–66.

Taylor, Irene. *Holy Ghosts: The Male Muses of Emily and Charlotte Brontë.* New York: Columbia University Press, 1990.

Thomas, Ronald R. "Dreams and Disorders in *Wuthering Heights.*" In *Dreams of Authority: Freud and the Fictions of the Unconcious.* Ithaca, NY: Cornell University Press, 1990, pp. 112–35.

Thompson, Wade. "Infanticide and Sadism in *Wuthering Heights.*" *PMLA* 78 (1963): 69–74.

Tillotson, Geoffrey. "Charlotte and Emily Brontë." In *A View of Victorian Literature.* Oxford: Clarendon Press, 1978, pp. 187–225.

Traversi, Derek. "*Wuthering Heights:* After a Hundred Years." *Dublin Review* No. 449 (Spring 1949): 154–68.

Trickett, Rachel. "*Wuthering Heights:* The Story of a Haunting." *Brontë Society Transactions* 16 (1971–75): 338–47.

Twitchell, James. "Heathcliff as Vampire." *Southern Humanities Review* 11 (1977): 355–62.

Vargish, Thomas. "Revenge and *Wuthering Heights.*" *Studies in the Novel* 3 (1971): 7–17.

Visick, Mary. *The Genesis of* Wuthering Heights. 3rd ed. Gloucester, UK: Ian Hodgkins, 1980.

Wallace, Robert K. *Emily Brontë and Beethoven.* Athens: University of Georgia Press, 1986.

Watson, Melvin R. "Tempest in the Soul: The Theme and Structure of *Wuthering Heights.*" *Nineteenth-Century Fiction* 4 (1949–50): 87–100.

Weissman, Judith. "Charlotte and Emily Brontë: Masters and Mad Dogs." In *Half Savage and Hardy and Free: Women and Rural Radicalism in the Nineteenth-Century Novel.* Middletown, CT: Wesleyan University Press, 1987, pp. 76–99.

———. "'Like a Mad Dog': The Radical Romanticism of *Wuthering Heights.*" *Midwest Quarterly* 19 (1977–78): 383–97.

Widdowson, Peter. "Emily Brontë: The Romantic Novelist." *Moderna Språk* 66 (1972): 1–19.

Williams, Anne. "Natural Supernaturalism in *Wuthering Heights.*" *Studies in Philology* 82 (1985): 104–27.

Williams, Gordon. "The Problem of Passion in *Wuthering Heights.*" *Trivium* 7 (1972): 41–53.

Yaeger, Patricia. "The Novel and Laughter: *Wuthering Heights.*" In *Honey-Mad Women: Emancipatory Strategies in Women's Writing.* New York: Columbia University Press, 1988, pp. 177–206.

ACKNOWLEDGMENTS

"Emily Brontë" by David Cecil from *Early Victorian Novelists* by David Cecil, © 1935 by The Bobbs-Merrill Company, renewed © 1962 by David Cecil. Reprinted by permission of Macmillan Publishing Company and David Higham Associates.

"Books in General" by V. S. Pritchett from *New Statesman and Nation,* June 22, 1946, © 1946 by New Statesman & Society. Reprinted by permission of The Observer Ltd.

"On *Wuthering Heights*" by Dorothy Van Ghent from *The English Novel: Form and Function* by Dorothy Van Ghent, © 1953 by Dorothy Van Ghent, renewed © 1981 by Dorothy Van Ghent. Reprinted by permission of Holt, Rinehart & Winston, Inc.

"Emily Brontë" by J. Hillis Miller from *The Disappearance of God: Five Nineteenth-Century Writers* by J. Hillis Miller, © 1963 by the President and Fellows of Harvard College. Reprinted by permission of Harvard University Press.

"Emily Brontë: The Woman Writer as Poet" by Inga-Stina Ewbank from *Their Proper Sphere: A Study of the Brontë Sisters as Early-Victorian Female Novelists* by Inga-Stina Ewbank, © 1966 by Inga-Stina Ewbank. Reprinted by permission of Harvard University Press.

"A Fresh Approach to *Wuthering Heights*" by Q. D. Leavis from *Lectures in America* by F. R. Leavis and Q. D. Leavis, © 1969 by F. R. Leavis and Q. D. Leavis. Reprinted by permission of Random Century Group.

"*Wuthering Heights*" by Robert Kiely from *The Romantic Novel in England* by Robert Kiely, © 1972 by the President and Fellows of Harvard College. Reprinted by permission of Harvard University Press.

"The Adolescent as Heroine" by Patricia Meyer Spacks from *The Female Imagination* by Patricia Meyer Spacks, © 1972, 1975 by Patricia Meyer Spacks. Reprinted by permission of Alfred A. Knopf, Inc.

"*Wuthering Heights:* The Love of a Sylph and a Gnome" by Avrom Fleishman from *Fiction and the Ways of Knowing: Essays on British Novels* by Avrom Fleishman, © 1978 by the University of Texas Press. Reprinted by permission of University of Texas Press and the author.

"Looking Oppositely: Emily Brontë's Bible of Hell" by Sandra M. Gilbert and Susan Gubar from *The Madwoman in the Attic: The Woman Writer and the Nineteenth-Century Literary Imagination* by Sandra M. Gilbert and Susan Gubar, © 1979 by Yale University. Reprinted by permission of Yale University Press.

"The Problem of Boundaries in *Wuthering Heights*" by Elizabeth R. Napier from *Philological Quarterly* 63, No. 1 (Winter 1984), © 1984 by the University of Iowa. Reprinted by permission of *Philological Quarterly* and the author.

"The Male Part of the Poem" by Lyn Pykett from *Emily Brontë* by Lyn Pykett, © 1989 by Lyn Pykett. Reprinted by permission of Barnes & Noble and The Macmillan Press Ltd.

"The Rejection of Heathcliff?" (originally titled "*Wuthering Heights:* The Rejection of Heathcliff?") by Miriam Allott from *Essays in Criticism* 8, No. 1 (January 1958), © 1958 by the

INDEX